Career

Careershift

How to Plan and Develop a Successful Career

BRIDGET WRIGHT

PIATKUS

© 1992 by Bridget A. Wright

First published in 1992 as *Which Way Now?* by
Judy Piatkus (Publishers) Limited of
5 Windmill Street, London W1P 1HF

Reprinted 1993
Revised edition 1996
This updated edition 1999

The moral right of the author has been asserted

*A copyright record for this book is available from
the British Library*

ISBN 0-7499-1930-2

Designed by Paul Saunders

Printed and bound in Great Britain by
Mackays of Chatham PLC, Chatham, Kent

CONTENTS

ACKNOWLEDGEMENTS

At last the deed is done, the last word is written. This could never have been achieved without support from Peter, Claire and Simon. Thank you for your help and putting up with all the take-aways.

Also, to the numerous people I meet in the course of my work, including Peter Turner who gave me the opening quote. Thank you all for providing me with a wealth of information and ideas. All the illustrations in this book are genuine, only the names and situations have been changed to protect confidentiality.

PREFACE TO THE THIRD EDITION

'The future is yours, work positively to achieve your own success' are the last words of the preface I wrote for the second edition of this book in 1995. The first edition was created at the beginning of the 90s. As we all wait for the new century the words and concepts found within these pages seem even more appropriate—after nearly ten years.

Taking control is currently in vogue, a catchphrase of the British government and a principle behind many of their policies. Prime Minister Tony Blair believes that individuals should take more responsibility. This is a great idea, but the question I'm constantly asked by clients is *how*? Some people will grasp the idea with ease, many will start full of enthusiasm only to be knocked back at the first obstacle. Others remain confused and perplexed about the whole topic.

The world of work is still a frantically changing place but sadly the issues created for employees by this change remain much the same. Stress, uncertainty, low morale, lack of direction, poor motivation and no confidence are problems that prevent employees from performing to their greatest potential. Something that *has* changed in the last few years is my view of how we should help to combat this wave of negative feeling that is engulfing many of today's work force.

Five years ago I saw signs that employers were beginning to acknowledge that the way forward was to encourage employees to take responsibility for their own progress and provide them with the opportunities and support to achieve this control. A few companies now see the value in this approach for their business but sadly it is still only a few who really understand what this means and are fully committed to making this investment. Many are still only paying lip service to the concept and not backing the words with support or resources. The majority are still ignorant of the wealth that lies before them, locked inside their work force.

My experience, during the last five years, has led me to revise my thinking and return to the view I held at the beginning. We cannot wait for employers to wake up to the lost opportunity staring them in the face. You must take control of your own future in terms of career or work. It is too valuable to leave it to the whim of your employer. The reason for this change in my thinking is that I am now working with more and more people who have so much of their self-worth invested in work that when things go wrong it has a devastating effect on their whole being. The process of self management is too important to leave to someone else to sort out. *You* must take control and work things out yourself.

If your employer is forward thinking in this area, take advantage of the opportunity and learn whilst you have the chance. Remember that employers can change and you may even choose to leave the organisation to gain some wider experience.

Any positive action, however small, will create a positive result. This may not always be in the way you expect or envisage, but it will enable you to move forward. The power of this small activity, this first step to taking control, has always astounded me in the work I do. The number of times clients report back, 'You'll never guess what happened . . .'. Oh yes I can. The truth behind the saying *action breeds action* never ceases to amaze me.

You can start today by acknowledging that you are a valuable asset. In fact you are your own **most** valuable asset. You own nothing more valuable than yourself and your skills. You need to take care of yourself and pay yourself some attention—most of all nurture yourself so that your value is always increasing. Please don't allow yourself to wake up one day and find that someone else is delivering the message to you that says you are finished. That you have no value in this organisation any more. Take control *now*—you will be better motivated, have more energy and discover that you *are* of value. Believe me, it's true. You have a depth of hidden potential that will amaze you—and your boss. Start today. The future is yours. So work positively to achieve your own success.

Bridget A. Wright
Freelance Careers Consultant, Mentor and Coach
to individuals and organisations
Chadlington
Oxfordshire

November 1998

PREFACE TO THE FIRST EDITION

I believe we stand at the crest of an exciting time. Many may disagree, pointing to high unemployment, a depressed housing market and an economy which is 'bumping along the bottom', with all the political uncertainty that brings. These are all external factors, however, for the exciting crest relates to individual empowerment. The last 10 years has seen the encouragement of individual enterprise, but unfortunately little has been done to give the individuals the required knowledge, tools or techniques to achieve this successfully. Those that have succeeded have acquired and developed these skills for themselves. This is where the real excitement is to be found.

Watching people find and develop their latent potential is a very powerful experience. Career management can do that, but you need to value yourself and understand that you do have potential. This can never come from the outside.

Potential is a very important concept. How many of us are under-achieving, only utilising a small percentage of our full potential? If you ask around, many people will agree that they feel frustrated by under-performance. If you are one of those people, don't wait for someone else to release you from your prison, take the first step yourself.

Give yourself permission to be selfish for a short time, while you attend to your own needs. Invest some time, effort and maybe a little money in *you*, your most valuable asset. It will certainly be a wise move which will yield some amazing returns.

The return on your investment will really depend upon what your ultimate goal is. If money is the goal then you can progress to achieve this, but you may have to be prepared to take a step down or sideways to achieve the final result. If satisfaction is the aim, then you may have to learn new skills to help you move into a different role, discipline or function.

Whatever action you take, as long as you do your groundwork and are fully prepared, you will be moving towards your goal. Don't set yourself giant tasks immediately, but work at smaller parts of the whole, because action will follow action, and success will bring success. Positive energy will always create more energy.

Energy is certainly something you will need in abundance because many of the actions related to career management need to happen on top of your present hectic workload. But with good prioritising and a commitment to your own development, it becomes easier. Also, as things progress, work and career management can go side by side. If you are working in a partnership with your organisation there are dual returns: some for you, some for the company.

The return on your investment will be directly related to your own effort. Nobody else can do the work. You can build in encouragement, and pay for professional support if you want to, but unless you put in comparable effort you will never achieve success.

What is guaranteed is that success is within your reach. Career management is a very powerful process, which more and more people are discovering as the answer to some of the important issues of the moment. It works, so all that remains is for you to start the process, and may I wish you every success for the future, because you are your own success.

INTRODUCTION

'What keeps you awake at night?'

Your future will certainly be one item on a list of issues that cause you concern and this is almost certainly going to be related in some way to your work, your career, your job, earning a living or employment. Very few people are able or want to be totally idle for 24 hours of every day.

The issue that really frightens many people is change; many don't like it and many more don't really know what it is about – but the fact is that change is around you everywhere.

Career experts are now forecasting that employees working over the next 20 years will have to retrain three or four times in the course of their careers.

Are *you* ready for that challenge?

Do you feel vitalised by the prospect of learning new skills, new methods of working, experiencing different cultures and diverse environments?

Your answer to this question should be 'Yes'. This book will help you to make the transition from the old traditions to a new way of thinking about the issues relating to you and your world of work.

Someone said to me recently that an employment contract used to be like a wedding licence, upholding values of honour and loyalty 'until death us do part'. Today the bond with an employer is nearer to that in a dating relationship. This, I believe, is very true and illustrates how things have changed. In my view these changes are a healthy move forward which shifts the burden of responsibility from the employer to the employee, from the company to the individual, from someone else to you.

Today you need to strive for a balanced working relationship, with you firmly in control and your employer sitting beside you. An analogy of a rally car fits well here – you drive, with your boss in the co-driver's seat. In the past it has been more akin to a coach journey; your boss in the role of driver, navigator, courier and tour guide, and you as one of the passengers. The ticket in your hand has a destination, but the coach has had to stop to let some people get off. The passengers on the roadside feel abandoned, confused and uncertain. You ask yourself, 'When the coach stops next will I be asked to leave?' The present economic climate makes this burden of responsibility too heavy for one boss to carry, but few people have been able to respond to change fast enough.

Moving to the position of taking responsibility for your own career is exciting and positive, but it is not easy, nor is it achieved in a flash. It is an ongoing process which continues throughout your life and provides many benefits which you may never have realised were possible.

Change is about taking risks and understanding that sometimes you win and sometimes you lose. The art of being successful in this area is to maximise the wins and minimise the losses. This book will help you to achieve that balance, but you must accept that it is a balance. You cannot win all the time and failure is not a disaster. When you fail you need to accept your fate and learn from your mistakes.

This is a very difficult principle to accept and often it is not helped by the situations or culture you find yourself in. Many organisations punish failure, often at a subconscious or unspoken level, thus constructing a vicious circle that obstructs change. You may not be able to alter an organisational culture overnight, but it certainly helps to understand that what people say is not always what they mean.

Change is uncomfortable and the more you fear it the more uncomfortable it becomes. What you are about to embark upon is a way of helping you manage change, take risks, and to know you have the tools, techniques and strategies at hand to assist.

This book is about realising your full potential (in your own eyes) and achieving what you want. You have a great deal of untapped potential which is often in areas totally unknown to you. This book will help you discover things about yourself and to see how you can apply them to the world of work, leisure, home, hobbies, family . . . in fact, whatever you want.

From my experience of working with many people who have faced numerous questions about their future, I have devised a process which has proved helpful in first achieving a desired result and secondly in maintaining progress. The process is called career management and the following model explains the phases which contribute to successful results.

Career management is rapidly gaining acceptance from organisations as they seek new ways to answer many of the urgent problems that face them. From my experience of working in this field with many large organisations, the ingredient that has so often been neglected is input from an individual, information about an individual's needs, aspirations, values and skills, as seen from their perspective.

Career management attempts to address some of these issues, but it is a complex activity because there are views from both the individual and the organisational standpoint which are made even more confusing by factors like family constraints and the reality of the economic situation.

The model is made up of four phases. To take responsibility for your own career successfully you need to work through each phase, at a speed that suits your own situation. But remember that career management is a process, so once you have worked through the model it should become your framework for the future. The only successful monitor as to whether you are taking responsibility for your own career management is to be able to recognise which phase your career is in at the moment.

PHASE 1 is about taking stock, collecting knowledge about yourself and testing this against reality to ensure you are on the right track.

PHASE 2 is about exploring options in a creative way, breaking down the traditional views about careers.

PHASE 3 is about setting and achieving objectives through communication, both verbal and written.

PHASE 4 is the most important because it contains the key to success – monitoring and maintaining progress.

Each phase requires a certain number of tools or techniques, knowledge, information and materials. What this book will provide is a guide to how you progress through the model. A word of caution – you must start with Phase 1 and move forward logically. Jumping from one phase to another will not give you the rock-solid foundation you need to survive.

Also, you have to do the work. Nodding your head in agreement with statements you read is not enough. Vaguely thinking, 'Yes, that sounds like me' or 'No, certainly not', will not produce success. You actually have to participate and be extremely well disciplined, but you only have to do the initial exploration once, and committing your thoughts to paper has two great benefits.

1. The action of writing your thoughts down on paper gives them structure and form. You can actually see what is real, and this action is vitally important in the process of taking ownership of what you have done. How can you know what you think until you write it down?

2. Once on paper it is recorded for future reference, and you will, on occasion, need to look back to refresh your memory, confirm your feelings or assess how things are progressing.

Shopping list

These are the materials that you will require to start your own Career Management portfolio.

Large A4 arch lever file (4 holes)
A4 paper (4 holes)
A4 dividers (how many will depend on how you plan to organise your work)

Spend some time thinking about how you work best and how you can plan your time. Make a contract with yourself to spend a definite amount of time on your career management on a regular basis. Choose a style and format which reflects you. *It is essential that you always moderate everything to suit yourself.* Following blindly will not reap the ultimate benefit. Assimilate everything, digest for a while to assess the true value for you, and discard everything that does not fit with your own character. Acting in a manner that does not truly fit your style will be spotted immediately. Nobody is looking for a herd of clones. What is of real value is to be able to reach your own decisions and know why you think that way.

How to use this book

This book is not designed as a work book because the idea is to encourage you to use the material in your own way and to think creatively about how you can adapt the ideas.

After reading this introduction you may be very clear about the career issues that are facing you and be eager to get started. On the other hand you may need some more background information to build a better picture of your own situation. From here there are two options open.

Option 1 Get started immediately and move directly to Chapter 4 where we examine self-knowledge.

Option 2 Read on in logical sequence.

If you choose Option 1 you will need to return to Chapters 1, 2 and 3 later because they will give you a clearer context and a better understanding of the issues. This is vitally important in building the rock-solid foundations which you will need for your future success.

After you have completed your chosen option, *Which Way Now?* will become an important reference book for the future. Keep it near you and refer to it often.

CHAPTER 1

BACKGROUND

Companies can no longer offer their employees cradle-to-grave job security. They are no longer able to take a school leaver or graduate and offer to guide them right through their career until retirement.

This fundamental truth has been dawning on many companies for several years, although they have taken some time to admit it, either to themselves or to the outside world, but the majority of individuals have still not grasped what this is going to mean to them.

Companies can no longer take responsibility for building the long-term careers of their staff. Individuals themselves are going to have to take more control. For most of us that means a complete change in the way we think and act, *'change'* being the key word for everything which is happening to us in the world of work at the moment, and the key to everything we are going to talk about in this book.

Coping with change is hard for everyone, but it is a great deal easier if you are the instigator of those changes or, if that is not possible, if you are able to see them coming and plan accordingly, preparing yourself and working out what your options are going to be.

Many of the most influential management thinkers are writing books about how companies can help their people to cope with change, but it is wise if you can learn the secrets for yourself, so that you can be proactive, rather than reactive, able to shape your career to fit *your* needs, rather than being buffeted about as the company tries to navigate the rough seas of change.

The historical pattern

Throughout history most people have had their careers governed by others; in feudal times the faithful family retainers worked in the homes and fields of farmers and landowners in times of peace. Soldiers marched around the world at the behest of their kings, princes and generals. Loyalty was basically exchanged for protection, which the aristocrats were able to offer in a dangerous and uncertain world.

With the arrival of the Industrial Revolution the power of the employers became more concentrated than ever, with the big manufacturing companies replacing the aristocrats as the major employers, developing an endless appetite for labour. They needed the unquestioning loyalty of people willing to go down mines or work in appalling factory conditions for little money. The last thing they wanted were people who thought for themselves or showed any signs of wanting to take their personal destinies into their own hands. They needed people's muscle power, not their brains. And they needed to know that their employees would be there to do the work, not that they necessarily wanted to be there or were happy with their jobs.

To help ensure that their people remained loyal to them, and to lock them into their jobs, some employers became known for being philanthropic. Bournville, for instance, looked after every aspect of their employees' lives, not just their work. They built a complete village for them, ensuring good housing, good diet and access to good medical facilities, giving the company control over every aspect of the lives of their employees and their employees' families.

The Technological Revolution, linked with a decline in industrial and manufacturing demand, has refocused the needs of the employers. Now, at long last, companies are realising that their most important assets are the knowledge and skills of their staff. Those workforces with the highest level of knowledge and skills will make their companies successful. *Fortune* magazine told us recently, 'there are no products, only services'. By that they meant that companies have had to become more service oriented because they can no longer rely on keeping a technical advantage. If all products are equally good, then it will be the skills, intelligence and motivation of the staff which will make the difference between winning or losing an order.

Added value to basic products and services

It is all about 'added value', which means taking a basic product and making it superior to the competition by providing extras. If, for instance, you are selling a word-processor, you could add value by providing training in how to use it, courses to show how to bolt on extras and prompt customer service for when the machine goes wrong. Added value is generally related to enhanced people skills.

Good times and bad times

Throughout the periods of growth which followed the Industrial Revolution many companies were able to keep their promises to their employees. In the best companies a 'virtuous circle' was set up; because they offered the best career prospects they were able to attract the best people, which led to a greater degree of success in the marketplace, which allowed them to continue to improve the standards of employment which they could offer their people. Rewards were linked to promotion, and salary and benefit increases.

It happened in every boom sector – the oil boom led to the growth of paternalistic giants like Shell and BP; the retailing boom has led to the exceptional career opportunities offered by companies like Marks and Spencer and the John Lewis Partnership; the information technology revolution led to IBM becoming the biggest and most powerful company in the world, able to offer its people the best of everything.

But every sector is subject to cycles, and just as these philosophies of paternalism flourish in times of growth and prosperity, so they begin to collapse during times of recession and contraction. Any company which has a philosophy of never firing employees, for instance, will eventually end up with a thick stack of dead wood. It may be high-calibre dead wood, but it is still an overhead which has to be cut back when times are hard.

It happens in every sector, and every time it occurs the shock is enormous, both inside and outside the companies. In 1991 we heard the news that Marks and Spencer were going to be laying people off in large numbers. Not only were people within the company horrified at this perceived betrayal of trust and loyalty, but the outside world, which had perceived for so long that the company nurtured the careers of its employees, was also shaken and disappointed. In the same year one of the world's biggest computer companies asked for early retirement volunteers, and it was reported that 17,000 people stepped forward, anxious to abandon ship.

The days when any company could afford to take a paternalistic attitude towards staff are now over. Things are changing fast, and someone whose skills make them a valuable employee today, could find that their skills are out of date tomorrow through no fault of their own. Technology is simply moving too fast to be able to predict what will happen in 5 years' time, let alone the 30 or 40 years that someone might traditionally have spent working for a company.

Job security

Job security is a thing of the past. Everyone knows of someone close to them who has experienced redundancy. They may be of any age when it happens, and for some it is an experience which is to be repeated twice or even three times during their careers.

The City and financial institutions have been considered highly secure in the past, with someone joining a bank straight from school or university and then working their way steadily to the top, well looked after from the post room to the board room. Things have changed, profits have plummeted and automation has been a major contributory factor in the cutting of staff.

Public sector employers were also traditionally known to provide highly secure employment. When someone went in they knew they had a job for life. Because organisations were so large they were able to move people around and give them a broad range of experience. But just as private companies have had to cut back, so the public sector has been forced, by government scrutiny of their budgets, to cut costs, putting work out to private tender and ensuring that every aspect of their operations is cost-effective. People, therefore, who have always been cosseted within this environment, suddenly find themselves having to rethink their whole lives.

The initial reaction to these problems has, quite naturally, often been to treat the *symptoms*. Outplacement consultancies, for instance, have sprung up to help companies to assist their people to find new jobs; massive retraining schemes have been undertaken and a host of professional advisers have appeared on the market to help the unemployed with everything from writing better CVs to setting up their own businesses.

The fundamental *cause* of the problem, however, has still to be addressed by most people, and that is our attitude to careers. Until we understand ourselves and the way that we fit into the world of work, we cannot hope to be truly secure, nor can we rely in the future on achieving success in the traditional ways.

The future

There are a number of management gurus around predicting how things are going to be by the year 2000, from Tom Peters to Professor Charles Handy. While many of their opinions differ, there are some broad predictions which seem to run in parallel.

Organisations, for instance, are already becoming much flatter, with layers of management being stripped out and decision-making responsibilities being pushed much further down the ladder. This is a trend which is gathering speed as companies are forced into being more cost-effective. Fewer people are consequently needed to achieve the same results. The people who are left, however, do have to work much harder, with 'burn-out' being expected at a much earlier age.

The resulting work structure has been described by Charles Handy in his book, *The Age of Unreason*, as 'the shamrock', with one leaf for the 'core' of the business, the second leaf made up of contractors, either self-employed or running their own small businesses, and the third being the flexible labour force, brought in only when there is a demand for their skills.

The predicted career pattern for the future is that you will be recruited into a core business from university or some type of vocational training in your early to mid 20s. Here the pressure will be intense because everything will be cut back to the most minimal requirement. Time spent in the core will be relatively short, either until your skills have become outdated or you have reached 'burn-out'.

This will trigger a move, maybe to retraining or to working in a more flexible and less pressurised way. Perhaps you might end up acting as a freelance consultant to a number of core businesses or running your own niche type of operation, or spending time in training others, giving time to the voluntary sector, or pursuing some creative activity.

Someone, therefore, who has worked at the core of a company in the marketing department might move out in order to become a public relations consultant, a copywriter, an organiser of corporate hospitality or any one of a number of related fields. Equally, the same person might make a complete change and decide to run a hotel somewhere or perhaps a market garden. These sorts of changes in direction will soon become commonplace – in fact it is already happening.

As organisations become flatter people will not face the same challenges of climbing to the top of the tree, which previously kept them occupied throughout their careers. In fact, there will be fewer and fewer key positions. At Unilever, for instance, there are only four grades between graduate and chief executive.

People will therefore need to look for other ways to stimulate their interests and their ambitions. This problem already arises in the academic world. In universities there are only four levels between junior lecturer and professor. Staff who are stuck on plateaus for long periods remain motivated by doing research work, taking sabbaticals, travelling or writing.

A similar pattern will need to emerge within companies if they want to keep people motivated and realising their full potential. They will have to have some extremely creative ideas because the traditional goals have been strong motivators. All this requires a complete change of attitude on the part of organisations and employees equally.

CHAPTER 2

CAREER ISSUES

So what are some of the career issues that make you feel uncomfortable at work and alert you to the need to do something about your situation?

Professor Cary Cooper, a psychologist at Manchester University, has conducted numerous research projects into stress. He has found that certain ages in your life are 'borders' through which you have to pass. These phases bring about changes in feelings, attitudes, needs and values which affect how you react to different things. Borders can have a significant influence on your career and raise a number of issues which make you feel unhappy, discontented or perplexed. Often we are uncertain about what these inner feelings mean.

From my experience, people often make career moves without knowing the real reason why they are doing so. You may think that the problem is lack of promotion opportunities for instance, but the real issue may be boredom or lack of stimulation. If you don't know what the reasons are there is a danger that you will repeat the same story over and over again.

The recession of the late 1980s and early 1990s in Britain halted job movement. With the upturn in the economy more jobs are now becoming available and there has been a panic in the recruitment world. Some people have made bad career moves because they have not been totally clear about the real reason why they should move.

This chapter should help you to identify some of the real issues which are making you feel uncomfortable at work, and will help you to open your mind in order to explore the alternatives and avoid some of the pitfalls.

Are you taking the wrong direction?

This issue most often raises its head early on in a career, probably when you are in your 20s. Your 20s are an especially significant borderline, because it is a time when you are faced with many important decisions that will affect you for many years. Other people are already beginning to see you in certain ways, e.g. 'Clare's very practical', 'Ann's extremely good with people', or 'Jason's exceptionally gifted with figures'. Already you are beginning to be pigeon-holed into a certain way of thinking and before long you can find yourself swept along on a wave that doesn't really feel right for you, but because you cannot see other, related alternatives, you go with the swell.

It is all too easy to be pushed into taking career decisions as soon as you finish your formal education, or even earlier, which for many people is too soon to have a clear picture of what they want or what they are best suited for. The danger then is that having taken certain decisions, and made some progress, you may be loath to give up the ground you have gained, or simply not have time to think about what you really want. If you don't face up to the issue at an early stage, it can lead to greater unhappiness later on.

Jane, for instance, was always good at art and she had a keen interest in fashion. At art school she enjoyed her studies and did well, achieving a good first-class degree. She easily found a job in the fashion world because she had flair and talent. Before long she was earning good money and had developed an exciting and lavish lifestyle. Underneath she began to despise the rat race with its shallow values, but she was trapped. Her answer was to work and play harder in an attempt to lose herself and forget the nagging unhappiness. This could only make the problem worse. She should have stopped to evaluate the situation, take stock and maybe change role before it was too late.

Stephen took a different direction. He had been good at a variety of subjects, but when it came to choosing A levels, his school had a strong tradition in the sciences and he was channelled into chemistry, physics and biology. He achieved three A grades and went to university to read polymer science.

His career started as a graduate trainee with a large chemical company. He progressed rapidly down the technical path and was extremely successful, discovering an amazing new process. Although he was outwardly successful he felt trapped in such a narrow, specialist furrow. He wanted to widen his experience, but traditional career paths in the industry did not allow for this transfer between different functions. In his early 30s Stephen made a very brave career change, leaving the chemical multinational to join an American fast-moving-consumer-goods (FMCG) company as a brand manager.

Unlike Jane, Stephen took the step to evaluate his career needs and make the appropriate changes, which brought him greater fulfilment and happiness.

In this case, Stephen's career change was certainly made easier by the salary increase which he received, but this is not generally so because lack of experience usually warrants a drop in salary which, hopefully, can soon be rectified if finance is an important career need.

Regular self-assessment will help to ensure that you are going in the right direction. If you feel you are going in the wrong direction you could take some expert advice and try to clarify in your mind what the right direction would be. You must not be afraid to take the necessary steps. Turning a blind eye to the situation will not improve it. Inaction will build up the problem until it becomes a crisis issue.

Are you rising too far, too fast?

It is sometimes possible to go too far, too fast, finding that you have achieved more than your peer group, and that you are suddenly asking yourself 'what is there left to do now?' Many of the satisfactions which careers offer come from setting goals and then achieving them. If they are all achieved too easily you can be left with a feeling of anti-climax.

Mary-Jane was the communications director for a high-profile media consultancy. She had always been a high achiever, with exceptional results at school, an Oxford entrance exam and a First in French. During the milk round she was offered a number of jobs, but decided to accept a position with an advertising agency. She was highly successful. Her career flourished and she was head-hunted into three positions during the next 10 years. She worked incredibly hard and was recompensed lavishly.

Outwardly, she was a shining example of a woman who had succeeded and was destined for an ever-increasing, highly visible, career profile, but suddenly she stopped. She was 39 years old and she felt that her life was out of balance. Having moved up so fast she hadn't had time to attend to the other aspects of her life. She had achieved everything she thought she wanted, so what should she do next? Her priorities had changed but because she had been moving up so fast she hadn't been able to adapt her life to satisfy these changes, or even to notice that they were happening.

The answer to this type of situation will depend upon what the individual wants from life. It requires a radical rethink of your values and some research into the various alternatives open to you. It may then require a complete change of direction, or it may mean a change of emphasis to other aspects of your life outside work.

Have you reached a plateau?

This is a problem which has traditionally struck people during their 40s, when they have progressed as far up a company as they are likely to go and yet they can see another 20 years of working life ahead of them. In the future, however, the plateau is likely to be reached much earlier and much more frequently in everyone's careers.

As organisations become flatter people will reach ceilings more quickly because the ladders to the top will be shorter. An entire career is unlikely to be spent scrambling to the top of a company if there are only three or four layers of management to get through.

15

The first step is to understand what is happening. Only when you have realised that you are not going to get any further where you are, can you begin to look at alternatives.

You have to decide whether you are prepared to undergo a change or whether you would prefer to stay where you are. If the thought of embarking on a new career, with a new set of people, in a new field, is too daunting, then you have to look at the possibilities within your existing environment. Do your current employers have anything else which they could offer you?

Many people are frightened to ask, believing that if the answer is 'No' they will have shown that they are dissatisfied with what they have got, and will be shown the door. In reality many companies are pleased to have employees who are looking for new challenges, but who still want to stay with the organisation.

The problem here is that employers who are used to seeing you wearing one hat may have trouble imagining you doing something else. If you have always worked in finance and you would like to have a go at selling you may have trouble convincing them that you can do it. It is, however, often easier to try to persuade your present employer, as an initial step, before starting to look elsewhere, because you have a track record which is known. People are generally more inclined to take a risk with someone they know.

Alternatively, it may be that there simply aren't any other opportunities which would suit you within your current organisation. If that is the case and you still don't want to move, then you are going to have to accept that your job is not going to be the part of your life which offers you the greatest challenges and excitements. You will then have to look at your whole life, analyse your values and skills, and look for other avenues of stimulation – perhaps through learning a new skill, voluntary work, a new hobby or secondment to another organisation.

Are you bored?

Many people believe that it is the responsibility of the organisation for which they work to keep them stimulated and interested in their jobs. In fact, this does not have to be the case.

All too often people start looking around for new jobs simply because they feel bored with what they have. They don't actually work out why they are bored or whether there is anything they can do about it themselves. Moving on is not always the answer.

Dawn worked as an administrator. She was highly competent at her job and felt that she could not progress in any particular direction. She was full of complaints about how 'they were not interested in her' and 'they didn't offer her any new challenges'. She was totally apathetic towards her job, a feeling she had not experienced before, being generally very competent. The situation was becoming serious and beginning to affect her health. She had started taking days off work because of her feelings of inadequacy.

When she analysed her skills and values, and worked out what she truly wanted to do with her life, her current job fitted her perfectly, so all she had to do was find a new challenge.

She thought about what really interested her and identified an area of innovation that would provide a new challenge. She planned a campaign strategy which was enthusiastically presented to her boss, who was immediately impressed by this revitalised member of staff. Her suggestions were discussed further and were eventually implemented, with benefit to both the organisation, the staff and Dawn herself.

Suddenly she was motivated and enthusiastic about her work again and dying to get on with it. The boredom was gone and yet she hadn't had to throw away any of the experience, achievements or track record that she had already attained, by moving elsewhere.

Another example is *Heather*, who was working as a secretary. Her boss felt that Heather had a lot of potential, but was likely to leave the company for the wrong reasons. Her complaints were also typical; she felt that no one was interested in her and that all the boring tasks were dumped on to her.

It wasn't until she began to talk about her situation that it dawned on her that she had the power to do something about it herself. With thought she could easily pass one or two of these grotty jobs on to others, spreading the load and leaving herself free to take on new challenges. As long as she saw herself as a victim and was 'whinging' about how other people treated her, she couldn't change anything, but as soon as she started to take control she was able to do whatever she wanted, and went on to develop her job, adding wider and more interesting aspects which she saw as beneficial to her future.

If you have become bored with your job it may be time to look at your needs and priorities, and how they can be satisfied in your current position, rather than immediately looking around for a new job.

Have you been made redundant?

Redundancy is very different from other career issues you may face because it forces you to be reactive rather than proactive. With other issues you have a degree of choice as to whether or not you do something about your situation. Deciding not to act may well be the wrong decision to make, and could actually result in redundancy in the long term.

When you are made redundant you *have* to do something and in many cases people do the wrong thing. They are panicked into taking short-term decisions, because they do not allow enough time to assess the best possible course for them.

I believe that if more individuals practised career management, redundancy could become a thing of the past. People are not made redundant; it is their skills and their jobs that are not required. The skills become surplus to requirements, which means it is time for the people to discard them and get new ones. If you are managing your career correctly you will be constantly assessing whether or not your skills fit with market needs, and you will begin to understand warning signals if things are going wrong long before anyone starts discussing redundancy.

Andrew's 20-year career had been with an organisation which upheld a no-redundancy policy, but he gradually realised that this was no longer realistic in the present economic climate. He started to look at his own situation, assessed his skills and saw that he needed to update and widen his skills base. He studied for a second degree part time and added a vocational qualification, outside his present function, to his repertoire.

This involved a heavy commitment of his own time, but he is now well equipped to move from his present employment to something new when the time is right. Stories like Andrew's will become more and more common in the future.

Once you sense those early warning signals you can begin to be proactive in redefining your job, retraining to make your skills more suitable, or looking around for something new.

Given, however, that this ideal situation will take time to be attained, and that most people at present are only jolted into thinking about their careers when something goes wrong, redundancy will continue to be the single most traumatic career issue for most people.

If, or when, redundancy does happen, it has to be viewed in perspective and seen as an opportunity to move forward, not as a failure or defeat. All too often people who are in this situation rush around trying to find a job exactly like the one they have just lost. The chances are, however, that if that job was no longer relevant in their previous organisation, it may also have a short lifespan in another company. At the very least they will need to add some new or updated skills to their portfolio before trying for a comparable position.

There are obvious exceptions, such as jobs that disappear due to takeovers, resulting in a duplication of posts. In such cases there may be no reason why you shouldn't look for something identical in another organisation. In most cases, however, redundancy can be a time to look carefully at your skills and values, and decide where you want to move next.

Rather than making 'finding a job' your first priority therefore, if you have been made redundant you should start by finding out about yourself and about the alternatives which are open to you. You can then make a long-term plan and set about improving your life, rather than merely repairing the damage and sailing on as before.

For many, redundancy has turned out to be a very positive experience, providing the stimulus they needed to move in another direction. While working as a redundancy counsellor I met many people who found that, once they had dealt with the initial trauma, they moved forward in a positive way, often benefiting from the outplacement experience, and gaining both financially and personally.

Although we often hear about the success stories, it is important to remember that, for many, redundancy is something from which some people never recover. They never regain their shattered self-respect. Many families have been torn apart by the stress of someone job-hunting year in and year out and they are finally defeated by endless rejection.

When you analyse some of the reasons why individuals never recover from the redundancy experience, it is often because their value system has been destroyed. They believed in a job for life, society promoted that view and organisations took control, promising security in return for hard work and loyalty. As attitudes change in this area and people begin to understand that nobody is owed a job indefinitely, the number of serious casualties of redundancy should decrease. As you read on you will discover some helpful strategies to enable you to work with the many changes that may face you in your career.

Is your corporate culture changing?

Every company has a culture, but most of us take it for granted until something goes wrong. If you fit perfectly into the culture of the organisation that employs you, you will not stop to analyse it, you will merely be aware that you like the people around you and agree with the way things are being done.

Where things often go wrong is when a new boss arrives; 'a new broom' who 'likes to do things differently'. When the style of operation changes some people are almost bound to start feeling uncomfortable. They won't necessarily realise what it is that has caused the problem, they will just know that they no longer feel they 'fit' into the company in the way they did before.

It is important to know and recognise what your needs are. What sort of culture are you comfortable in? What makes you uncomfortable?

These are hard questions to answer, since it is often the unspoken things which mean most to you. Are you, for instance, comfortable in a company that has a rigid structure or do you prefer just to get on with things? Do you find that a large number of meetings makes you feel secure or insecure? Would you prefer to have a boss who likes to keep control of everything or do you like to take your own decisions and your own risks? Do you prefer working exclusively in one area or do you seek variety?

All these things will become important if your environment is gradually changing. It is far better for you to understand how things are changing and to plan what you are going to do about it before there is a confrontation.

In his book, *The Age of Unreason*, Charles Handy tells the story of a frog which, when put in cold water, will not try to escape when the water is heated gradually. It will stay there until eventually it is boiled to death. If the same frog was dropped straight into boiling water, however, it would hop straight out again. In other words, if change is gradual enough we will adapt to it and grow used to it, even if it is not the best thing for us – we may not even notice it is happening. A sudden shock, or 'discontinuity' as Handy calls it, may seem like a catastrophe at the time, but if it causes you to take evasive action it can be beneficial.

You often hear people saying, once a crisis has passed, 'Well it all turned out for the best in the end'. What seemed like a disaster at the time may be necessary to jolt you out of your apathy or to open your eyes to just how badly things are going. It happens in personal relationships in just the same way, with one partner assuming that everything is going all right until the other suddenly gets up and leaves.

It may be that there is room for some change and adaptation. Alternatively, it may be unreasonable to believe that you will ever be happy in that particular changed environment and you should start thinking about making a change before a cultural clash damages your career. If you know what it is that you need from your work, you will be able to make your needs known to those around you, and if they cannot accommodate them, and you cannot make the necessary compromises, then it is time to move.

One thing is definite, if you begin to feel uncomfortable at work, ignoring the situation and hoping it will pass is not the answer. The status quo will not return. 'Times are a-changing' and we must recognise this fact.

Do you/don't you play office politics?

Anyone who claims that they don't believe in office politics is making a serious admission of naïvety. Anyone who knows that they exist but chooses to ignore them, does so at their peril.

Research conducted by Henley Management Centre and Pauline Hyde and Associates in the 1980s to identify if people being made redundant had anything in common, revealed what they called the 'N' factor. Based on psychometric tests, the research revealed that a high number of redundant people were free thinkers, talented entrepreneurs and doers, but politically naïve. They were people who wanted to keep their heads down, to get on with the job and did not realise that while they were doing that, other people were playing political games around them.

Everyone has to learn to understand the issues around company politics. They need to be aware of what is going on around them and to find ways in which they can fit in, and to be aware that during periods of change company politics are at their deadliest.

Paul, for instance, couldn't understand why he had lost his job because he was skilled, conscientious and successful. When he analysed the situation in more detail he admitted that many of his colleagues, including his boss, liked to go to the pub after work. Because he didn't like pubs and because he had a long drive home, he had declined to join them.

Not only had he rejected his boss and peer group by doing this, but also formal meetings were not part of the department's culture, so he had ensured that he was not around when important group interplay was going on and information was being communicated. He lost touch with what was happening in the department and so was eventually eased out. Paul paid the expensive price of ignoring and rebuffing the departmental culture. Initially he said that he couldn't 'play' the company politics, but after much discussion he understood how foolhardy it can be to ignore them totally.

If you find company politics difficult you need to know more about yourself so that you understand to what degree you are prepared to 'play'. It is also about improving your own self-awareness, which will then automatically enhance your awareness for what is going on around you in your situation.

Is the grass always greener?

Anyone who is dissatisfied with their job in any way tends to think that everything will be better if they move to another company. They think they will earn more, be treated better, have better opportunities and all the rest.

In reality, most people who are dissatisfied with what they have in one company, tend to carry those dissatisfactions with them. Instead of analysing what it is that they are really dissatisfied with in their existing situations, they move on to something new. People are attracted to the familiar; they tend to choose companies or situations which are similar to the ones they have just left. And when the 'honeymoon' period is over they find that they are in exactly the same position as before.

Jane spent the first eight years of her career jumping the fence to greener pastures. After her sixth job and a warning that she was becoming a 'job hopper', she began to see the light, and to understand what the problem really was. She always needed a challenge and when she achieved the set targets in one job she looked around for the next mountain. Unfortunately, she only knew one mountain range and quickly became accustomed to its climate and terrain. When she moved to a new discipline and started to use a new range of skills which stretched her in different ways, she became more satisfied and her boredom syndrome passed.

If you find that you are constantly looking over the fence at other pastures, believing that they offer you more than you have at the moment, start by working out exactly what it is that you are dissatisfied with. Then consider if you can do anything to put those problems right. Supposing, for instance, that you are a secretary and you are hoping for promotion to something more interesting. The chances are that an employer who already knows that you are hard-working, creative and friendly, is more likely to give you a chance than someone who has nothing to judge but a written account of your past record, which shows that you are only experienced in secretarial work.

In career management terms, moving jobs should relate to a positive reason for making the change, i.e. you need to gain more experience in a different organisation or discipline, or to expand your skills, not to a feeling of pique because you are not receiving what you want.

Are your values/needs changing?

Are you fed up with toeing the company line?

People's values change as they mature. Things that seemed enormously important at 25 are less important when you are 55. All through your life you are discovering new things about yourself. The more things you experience the more other things come into perspective and the less important they seem. They may be changing so gradually, however, that, like the frog in the boiling water, you don't notice until it's too late.

Research conducted into the attitudes of men at 'around 40-ish' towards work (there has been nothing comparable done on women yet), shows that there is a tendency for men of that age to grow tired of toeing the company line and to start to be more concerned about being an individual. At this age, however, they often have high incomes and expensive lifestyles, which can mean that they are trapped in jobs which they thought they wanted 10 years before.

The result is that a number of men at this age can go off the rails and experience a mid-life crisis, or they can leave their jobs and go off to do something totally different which they find fulfilling, despite a possible drop in their status or earning power.

Values usually only come into question when something goes wrong, e.g. a new boss won't give you the freedom to take the decisions that you used to, or you are very creative and the culture at work doesn't allow you the scope to make changes. If you are clear from the start what your values are you will be able to make better judgements about the jobs and conditions which will work for you. Losing or neglecting one of your values will always be painful.

Monitoring your work values can help you avoid the reactive situation, giving you insight and some pre-warning that things are changing for you. When this is evaluated against the company or job situation it can give you some clues, in advance, of what might be the right course of action.

Do your work and family balance?

The area which causes the most conflict for people in their careers is the balance between working life and family life. As people start having children they tend to want to spend more time with them and to resent employers who make unreasonable demands on their time. These are the same employers who might have seemed dynamic and exciting a few years before, offering opportunities for growth and stimulation. It is a problem which besets everyone, even those with the most exciting jobs.

A survey carried out by the Centre for Business Psychology at the University of Manchester Institute of Science and Technology, found that the single most stressful feature in the lives of 120 chief executives who represented the largest industrial companies in Europe, was that their jobs seriously interfered with their family and private lives.

This issue will grow more troublesome as organisations become leaner and more efficient. Everyone with a job inside an organisation will have to work harder, but there is at present a debate about whether this means working longer hours. Some companies are exploring the effective deployment of time. One German company based in Britain is questioning closely any executive who regularly stays in the office after 6 p.m.

The family/work balance will become more and more of an issue, as will the quality of life debate. Knowing how you relate to these issues prior to crisis time will help to give you advance warning and perhaps some insights into making minor adjustments in preparation.

Do you want to be a high flier?

When a company marks someone out as a potential high flier, that person is usually young, flattered and willing to allow the company to map out their future for them. At the beginning they probably do think that this is the best way to go, although even they may feel pangs of concern if too much control over their own future is taken away from them.

As they are pushed along in the fast lane they are often not given time to think about themselves and what they really want from life, and many of their options are lost because they do exactly as the company wants.

It all works out fine until the high flier starts to have doubts, or changes come about in their values which make them question what they really want. If they do begin to question their situations they might find that the alternatives open to them are more limited than to someone who has travelled more slowly up the corporate ladder, but has retained control over their own destiny.

Tom had been a high flier all his business life, eventually becoming managing director of a famous 'blue chip' company. He had experienced success all his working life. Sadly he discovered right at the end of his career that he had in fact never made a career decision himself; all his decisions had been made by other people and he had just gone along with their advice and suggestions without questioning them. Looking back, he felt he had always done things that came easily, that he had never really been stretched to his full potential or given the freedom to develop new skills.

It is hard to resist such flattering attentions early in your career, and it requires considerable strength of character to ask yourself continually if your values are being satisfied when everything on the surface appears to be going so well. However, taking stock and assessing your objectives can ensure that your needs are being accommodated as well as your organisation's.

Is age a problem?

Age is only a problem in the context of changing values. A job you are doing quite happily when you are 20 might seem less appropriate 30 years later.

During the 1980s there was a fashion for youth and many companies started to get rid of everyone over 50, or even over 40. The errors of that philosophy are now beginning to be recognised and employers now realise that age and experience probably mean that people have more to offer, not less. There is also the problem, when losing all the older people, that there are no role models left for younger staff to follow.

Role models are very important in career terms, especially in the development of junior staff. We all learn from the example of others. If there is nobody above us to 'copy', we cannot assimilate the cultural values of the organisation.

People generally say that age is an issue for them when they don't feel they have enough to offer, e.g. 'I'm 45 years old and I've only ever worked for one organisation'. But really age is only an issue if you are obsessed by your advancing years and you truly believe it is a problem. It is the only thing in career terms that you can do nothing about; it is a fact of life.

You have two options available, the positive view that age brings a wealth of experience, or the opposite – that you are a has-been. If, during your career, you have been open to change, then your value is that much greater because you can easily demonstrate your ability to be flexible. If this is not the case then it's certainly not too late to learn if you are willing to change your attitudes and adopt a more flexible approach.

If you are able to be flexible then age will not be a stumbling block. It may not be easy and you will have to persevere, but if you have a flexible and determined view that you do have valuable skills to offer, you will be a success. Negative thoughts bring about negative results.

Are you too good at your job?

Sometimes being too good at your job can be a career block. If you are good at selling, and contribute a lot to your employer's bottom line, they are going to be very reluctant to move you on to something else.

It may be that they are right, and that you would be better to come to terms with your limitations and stick to doing what you are good at. If, however, you have thought long and hard about it, and you still want to make it clear to your employers that if you don't get the opportunity from them you will look for it elsewhere, which is often a very difficult matter to raise. You might offer to go back to your original job if you do not prove to be as successful at the new one as you believe you will be. Or you could strike a balance between spending some time with the old job and some time developing a new skill. This may be linked to imparting your strengths to other employees.

Is there no way up?

Sometimes it becomes obvious that you are not going to get any higher until someone above you leaves the company or dies. If everyone is healthy and under 50, that may suggest that it is time for you to look for a new ladder to the top. If climbing higher is what you want to do you may have to rethink your strategy by making a sideways move, possibly even taking a temporary drop in status or salary before you can get your career moving again. To do this you need to have a clear idea of what your skills are and how transferable they are.

But moving up may not always be the right answer. More and more, as tiers of management are stripped from organisations, 'up' is no longer always possible. So you may need to consider other alternatives.

People can feel extremely frustrated if they believe they have the potential to do more, but they can't seem to get out of the rut they have fallen into. Often the problem will arise when an employer likes to label people – a 'secretary', for instance, is just that and nothing else. This was the problem with Lynne. Because she was so good at being a secretary, her boss felt very threatened whenever she talked about wanting to become a consultant. He relied on her so much in her current role that he refused to listen to any of her frustrations.

These frustrations are often caused by the fact that most people just drift into their careers. They do not make conscious choices and so many end up thinking 'There must be something else to life, there must be more I can do.' If career management was something which young people were encouraged to think about at the beginning, they would be less likely to get themselves into these culs-de-sac, which waste time and potential and cause frustration and unhappiness. They would be able to find instead something that fits their values and skills.

Do you lack qualifications?

Often people feel that a lack of qualifications is a barrier to getting any further in their careers. As you get older, however, experience becomes more important than exam results. People who get hung up about qualifications need to confront the issue and decide if it is important for them. If you truly believe that your lack of paper qualifications is making you feel inadequate, then you simply have to do something about it, whether it is through the Open University, evening classes or correspondence courses. There is no point in wasting time and energy complaining about it if there is something you can do to remedy the situation. Anyone who doesn't act to put the situation right is failing to take control of their own career, and is allowing other people to block their progress,

If you feel that your lack of qualifications is a problem, look closely and consider if it is the real issue. Many times it is a screen for lack of confidence. Not knowing your own worth can make the feeling worse, and not having the right qualifications is a good, safe label to pin on yourself to prevent action.

When should you take a career break?

Career breaks for having and bringing up children are becoming more of an issue all the time. In the past, women had these breaks thrust upon them, and they just took them without looking at them in terms of their career. So now there are a large number of women wanting to return to work after an enforced career break of anything up to 10 or 15 years. Often they have done nothing during these years to keep up their skills. They just left work, looked after children and suddenly decided that they wanted to go back to work again. They all assume that looking after children will have no relevance to the job market, but actually the skills that they use in organising, planning, budgeting and running a home are important and relevant.

What they tend not to keep up to date with are the technical skills and knowledge about what has been happening in their industry sector. This gap in their knowledge could be avoided by simply staying in touch, continuing to read trade magazines, and perhaps even attending a few seminars and conferences.

In career terms everyone is quick to label and with each label there are a number of assumptions and prejudices. These barriers need to be broken down if the goal of transferring skills is to be achieved. One helpful move is to understand skills in a generic way, rather than sticking to functional labels. This can certainly help a housewife and mother because when she analyses the skills she has utilised in the job in a generic way, she will often find that she is far better skilled than many financial controllers, personnel officers, distribution clerks and administration managers.

In the future women will be more able to plan for career breaks. They will be able to decide when they will take the break and how they will do it. They will then need help in planning what they are going to do and finding out what things they need to consider before making decisions.

It is likely that men will also be given more opportunities to take this sort of break. It is already happening in America and Europe, where some employers are allowing 'Daddy breaks', albeit short ones, so that men can be at home to help during the crucial months after the birth.

Are you committing career suicide?

Certain people dig their own graves in career terms because they are not prepared to face reality. *Ted*, a highly qualified and experienced technical expert in a chemical company became a casualty of a company merger. But this was not the only reason for Ted losing his job; he had made a significant contribution to his own demise.

He had not kept himself up to date with new advances in his highly specialised field, nor had he widened his skills base to gain current management skills. All his efforts were channelled into working in the old ways, using traditional and tested methods. When challenged about this by his manager he became very defensive, dug his heels in and clung even more tightly to the past. Gradually he became more and more of a dinosaur in the new and changing culture.

On reflection Ted could see what had happened, but he strongly believed in the responsibility of the organisation to advance and enhance its staff. It had never occurred to him that he had any input into the situation.

'Whinge mode'

Almost any of the career issues examined above can send us into 'whinge mode'. Instead of doing something constructive to put things right, we blame everyone and everything around us.

Do you find yourself saying any of the following?

'Nobody understands how hard I work.'

'My boss doesn't let me do anything off my own bat.'

'I'm good at marketing, but nobody lets me do it.'

'I never get any of the exciting jobs.'

'I have lots of ideas but nobody listens.'

Nothing alienates colleagues or superiors more than a constant stream of negative statements. People very quickly turn off, and you get excluded from any forward planning or positive thinking. You begin to seem like a loser, then you act the part and before too long your feelings become a negative reality.

If this is you, then stop whinging and start to discover why you are so unhappy. Then you can take action yourself. A positive suggestion will always get a fair hearing if you know the right way to present it. You may not achieve total success, but there is a good chance that you will move a situation forward in some way. Complaining is such a waste of energy.

Next time you experience emotions of anger or frustration because you have to tackle another unpleasant task, just measure how much energy is being used and notice the draining feeling as you sit behind your desk. All this valuable drive is being utilised to no result. Positive action needs energy, but because of the nature of the activity it creates more energy. Negative action, on the other hand, drains energy until there is nothing left. In very acute situations this can lead to taking days off because you are so tired, and eventually somebody else takes charge and makes decisions which are out of your control.

These are some of the issues which can crop up in everyone's career at some time. For some people they will become enormous problems which will spoil large chunks of their lives, while others will be quicker to diagnose their problems and to act to put them right. Hopefully some of the examples cited will have helped you to gain more insight into your own situation.

A problem shared

If you identify with any of the above issues at this moment, it may be wise to talk about the situation before taking action, because sharing a problem can often help you get things into perspective, and maybe to see a course of action previously hidden. Using a sounding board to allow you to air your career issues is a valuable activity, but you must be careful to whom you choose to speak. Consider what agenda the other person will bring to the conversation.

Speaking to someone from your company has the advantage of the person understanding the situation and the context, but there are always issues about confidentiality to consider. An outsider will tip the balance the other way. If the issue has major implications for your career, it may be a good idea to seek professional guidance and you will find that the investment will certainly yield a good return.

Is your career already planned?

'Oh, my career is well thought out,' you may say, 'I went on two training courses last year, and I've got my eye on the boss's job, and he should be retiring in a few years, or getting kicked upstairs even sooner than that. I can see clearly where I'm going, don't worry about me.'

Wrong, danger signals!

Training courses are usually functionally based, and they are more than likely related to the job you are doing now, chosen to help you do it better in some way. They are unlikely to be related to your own long-term development. But suppose you are actually in the wrong job altogether? Then going on courses is merely distracting you from the fundamental truth that you should be somewhere completely different, doing something else entirely.

Training courses paid for by companies are usually to do with your job and not very often to do with you. Also, they are often not well thought out or planned to suit your individual needs. I recently heard about a managing director who realised that the training budget in his company was very low, so he approached a training company and purchased a job lot of programmes, which were then given to all the managers in the company, with no discussion with individuals as to whether they needed any of the training. Although this is an extreme example, this sort of approach to training is all too common in companies, who believe that you can buy it by the pound.

And all this stuff about getting the boss's job; are you just assuming that they are going to give it to you when it becomes available, or do you have a guarantee in writing?

Suppose they decide to make you redundant before the boss retires? Suppose they decide to restructure the company when he does go, making it unnecessary to replace him at all? Or the company may be acquired by or merged with another operation, making you surplus to requirements.

Even if things do go as you plan, are you sure that you want to do the boss's job, or that you are capable of it? Just because it is the next step up the ladder doesn't mean that it is right for you. You might be fundamentally unsuited to it.

Remember . . .

- We all have certain unanswered questions about our future.
- What many of us neglect to acknowledge is that we have far more potential and power than we know.
- Whatever your issue is, you can find a positive solution if you are prepared to take control.

3

WHAT IS CAREER MANAGEMENT?

Career management is a philosophy, a way of thinking, an attitude of mind. It is also a process through which you move. For many people it requires a radical change in their thinking about themselves and their work.

It is not a formula which anyone can pick up and put on, like a new suit of clothes, it is a formula which, once experienced, will begin to change the way you view yourself and the world around you. Career management is something which is going to be with you throughout your life, just like the management of your personal finances or your family relationships. It is something which grows and develops with you, and the more effort you invest, the greater will be your success.

Start by asking yourself this question: 'How much time and money have I invested in my career during the last 12 months? The chances are that your answer is 'Not much'. You should almost certainly be investing far more in your most valuable asset – *yourself*.

If you have children you are probably investing money, time and effort into making sure they get the best education. You are probably taking equally great care with your home and your health. By doing all these things you are recognising the importance of these elements in your life and the lives of those around you.

You will probably also make financial investments in the form of insurances and pensions in an attempt to give yourself some security for the future. And we have all heard of the great race to buy shares whenever another public body is privatised by the government.

Yet your career is probably the most important thing in your life, and in many cases the happiness and prosperity of your family will depend upon you having a successful one. How much are you investing in this valuable asset?

If your career goes wrong the repercussions will not only be financial. If things are not going well for you in this crucial area you are likely to become frustrated and dissatisfied with every other aspect of your life. It is in your interest, and also the interests of all around you, that you follow a career that is not left to chance.

On average a career spans 44 years and totals some 82,720 hours of a lifetime. Although work is likely to fill almost half an adult's waking hours, most people give it very little strategic thought.

They leave it to chance because they believe that there really isn't anything else they can do and they take a fatalistic approach right from the start. When students finish their education the career guidance available to them is generally scant. The choice of industry or profession is made because there are vacancies around at the time, or they take the first job that is offered to them. In some cases it is even more haphazard than that, with a first job being offered on the strength of some friend or relative putting in a good word.

Most people spend more time on deciding where to spend their two-week annual holiday than they devote to major career decisions.

Instead of finding out what they can do and then looking for jobs which will give them the opportunity to exercise and develop their skills, people stumble into the first thing they are offered and then try to mould themselves to fit the situation in which they find themselves.

They often only change direction when forced to by outside circumstances, like being fired or moving to a different area. Sometimes they move on for no better reason than that they feel like a change of scene.

In certain cases young people may give some thought to their future working life right at the beginning, when they are choosing a company to work for or a discipline to follow, but that is when they know least about themselves and the real world, and how they are going to fit into it.

...n at the start of a career, at either school or university, ...guidance still tends to be anecdotal. Young people will hear ...ead about people who do certain jobs and are then expected to make a 'divine' decision as to whether that job will suit them. Little real help is given to enable people to make the right match.

In most cases they will invest massive quantities of time and effort into getting the right qualifications for the first job on the ladder which they think will lead them to their desired goals, and will then do virtually no research into themselves or the marketplace before making a decision on which first step to take. They will then follow the path down which this immature decision leads them for the rest of their lives, often feeling frustrated or wondering if there is something else they could have done.

During my years of career counselling I have been forcibly struck by the number of people I have met who say, 'I'm sure I could do something else, but I haven't got a clue what'. I said it myself after 3 years in my first job, but it took me another 11 years to find the answer.

Some people choose a career simply because it provides a large enough income for them to pursue other interests, *Nick* worked for an insurance company, but his real love was the Territorial Army, having been turned down for the regular army on health grounds. He understood where his strengths and values lay, and accepted the reality of his situation, with all its constraints. He was therefore willing to work at a job he didn't particularly enjoy, provided his employers were willing to give him time off for TA activities. He was, in effect, playing at insurance and working at the Territorial Army.

Doing this may or may not be a good trade-off, depending on the degree of compromise involved and the personality of the individual. For most people the chances of making good money are greatly enhanced by being in the right job for their skills, personality and values.

There is seldom an ideal answer to all your career requirements, since there will always be some compromise involved, but by approaching the whole question of careers in a serious, dare I say, scientific manner, the chances of making major errors of judgement are greatly reduced, and the chances of personal contentment and commercial success are maximised. The cost of compromise must never be too high; it must be an even balance for both the employee and the employer or there will be frictions.

How compromise is achieved

Before you make any investment you need to find out what you are investing in, research the market thoroughly and look at all the alternatives in detail. A similar sequence of actions is needed when it comes to investing in your career.

To help you undergo this process I have developed the career management model, which demonstrates the phases that are involved and the sequence which needs to be adopted. A measure of successful career management is the ability to know which phase you are in at this moment. It is a fluid process and you will move in and out of phases as needs and situations dictate.

The career management model

Phase 1   Data collection

The first research must be into yourself. If you do not know yourself you cannot possibly decide what would be the most suitable thing for you to do. You have to do some internal research to find out what you want to do and what you are able to do, analysing your skills, strengths and achievements.

You then have to look at your values or needs. Very few people have ever bothered to analyse what their work values are, or what is actually important to them or contributes most to their happiness.

You also need to assess what limitations, constraints and weaknesses there are to your ambitions, and learn to accept them if there is no way to overcome them, or even turn them into strengths.

The essence of successful career management is to establish a firm foundation on which to build. This rock-solid base will enable you to act in a positive manner, no matter what is placed in front of you. Without this fundamental core you cannot move forward. Remember, career management is a *process*. Unless you get this first phase correctly in place from the start you will always be bothered by emergency repair jobs which will occur at a vital moment when you least want to show weakness or fault in the structure of your career. Time spent now in Phase 1 of the career management model will reap untold rewards in the future.

Phase 2   Exploring options

Once you have collected all the information about yourself and your situation you are then better prepared to start assessing the alternatives which are open to you, and researching the world of work from a vantage point of knowledge. It is important to view your skills and achievements as a 'product' which you are going to market. A major Plc about to launch a new brand will invest large amounts of cash in market research, evaluation of the competition and advertising campaigns. Career management is no different.

Phase 3   Taking action

Once you have a clear idea of what it is you are looking for, and an understanding of the marketplace in which you are going to be selling your services, you can then actually go out looking for the right situation. This, however, is where you come into direct competition with everyone else who is chasing the same goals. Most jobs will involve you in competing against others. There are techniques, which I will cover in Chapter 6, to help with an effective job search, but the secret is to have done all the preliminary research work thoroughly, because then you will have a very real advantage over everyone else.

Phase 4   Maintaining progress

Once you have achieved success you cannot stand still, you have to ensure that events are not overtaking you. This is where most people neglect their careers, doing little to maintain or enhance their advantage. Unfortunately this is the most difficult area in which to achieve success, mainly because we give little value to our own development. We price our own progress very low. The organisation, customer, client and boss generally come first.

No end to the process

Once you have started to understand the philosophy of managing and owning your own career, you will see that it is a process which never ends. Just because you have managed to land a job which suits you this year, doesn't mean that you can sit back and relax for the rest of your life. Both you and the job will be continually changing, and what suits you this year might be totally unsuitable in two years' time.

The only guarantee of continuous success is effort and commitment. There will always be a direct relationship between input and results. The harder you work the greater will be the rewards.

To ensure success you must progress through the career management model in a logical and systematic manner. Behind each phase are a number of tools or techniques which are especially useful to that specific phase, although there are a number that are general to the whole process.

Core techniques

There are certain core techniques which are extremely useful when applied to career management.

Active listening when discussing your career
   reflecting
   paraphrasing
   asking open questions
   being non-judgemental
Focusing
Exploring new perspectives and alternative frameworks
Empathy
Sharing experiences
Divergent thinking
Decision-making
Problem-solving
Knowledge of resources
Goal-setting

These core techniques will be explained in more detail as you progress through the four phases.

To gain a full understanding of career management you need to understand first the philosophy, which is about taking responsibility for your own career and entering into a partnership with your superiors. Secondly, you should understand the principles which underpin this, involving:

- self-knowledge;
- ownership;
- empowerment;
- proactivity.

To implement the philosophy requires a raft of skills at each phase of the model, but these generally fall into the following areas:

- identifying potential;
- raising self-awareness;
- handling change;
- facing reality;
- enhancing confidence;
- transferring skills;
- taking action;
- extending vision.

Remember . . .

- Career management is about you taking responsibility.
- Given future predictions, there really is nobody you should trust with your most valuable asset.
- Your potential is greater than you know.

PHASE 1

CHAPTER 4

SELF-KNOWLEDGE

What you need to know

Self-knowledge is an important part of Phase 1 and the foundation stone of a successful career. Without it it is impossible to take control or be responsible for your own destiny. It is also important for other aspects of personal happiness and fulfilment.

- Until you know what you are capable of, you cannot make valid choices, market yourself or negotiate to achieve what you want.

- Until you know yourself you can't possibly make decisions about the best courses for you to follow to achieve success.

- Until you know, and like, yourself it is difficult to form relationships with other people.

Many people make the mistake of believing that all the ingredients for their success lie in the company around them, whereas in fact they all lie within yourself as an individual. A company is just a collection of individuals who, hopefully, share common goals. Each individual has to contribute to the overall effort, but success is down to the individual, not some magic formula held by the company. You therefore need to know what you have within you which will be useful in achieving the common goals, as well as your own goals. To discover what this is you need to explore in some depth. That does not mean thinking about it for a few minutes and then getting on with other things, it means spending time and effort on the analysis.

Owning your own skills

Now let's start to explore. You need to find out as much about *you* as possible. Remember, 'knowledge is power', and the more you know about yourself the more control you will have over your environment.

The first step is to define what your skills are and then to 'own them'. This means knowing that you have them, knowing that they are good and not apologising for them.

You need to be able to say, for example, 'I am a good manager because I am able to initiate and motivate people.' That is different from saying 'I am a good manager because I have worked for Unilever for 20 years' or 'I am a good manager because I have an MBA'. You are a good manager because of what is within you, not because of your external circumstances.

Before you can own your skills you need to understand that they are an intrinsic part of you. No matter where you go or what you do, you always take them with you. If the company you work for ceases to function, your skills are still intact – you can walk out of your current job as the same person, with exactly the same skills to sell and nobody can take those skills away. If you believe that you only have these skills because you work for that company, you will feel that you have ceased to exist when your job changes.

Most people find this change of thinking very difficult, whether from modesty or because of traditional conditioning. They tend to say things like 'I've been successful because I was in the right place at the right time,' or 'I have been successful, but then I've always been able to work with the best people', or 'I just had some lucky breaks'.

By subscribing to the luck theory you are rejecting your own individual input. *Alan*, a very successful financial controller, attributed all his success to being in the 'right place at the right time'. He completely ignored the fact that he was extremely gifted. His IQ was in the top 10 per cent and he had achieved many successes, entirely as a result of his own skills. He took a long time recognising this, but until he did he could not completely take charge of his own career and move forward.

Overcome your modesty

So, begin by shaking off your modesty. First, start to recognise that this modesty exists and convince yourself of its worthlessness. If you begin by doing this in private you will begin to overcome the fear that you will be perceived as being boastful. Then, once you are more confident of your abilities, you will be able to talk about them to other people.

The British culture erects a difficult barrier in this area. We are a race renowned for our modesty. The Americans are much better at proclaiming their self-worth, so much so that they are known in Britain for being brash and 'over the top'. This is not what is advocated in career management. What is aimed for is an honest statement about what is fact, accurately presented by you to other people.

It will be very helpful to involve someone else at this early stage, as long as it is the right person. It needs to be someone you feel completely at ease with, and who you are not afraid will put you down. Ideally it will be someone who either knows you quite well or who has some career counselling skills.

Understanding your skills

Before you start to explore self-knowledge further, it may be helpful to clarify the meanings of some words which are frequently used in skills analysis. This will allow you to develop a common understanding and terminology.

Read through the words below *now*, but return to them as you progress your own analysis to ensure that you have a full understanding of the words you are using.

If at any time you do not agree with the meaning of any word explained in this book, do not hesitate to challenge it and find your own meaning, one with which you are more comfortable. This is very important – don't follow anything slavishly but work it out for yourself. This will give you ownership of your own success.

(The list of skills has been adapted from the Herrman Test).

Analytic The ability to break down things and ideas into component parts, looking at them closely in order to understand how they fit together, and why.

Artistic   Being skilful at painting, drawing, designing, music or sculpture, and getting enjoyment from your efforts. It also applies to the ability to co-ordinate colours, designs and textures successfully.

Conceptual   Being able to conceive thoughts and ideas and to take specific facts and see what they mean in a broader, more general and more abstract context.

Controlled   Being able to stay in charge of your emotions, holding them back when others might let rip.

Conservative   Preferring to maintain the status quo, whether that is because of tradition or because you believe in going with what has proved successful in the past.

Creative   Being able to come up with unusual and innovative ideas, and to combine things in imaginative ways.

Critical   Having the judgement to be able to evaluate things with a high degree of accuracy, such as the feasibility of an idea or product.

Detailed   Being able to pay attention to the smallest details of any project.

Dominant   An ability to control others by force of personality.

Emotional   Being able to show your feelings openly, and being easily moved.

Empathetic   Understanding and knowing how others feel, and communicating this.

Extrovert   Being more interested in other people and things than yourself and what is going on inside you, and being able to express yourself to others without difficulty.

Financial   Being able to handle everything related to money, from costs to budgets.

Holistic   Seeing the 'big picture' rather than the individual elements which go to create it – seeing the wood rather than the trees.

Imaginative   Having the ability to create mental pictures which are not obvious to other people, and so being able to find new and unusual ways of doing things.

45

Implementation   The ability actually to get things done, often with concrete measurements of the results.

Innovating   The ability to come up with new and unusual ideas and ways of doing things.

Integration   The ability to combine different elements into a unified whole.

Intellectual   Being able to acquire and retain knowledge.

Interpersonal   The ability to develop and maintain good relationships with other people.

Introvert   Someone who tends more towards inward reflection and less towards other people, making them slower to show their feelings and thoughts.

Intuitive   Being able to understand something immediately without a great deal of thought, research or analysis.

Logical   The ability to use deductive reasoning to work out what is likely to happen in the future.

Mathematical   Being able to understand and manipulate numbers to obtain the right results.

Organised   Being skilful at combining things in relationships that work.

Planning   Being able to see in advance what the best methods and means would be to move forward.

Problem-solving   The use of reason to reach solutions.

Rational   The ability to make choices using reason rather than emotion.

Spatial   An ability to understand and control the relative positions of objects in space.

Technical   Understanding and knowing how to apply engineering and scientific knowledge.

Teaching/training   Being skilled at putting across ideas and facts, and making them understandable.

Verbal Possessing good speaking skills.

Writer Someone who is able to communicate effectively through the written word.

ACTION

Write down a number of sentences beginning with the words 'I am', e.g. 'I am a manager', 'I am a mother', 'I am a wife', 'I am a salesperson'. Think of at least 10 of these, and if you can think of 20 so much the better.

Now do the same exercise with the words 'I can' at the beginning of each sentence, and then again beginning 'I am good at'.

Don't spend too much time deep in thought. Just give quick, crisp answers. If you get stuck then put the exercise to one side and return to it later. By the time you have finished you will be surprised by just how many things you can do and are good at. Once you have started focusing on these things you will being to get a picture of yourself, maybe including some aspects you had forgotten.

Also, during moments of doubt which may arise later in the process, you can return to this work to reaffirm your abilities and strengthen your confidence.

Writing a biography

It is very useful to write a biography of yourself, briefly recording the major landmarks from childhood to the start of your working career. This may include information about your parents, family, friends, school, hobbies, sports, relationships, holidays, part-time work, clubs, social activities and anything else you can remember.

You can include as much detail as you feel is relevant and go back as far as your memory allows. An important part of this exercise is to examine how decisions were reached during your formative years and to act as a memory 'jogger'. There may well be patterns in your behaviour during these early years which have continued in your working life. Seeing and understanding these patterns will help you to focus on which paths might be open to you in the future.

Alternatively, there may have been areas in which you were especially creative and which you enjoyed, that you have since cut out of your life. It is easy to forget certain aspects of your past, some of your likes and dislikes, and your abilities and strengths. Some may have become so refined and developed that they bear no resemblance to your original skills or interests, others may even have been blocked out completely.

Many people become so wrapped up in the day-to-day problems of their working lives that they forget what their dreams were before they started out. Remembering that you once wanted to be an artist, a librarian or a policeman will give you a chance to analyse what it was that was attractive about your choices, and to see if anything about your current job satisfies the same criteria.

How you record your biography doesn't matter. You may want to write it in essay form, or just record points. Some may find it helpful to draw a 'Life line'.

Drawing a life line

- Take a large sheet of paper (A3 or larger).
- Draw a straight line across the middle and mark the years along the bottom.
- Place a cross at your present age.
- Then map out the events of your life along the line.
- Put them above or below the line depending on whether they were high or low points in your life.
- This activity can be projected on beyond the present point to help you focus on the future, but you may need to return to complete this at a later date (see pages 91–2).

Here is an example:

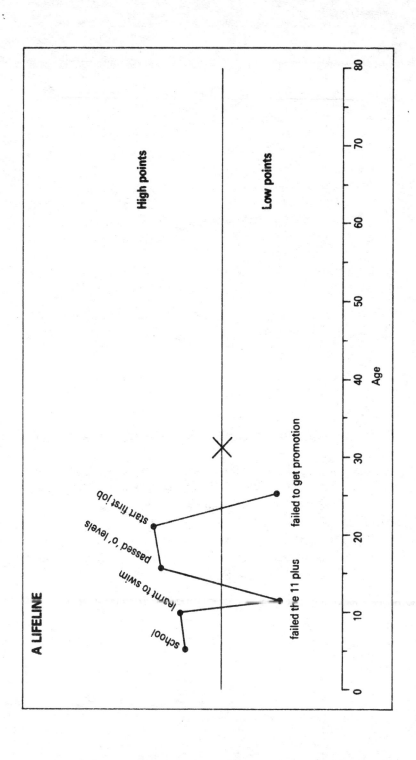

A LIFELINE

High points

Low points

Age

0 10 20 30 40 50 60 70 80

school

learnt to swim

passed 'o' levels

start first job

failed the 11 plus

failed to get promotion

Career path

Now move to your working career, and, using a separate sheet of paper for each job, record the following information.

- Your job title.
- The company name.
- The dates that you worked for them.
- Your salary.
- How you got the job.
- What or who attracted you to it.
- What your family or friends thought about the job.
- What you liked most about the job.
- What the worst elements were.
- Why you left.

When you have completed this for every job, read through what you have written to see if you can identify any patterns or repeated situations in your career path.

When *Bernard*, a board member of a large multi-national company, completed this exercise, he was astounded to realise that he had had no input into any of his career moves. All his career decisions had been governed by external influences. This made him question seriously what would have happened if he had taken more control.

This is not an unusual reaction. After counselling numerous individuals facing many different career issues, I have been amazed by how little they have influenced or directed their own career path. This has left each of them with a mass of unanswered questions – 'if only' is a commonly voiced regret. I believe that people need to understand themselves thoroughly before they can take control of their own career decisions and develop their full potential.

Areas of strength

Until now the activities have been of a general nature. It is time to start being more focused. The next action is to help you look in more detail at your strengths and skills.

ACTION

Answer the following questions by ticking the 'Yes' or 'No' box. They are designed to help you to identify where your strengths lie. Think about each of them, and try to imagine what your answer reveals about your strengths and weaknesses, likes and dislikes, and how they fit in with the realities of your job, or whether they are being wasted. There are no right or wrong answers; the questions are merely designed to get you thinking about yourself.

Section A

	Y	N
Are you actively interested in the arts?	☐	☐
Can you play a musical instrument well?	☐	☐
Can you act, sing or dance to a good standard?	☐	☐
Are you good at creative writing?	☐	☐
Can you write good, clear and correct English?	☐	☐
Can you speak well in a group?	☐	☐
Do you enjoy public speaking?	☐	☐
Are you an individualist in your dress and behaviour?	☐	☐
Do you often question other people's values?	☐	☐
Are you always concerned about how you present yourself?	☐	☐
Do you enjoy constantly changing situations?	☐	☐

Y N

Do you think a lot about your inner self? ☐☐

Section B

Do you enjoy helping others? ☐☐

Do you like listening to other people? ☐☐

Are you aware of other people's needs? ☐☐

Do you build strong relationships with others? ☐☐

Do you get on well with people? ☐☐

Have you studied psychology or sociology? ☐☐

Do you always try to see the other point of view? ☐☐

Do you ever discriminate against people? ☐☐

Do you enjoy teamwork? ☐☐

Can you put over facts and figures? ☐☐

Do you have counselling skills? ☐☐

Does helping others come easily to you? ☐☐

Section C

Can you mend anything mechanical? ☐☐

Can you use tools well? ☐☐

Are you good at manual tasks? ☐☐

Do you always want to know how things work? ☐☐

Do you always work out the answer for yourself? ☐☐

Are you computer literate? ☐☐

Can you identify complex faults and put them right? ☐☐

Can you build or construct things, large or small? ☐☐

Y N

Do you always question the accepted answer? ☐☐

Do you keep up to date with technical advances? ☐☐

Are you good at problem-solving? ☐☐

Are you highly skilled technically? ☐☐

Section D

Do you examine everything in detail before making a decision? ☐☐

Do you plan your work well? ☐☐

Do you assess the pros and cons of every debate? ☐☐

Do you always have to see the reason behind something? ☐☐

Do you deal with jobs in an orderly manner? ☐☐

Do you understand problems quickly? ☐☐

Can you use a computer to present data? ☐☐

Can you deal easily with mathematical and statistical data? ☐☐

Do you prioritise your work tasks? ☐☐

Do you manage your time well? ☐☐

Do you work in a well-organised environment? ☐☐

Do you enjoy working with detailed information? ☐☐

Section E

Do you help people to develop their skills? ☐☐

Do you look closely at the way your company is run? ☐☐

Are you a good manager/supervisor? ☐☐

Y N

Would colleagues say that you were a good leader? ☐☐

Do you recognise and use the talents of others? ☐☐

Is the setting of targets very important to you? ☐☐

Can you delegate work to others? ☐☐

Do you watch how other people work? ☐☐

Do you keep up to date with new management skills? ☐☐

Do you read management literature regularly? ☐☐

Do you always plan your campaign carefully to get the resources you need at work? ☐☐

Section F

Do you like experiencing new situations? ☐☐

Do you have a good network of contacts? ☐☐

Are you a good listener? ☐☐

Can you get people to think about different angles? ☐☐

Are you aware of what people want to hear? ☐☐

Can you sell/market? ☐☐

Do people often look to you to show the lead? ☐☐

Do you always know how things should be done? ☐☐

Are you good at putting over your point of view? ☐☐

Do you usually win arguments? ☐☐

Can you influence people to change their behaviour? ☐☐

Can you easily adapt your approach to others? ☐☐

By thinking about these questions you should be able to build up a picture of your abilities.

Section A   Positive answers in this section demonstrate that you are good at self-expression.

Section B   This section demonstrates abilities with people.

Section C   Positive answers here show you are a practical or technical person.

Section D   These answers show you are a good manager.

Section E   These questions are designed to reveal whether you are a good organiser.

Section F   Positive answers here will show that you are persuasive.

You will be stronger in some areas than others, and you must identify which they are.

Acknowledging your achievements

Next you need to extend your search and look at your achievements. Because of the innate modesty in the British character, it is often hard to discern exactly what your skills are, particularly if you have been working as part of a group and claim that any success was as a result of teamwork, not your individual effort.

You have to look honestly at everything you have been involved with, and work out how much of the success of the project was due to external factors, how much was due to the skills of other members of the team and how much was due to your own skills. Remember you are only doing this for your own benefit at the moment; you are not trying to impress anyone and no one will judge that you are boasting. If you lie you are only lying to yourself. This exercise is only valuable if you are totally honest.

Therefore, in order to get an accurate picture of what your skills are, you have to look at what you have achieved and see how you did it.

Generally, while you are working, you have little time to think about things which have been successful. You simply heave a sigh of relief when they are over and move on to the next problem.

Occasionally an achievement will be recognised by others and praised or rewarded (usually only if it is something of major importance), but more often than not companies are quick to criticise when things go wrong and slow to praise when they go right.

Modesty prevents most people from voicing self-praise, but employers need to hear about the achievements of their employees because they provide evidence of what the employee is capable of and suited to, and demonstrate the added value that you provide.

Everyone has achieved something at work. By that I don't mean you have to have beaten a world record, received a Nobel Prize or invented a new computer language. It has to be something which *you* are proud of and value as important.

Unfortunately, many people firmly believe that they have achieved nothing during their working lives. *Philip* believed it was 'Just my job, something I do every day – nothing special' After long discussions with me he gradually began to admit that perhaps certain things had resulted from his contribution, but he was very unsure. He agreed to go away and do some more work on this aspect of his career management plan, but I knew he would not return.

For some people the belief that recognition of their worth should come from external sources, not from themselves, is deeply ingrained. It is understandable because many of our long-standing traditions embody the view that we should not 'blow our own trumpets', and modesty is seen as a very attractive characteristic.

I would like to stress that I am not advocating that you should brag and embellish your good points, but I do believe that you should accept the truth about your attributes and be equally truthful about your weaknesses. Without this understanding you cannot combat successfully the issues that will face you during your career.

Philip will remain frustrated about his lack of job satisfaction and promotion prospects, until he can really understand what he has achieved. Unfortunately this can take a long time to germinate fully in a person's consciousness, but, from my experience, once the seed has been sown it will grow, and eventually Philip will return to career management, wanting to move on to the next stage.

When you are thinking about your achievements do not limit yourself to your work. Think about home, hobbies, sport, friends and family as well. Spread your thoughts as wide as possible. It may be that an achievement outside work is more indicative of your greatest strengths than things which you have done in a job which has not stretched your capabilities particularly, or you may have taken a career break and feel that recently you have not achieved anything that would be relevant in a skills audit. This is a totally false perception.

Susan felt this way after a break from work of four years. She had been a research chemist and could see little relevance in her most recent activities with the local nursery school and the conservation group. Yet, as chairperson of the PTA (Parent–Teacher Association) for her child's nursery school, she had avoided a staff resignation over a very difficult incident between two parents. The matter was resolved with extreme tact, accurate people assessment and diplomacy, all skills which would not necessarily display themselves in her research work.

At first Susan dismissed her years of being a mum as insignificant, but with the help of a different perspective she began to see that everything has positive value. It is really a matter of your own individual perceptions.

An achievement could be:

- a new idea which you formed and turned into some sort of reality;

- results which improved as a direct result of something you did;

- costs you managed to cut, making a difference to profitability, or perhaps making a project possible;

- an activity which you managed to simplify or improve with your ideas;

- a crisis which you averted or dealt with in a beneficial way;

- something which you made – either a physical object or a project;

- something you have collected;

- a difficult or new skill you mastered successfully;

- a group which you led or organised, perhaps one which wouldn't have existed at all without your instigation;

- a problem which you solved;

- anything that had a happy ending, thanks to you.

By thinking about these achievements you should be able to identify your contribution and that will reveal what your skills and strengths are. Are you good at developing things, for instance? Or creating and designing, or identifying opportunities, taking decisions, implementing decisions, writing, presenting, contributing to a group, saving, making, originating or improving?

ACTION

Having thought about your achievements in a general way, you now need to make a list of six to eight achievements that you feel are important. Again, don't restrict yourself to work, but look at your whole life. Thinking in this wider context will help you to extend your thought process and perhaps consider something in a different light.

Your achievements can also be from any time in your life, right back to your early school days, as long as at least two of them are reasonably recent. It may well be that you were more stretched and challenged at school or university than you have been since, and as a result you showed more of what you are capable of then.

Think about each achievement in detail, recording the facts and then, most importantly, the role which you played in achieving the successful results. Write each one down on a separate piece of paper. *Now arrange them in date order, with the earliest achievement first.*

Searching for your skills

Skills are extremely valuable assets. I sometimes compare this exercise of searching for them with panning for gold. You have your sieve which all the water and mud pours through, and every so often a nugget will come to light. Some of these nuggets will shine immediately, while others will be tarnished because they have been neglected for a few years, but nevertheless they are of equal value and must still be treasured.

Now that you have recorded your achievements and ranked them in date order, the next step in the process is to unravel each achievement to identify which skills and strengths were used to attain the result.

First, we need to be clear about what we understand by skills and strengths. *Webster's New Collegiate Dictionary* defines a skill as 'the ability to use one's knowledge effectively and readily in execution or performance; a learned power of doing something competently; a developed aptitude or ability.'

A strength is a quality that is innate, something we inherited. (See pages 65–6.)

Skills can be divided into five categories:

- people skills;
- information skills;
- thinking skills;
- co-ordinating skills;
- initiating skills.

People skills

Communicating (a) written, (b) oral   Conveying and receiving information.

Motivating   Generating a willingness to work.

Negotiating   Persuading and bargaining to get agreement and commitment.

Counselling and coaching   Helping a person improve their performance by defining problems and gaining their commitment to action.

Delegating   Handing over work to a subordinate or peer in such a way that the person has the necessary guidelines and commitment to complete the task correctly.

Flexibility   Seeing yourself in relation to others and as others see you in different situations.

Advising   Recommending a course of action.

Managing and supervising Having executive control or authority.

Persuading   Inducing another towards your inclinations.

Instructing   Making known to a person what he or she is required to do.

Training   Bringing someone to a desired standard of efficiency.

Teaching Enabling a person to gain knowledge through instruction.

Using intuition   Attaining immediate insight without the use of reasoning.

Caring   Expressing feelings of concern or interest.

Information skills

Researching   Discovering new or collating old facts.

Computing Reckoning, generally with the use of high-technology equipment.

Observing   Watching and examining situations, people, trends.

Classifying   Assigning categories to a person, place or object.

Clerical   Copying, entering and record-keeping skills.

Numerical   Working effectively with numbers.

Diagnosing   Ascertaining the cause of malfunctions.

Calculating   Ascertaining mathematical problems.

Memorising   Remembering and recalling given pieces of information or facts.

Budgeting   Estimating the amount of money needed or available for a situation.

Surveying   Inspecting or investigating the condition or amount of a given subject.

Information extraction   Tracing and retrieving given facts or data.

Thinking skills

Decision-making   Establishing the purpose of a decision; evaluating and selecting a course of action which satisfies the decision and carries least risk.

Evaluating   Considering objectively how well each alternative meets objectives and what the risk areas are.

Validating   Establishing the truth of a situation by testing against reality; written/oral.

Analysing   Distinguishing the significant elements of a situation.

Generating alternatives   Creating a number of options to improve or overcome a worrying situation.

Designing   Creating a plan for a purpose or object.

Innovating   Making changes or creating new solutions.

Problem-solving   Overcoming difficult questions or tasks.

Co-ordinating skills

Planning   Identifying the key tasks to be accomplished.

Organising   Structuring, arranging and allocating resources so that they are utilised effectively.

Controlling   Setting up monitoring systems and taking corrective action where necessary.

Identifying priorities   Assessing the comparative level of importance of tasks.

Developing   Creating progress.

Administering   Managing or overseeing.

Assembling   Gathering together a collection of parts.

Construction/building   The skill of putting something together by following a plan of instructions.

61

Mechanical dexterity   Ability to work with machinery.

Initiating skills (achievement oriented)

Achieving   Identifying risks, and taking responsibility for actions. Gaining acceptance of and commitment to those actions.

Risk taking/speculating   The combination of initiative and judgement that together display a willingness to opt for great profits but high-risk probability.

Responsibility taking   The willingness to assume levels of authority and responsibility to achieve desired results.

Creating   Originating a concept, idea or plan.

Remember that these skills are not mutually exclusive, they are always interchangeable, e.g. communication skills can apply both to information and people.

ACTION

Using the grid on pages 63–4, take your first achievement and compare it against the list of skills, ticking those that have played a significant part in that achievement.

Do the same thing for your seven other achievements. This will help you to build up a picture of your skills in general and, most importantly, when you have worked through all your achievements the key skills will emerge. Any gaps in your skills will also become clear. You need then to address the question of how you improve any gaps. Is further training required or feasible?

Remember that you can't be good at everything and you must make the decision to concentrate on your key skills. As you progress in your career, knowing the skill areas in which you are weak is a great advantage because you can ensure that someone else in the team has the skills you lack. This is by far the best use of resources.

Skills	Achievements								Total
	1	2	3	4	5	6	7	8	
Written communication									
Oral communication									
Motivating									
Negotiating									
Counselling Coaching									
Delegating									
Flexibility									
Advising									
Managing Supervising									
Persuading									
Instructing									
Training									
Teaching									
Using Intuition									
Caring									
Researching									
Computing									
Observing									
Classifying									
Clerical									
Numerical									
Diagnosing									
Calculating									
Memorising									

Skills	Achievements								Total
	1	2	3	4	5	6	7	8	
Budgeting									
Surveying									
Information Extraction									
Decision Making									
Evaluating									
Validating									
Analysing									
Generating Alternatives									
Designing									
Innovating									
Problem Solving									
Planning									
Organising									
Controlling									
Identifying Priorities									
Developing									
Administering									
Assembling									
Construction Building									
Mechanical Dexterity									
Achieving									
Risk Taking									
Responsibility Taking									
Creating									

Strengths

Now you need to look at the following list of strengths, or innate qualities, and decide which of these you possess.

Ambitious Eager to achieve.

Calm Having serenity of mind.

Caring Feeling concern or interest.

Courageous Showing bravery or boldness.

Dedicated Being devoted to one's aims or vocation.

Determined Being resolute.

Diplomatic Having tact in personal relations.

Energetic Being vigorous in one's actions.

Fair Being considerate and just.

Fearless Remaining undeterred by danger.

Honest Being fair and righteous in speech and action.

Independent Not being dependent on others for opinions or conduct.

Intelligent Showing a high degree of understanding or being quick of mind.

Intuitive Having immediate comprehension without the use of reasoning.

Level-Headed Being mentally well balanced.

Open Being revealing and communicative.

Optimistic Having a hopeful disposition.

Patient Remaining calm under endurance.

Perceptive Displaying sensitivity and understanding.

Practical Being inclined to action rather than speculation.

Precise Being accurate.

Rational Being reasonable.

Resilient   Recovering readily or remaining buoyant in the face of adversity.

Resourceful   Being skilful in devising solutions.

Self-motivated   Stimulating interest oneself.

Self-reliant   Being able to depend on oneself.

Sense of Humour   The ability to enjoy what is amusing.

Sensitive   Being very open to external stimuli or mental impressions.

Sincere   Being free from pretence or deceit.

Sociable   Enjoying company and being communicative.

Spontaneous   Acting without external incitement.

Tenacious   Holding fast to one's actions or beliefs.

Thorough   Striving for perfection and paying attention to detail.

Trustworthy   Being reliable.

Visionary   Having imaginative insight.

The above are qualities you inherited at birth and they can be developed, but if they are not in your make-up from the beginning there is little you can do to change the situation. They are all strengths which are important in career terms. The list is not exhaustive, so you can add to it if you feel it is appropriate.

The definitions are given to help you clarify your thoughts, but don't feel constrained by the meanings. Add to and change them to suit your situation.

Using a similar grid to that used for the skills analysis can also be helpful to distil your key strengths. Remember only to tick the strength if it has played a *significant* part in the achievement.

Strengths	Achievements								Total
	1	2	3	4	5	6	7	8	
Ambitious									
Calm									
Caring									
Courageous									
Dedicated									
Determined									
Diplomatic									
Energetic									
Fair									
Fearless									
Honest									
Independent									
Intelligent									
Intuitive									
Level-headed									
Open									
Optimistic									
Patient									
Perceptive									
Practical									
Precise									
Rational									
Resilient									
Resourceful									

Strengths	Achievements								Total
	1	2	3	4	5	6	7	8	
Self-motivated									
Self-reliant									
Sense of Humour									
Sensitive									
Sincere									
Sociable									
Spontaneous									
Tenacious									
Thorough									
Trustworthy									
Visionary									

ACTION

Reality Testing

The actions you have taken so far have centred around your own personal views. The next important task is to validate your perceptions against another reliable source. This information can come from a variety of useful places. As one of the aims of career management is to broaden your horizons, it may be helpful to utilise at least two different sources, such as:

- a friend who knows you well in a non-work-related context;
- a work colleague.

Decide on at least two people who can be approached for 'reality testing' – more if you feel it would be appropriate, i.e. a manager, a peer and a subordinate.

Explain to each what you are doing in terms of career management. Share with them something about its philosophies and perhaps let them read some of this book, e.g. Chapter 3.

Then show them your skills and strengths grids and the key elements which have emerged. Ask for comments about how they view you in the light of what is being said by the skills and strengths analysis.

Record the feedback, especially if they add further dimensions which have not surfaced before. You may have overlooked something or taken a skill for granted.

An objective viewpoint is invaluable at this stage because when you are working alone you can become discouraged and bogged down by the complexity of the task. Encouragement from an outsider can provide a positive lift.

An outside view

It always helps with any self-knowledge exercise to involve someone else. However hard you work at analysing your own strengths and weaknesses, you are bound to have some illusions about yourself. You have, after all, had a lifetime of coming to terms with yourself and putting your best face forward. In order to get a rounded picture you also need to understand how others see you.

What you are *not* looking for is destructive criticism; you simply want the truth. So choose someone whom you trust to tell the truth regardless of whether or not it will hurt your feelings, but who has no reason to put you down needlessly.

When you have completed this action you should begin to experience the first signs of positive movement. When you have successfully finished your skills audit and shared it, you have the beginnings of a clear and honest picture of yourself. This is a definite plus in building your confidence.

When *Kelly* had completed her skills audit she reported, 'Next day I walked into work feeling 10ft tall. I really felt good about myself for the first time in ages.'

Also remember that once you have identified your skills they are yours for ever and nobody can take them away. They may become a little tarnished and need some minor attention, but fundamentally they are yours for life.

Career values

This aspect of career management generally makes the most significant impression on people, because it is the element which is given the least attention. As soon as they begin to consider career values it becomes clear how important and often neglected they are. Values are closely aligned to individual needs and this helps to explain why they are so important. If your needs are not being satisfied, then life can be very difficult.

With every decision you make regarding your career, your values should be on the agenda, with no apologies to anyone. It will help you to make decisions and it will lead to a far higher measure of contentment with any decision that you do take. You need to know what is important to you, what is unimportant and why.

People make value judgements all the time in all other walks of life. They decide what neighbourhood they want to live in, whether they want to have a big house with a big mortgage and splendid interior decor, or whether they think it is more important to have spare money for holidays or for educating their children. They make decisions about the sort of people they want as friends, and how much time they want to spend with their families, and what sort of car they will drive or whether they will ride bicycles instead. They design most of their lifestyle around their values, often without even thinking about it, but they seldom apply the same criteria to their career – perhaps because they believe that it is something beyond their control.

Yet your career takes up the majority of your waking hours and affects every other aspect of your life. If you aren't completely comfortable in the role you have been allotted through your work, it is unlikely that you will be successful. It may be that you have chosen your career instinctively to fit your values, but even then your values may change.

Assessing your values

Assessing your own value system is a focusing activity. It provides purpose and direction to your career and avoids the vague, unfocused attitude that a number of people display when it comes to their jobs. Many people hold the unstructured view that it is not their right to make these sorts of demands; that they are lucky to have jobs at all, and they should show their gratitude with hard work and loyalty. While hard work and loyalty are both values which may be prized by employers, they are not the whole picture by any means. By today's criteria company loyalty is really a myth. It is often a convenient smokescreen behind which people hide when they are fearful of facing the real issues. Loyalty is about our need to love and be loved. If this is centred upon a faceless non-entity, it smacks of feudal practices. Today's climate requires a more sophisticated attitude, one that has greater emphasis upon an individual's self-worth.

Let us consider some of the values that may be important to you in career terms:

Artistic	Place of work
Being an expert	Power
Challenge	Precise work
Choice	Pressure
Community	Professionalism
Competition	Promotion
Contact with	opportunities
people	Recognition
Creativity	Respect
Excitement	Risk
Fame	Routine
Family	Self-esteem
Fast pace	Security
Fortune	Status
Friendship	Success
Helping others	Surroundings
Helping society	Time freedom
Independence	Variety
Learning	Well-known
Money	employer
Morality	Working alone
Peace	Working with
Physical challenge	others

This collection of values is not finite. As you read through the list and the definitions that follow, you may think of others that you want to add. Feel free to add them to the empty column on page 71.

Every communication in which we engage is bugged by semantics. Is what I mean the same as your interpretation? So often the two are light years apart. To communicate effectively you need to check both meaning and understanding continually.

The following definitions of career values may help, but you will need to wrestle with your own understanding and maybe add some new words.

Artistic Do you value the opportunity to create through drawing, painting, making music or other artistic outlets?

Being an expert Do you like being an expert in your chosen subject, building an in-depth knowledge and being consulted by others and respected by your peers?

Challenge Are you stimulated by challenge, and do you enjoy being stretched and given new problems to tackle?

Choice Do you like to have the freedom to choose your work pattern and the directions you will go in?

Community Do you want a career which involves you in the local community, making you part of it and involving you with the lives of the people around you?

Competition Do you thrive on competition or do you hate it? Are you stimulated by the idea of winning out against other people, or do you prefer to travel at your own speed?

Contact with People Do you need to have people around you, or are you quite happy working on your own all day? Could you work from home alone for long periods? Do other people stimulate you into achieving bigger and better things, or merely interrupt and annoy you when you are trying to get things done?

Creativity Do you enjoy thinking up new ideas and ways of doing things?

Excitement Do you need to get a buzz from what you do now?

Fame Do you want to be famous? Would you like to be recognised in restaurants, or have people turn out to conferences specifically to hear you speak?

Family   A wish to share the demands and tribulations, as well as the joys, of family life may be a consideration in what sort of job you can take – as may a wish to escape them.

Fast pace   Do you like to be working fast, finishing one job and moving straight on to another with no time for boredom?

Fortune   Are you motivated by the prospect of building a fortune, either personal or corporate?

Friendship   Is it important to you to be working among people who are your friends rather than just your colleagues, or do you keep your friends separate from your working life?

Helping others   Do you like to work with other people, helping them to cope with problems on a daily basis?

Helping society   Is it important to you to feel that the work you are doing is of value to society, rather than just something to amuse you or earn vast sums of money?

Independence   Do you prefer to work in the way you want, without other people telling you what to do? Or do you need the discipline of having tasks set for you with deadlines.

Learning   Do you need to be continually learning new things and moving into new territories, or are you happier with the known and familiar?

Money   Is money important to you, either for the lifestyle which it buys or as a measure of your success? Or is it merely a means to survival and a way to afford to do the things you want?

Morality   Having regard for discipline, morals and ethics.

Peace   Do you require peace, away from hectic pressures and shouting colleagues, in order to feel happy, or do you thrive on the noise and distractions of a big office?

Physical challenge   Do you need a job which actually tests you physically, rather than keeping you in the office, using your brain, all the time?

Place of work   Is it important to you where you work? Do you, for instance, feel the need to be in a capital city with all its hustle and bustle, or do you prefer to be in the peace and quiet of the countryside? Do you have to work in the country of your birth, or near to your current home, or would you be willing to move anywhere for the right job? How far are you willing to commute?

Power Does the idea of power stimulate you or intimidate you?

Precise work Do you like doing work which requires great care and concentration on detail, or are you more comfortable and successful when you take the broad-brush approach and leave the details to other people?

Pressure Do you enjoy working to targets and having to beat the clock all the time? Does that sort of pressure make you get up in the morning or make you want to stay under the sheets?

Professionalism Is it important that your work, and that of the organisation, is of a high standard?

Promotion opportunities Do you need to be able to see where your next step is?

Recognition Is it important to you for the work which you do to be recognised, either by other people or rewards?

Respect Do you want to be regarded with honour and treated with consideration.

Risk Are you stimulated by an atmosphere which involves risk taking, or do you find it threatening? Are you able to cope with losing?

Routine Do you value a well-structured work environment where you know exactly what is expected of you and what is likely to happen each day?

Self-esteem Do you need to think of yourself in a favourable and valued manner?

Security Is security important enough for you to be willing to forgo some of your other values in exchange for a salary, a pension and a promise of regular work? Some people can never be happy unless they feel secure, while others are not willing to make the trade-off. This is a very important issue within career management. Job security will never have the same meaning as it did 50 years ago, and some people believe that it will never exist again, especially if they have experienced a difficult phase of unemployment. If you feel that security is important, perhaps it has to be carefully defined and rooted within your own control, not abdicated to an outside agency.

Status Is status important to you? Do you need to feel that you will be in a position which makes other people respect you? Do you need the visible attributes that go with a position of power, e.g. big car, large office, gold credit cards etc.

Success Do you need to feel that you are a high achiever?

Surroundings Is it important to you to work somewhere pleasant, or do you not notice your surroundings? Some people prefer to work from home with their possessions and family around them, while others are quite happy to work in an anonymous open-plan office. Some people are excited by the prospect of living out of suitcases and hotel rooms, while others feel the need for a private office, protected from the world by a ferocious secretary. Just as some people lavish a lot of money and time on the design and decoration of their homes, while others never even pick up a paintbrush or wheel out a lawn-mower, everyone's ideas of the ideal place to work are different.

Time freedom Do you like to be free of routine and able to work whenever you want, taking time off to suit you, your family and your other interests?

Variety Do you need a wide variety of tasks and people to keep you interested, or do you merely find that confusing and unsettling, preferring a regular routine of repetitive tasks which you know you can handle?

Well-known employer Do you like working for a blue-chip company with a name which everyone instantly recognises?

Working alone Do you prefer to work on your own, at your own speed?

Working with others Do you like to work as part of a team, with the camaraderie and shared responsibilities which that leads to?

ACTION

Most individuals have some conflicting values. You might, for instance, enjoy being part of a team at times and being independent at others, working at home part of the time and travelling the other part. What you have to do is work out which of them is the most important to you. It might help to grade them into three columns, headed 'Very Important', 'Important', and 'Important to Avoid'. You can then take the Very Important ones and put them into an order of priority.

You need to be selective and restrict yourself to a maximum of seven or eight values in each category. This will result in a number of values being left over.

It is also important to remember that values change over time, and that it is important to recognise the ones that are also Important to Avoid, since they may once have been Very Important to you and may have been the reason you chose your current situation.

Geoff was the chief executive of a large fmcg Plc, with access to fast, chauffeur-driven cars, helicopters, the company jet, five-star hospitality and an elastic expense account. Overnight this high status evaporated when his company became part of an acquisition. Initially it seemed like a disaster. But when he faced reality he realised it wasn't such a blow because his lifestyle had been keeping him from his family, and now he lists status as an Important to Avoid value.

What is salient about this example is that Geoff recognised and understood what his true values were, rather than fudging the issue and pretending that the flash lifestyle had never been important to him, at the same time as trying to regain it. If people aren't honest about their true values problems will occur in the future.

Once you have worked out what your values are, you can then start looking for a career that suits you, or you can look at your current job and assess how far that goes towards satisfying your needs. Many people can find that when they stop to do this exercise their job satisfies almost none of their very important values.

As you grow and develop, your values will change. Money and status, for instance, may have been very important to you at the beginning of your working life and halfway through they may still be important, but helping others or freedom may have crept past them into the Very Important category.

This means that you need continually to take stock of your values, especially if you are feeling uncomfortable about work. If you are unhappy it will almost certainly be something to do with your values. One or more of them are probably being neglected and you are beginning to feel the pain. Once you have identified the problem you have to decide if it is a passing situation which will rectify itself in a short time, or something that needs to be addressed with action.

One of the most important aspects of reassessing your career values from time to time is to understand the reasons why, when things are not going well. If you achieve this depth of individual insight you will avoid taking wrong or snap decisions.

Money and your career

Nothing in life is totally compartmentalised, nothing exists in complete isolation and your career is no exception. One of the most important impinging factors is money and your financial commitments. Many people are invisibly handcuffed to their present job because of financial requirements.

Hidden handcuffs

Salary packages often contain elements that make career planning or experience mobility very difficult. Mortgage subsidies, company loans and non-contributory pension schemes can all appear very attractive as part of an exciting job offer, but in career management terms they must be considered very carefully. The long-term implications need to be investigated.

Also, lifestyle requirements have to be explored, especially when a partner and/or family have to be considered. These all constrain, to some extent, future career goals and none so damagingly as debt. So many people are trapped in jobs where the interest and challenge has long evaporated. All that happens day after day is following the same dreaded routine. This can affect people in different ways: some become immune to the situation and act much like robots; others suffer a high degree of stress, which can manifest itself in various ways such as depression, alcohol or drug abuse, over-eating, under-eating or illness.

ACTION

As part of your own career management strategy you need to consider financial matters at an early stage. Don't leave it until a crisis emerges. You need to be clear about what your financial values are. These will be closely linked to your work values, but you must have clear answers to the following questions:

– How important is money?
– How rich do I want to be?
– What does rich really mean? (Give examples and figures to support your answer.)
– Do you want to make a fortune?
– How much will your fortune be?
– Why do you want money?
– What will it buy for you?
– Is status important to you?
– What do you consider to be important status symbols?
– Is security an important factor?
– How do you define security?
– What do you need to achieve this type of security?

When you have considered these questions you should begin to see how money rates in relation to your other values. Also be aware that your attitudes, values and circumstances change over time.

Consult your partner

Once you are clear about these issues for yourself, it is vitally important to share them with your partner or spouse, or anyone who may be affected by your views and values. From my experience this is something that is often not given enough attention. The sharing of information may happen at the beginning of a relationship, but it is often not updated. The values of one partner begin to change, and this is not communicated other than by assumption. You assume the other person must be feeling the same. You, for instance, may want to give up the money side in order to do something which is more fulfilling for you. Your partner, however, may value the money and status of your current job very highly and be unwilling to make sacrifices so that you can be happier at work. Sometimes these differences are insuperable, but usually it is a question of communication and negotiation.

All too often we are just unaware of the values which those close to us hold dear, or we may have completely the wrong impression. It may be that your partner had no idea about something on your Very Important list, and will be quite happy to find ways of making it a reality. It is very easy to take other people's feelings for granted.

Pricing your lifestyle

Also, questions of lifestyle must be considered within a long-term framework. Discussions need to be priced well into the future and the implications considered. In the past it has been assumed that career progression was measured by salary rises, year upon year. This can no longer be taken for granted. So, as you need to become more flexible with your career path, you need to consider a more flexible approach to finance.

Not everyone is a financial expert, able to keep abreast of constant changes and how they impact upon your own situation, but what you should have is a regular yearly update of your financial position. This is the only way you can monitor the situation and how it impinges upon your career goals. Waking up in 10 years' time to find that you cannot retire at 50 or develop that new idea that is bursting to see the light of day is not good career management practice.

Remember . . .

- Your skills are your most valuable assets.

- Nobody can take skills away.

- Get your values balanced.

- Know your skills, strengths and values, and you become a person of great worth.

- You must govern your finances, not the other way round.

- Your finances are closely linked with career decisions.

- Share your values with your partner, don't make assumptions.

CHAPTER 5

*F*LIPPING THE DOWN-SIDE UP

The final part of Phase 1 involves looking at your negative attributes and assessing whether these can be turned into positive benefits, or whether you need to face reality and accept what is true or unchangeable.

These actions start with work that you must do yourself, but to make sure you are compiling an accurate picture it is vital that you confirm your analysis by checking it against external contributions from friends, colleagues, senior management and maybe the results of psychometric exercises.

Alan Hamilton from Hamilton and Associates, a management development consultant, maintains that our weaknesses are really our unexploited strengths. Imagine if that is really true, how much potential could we release?

Everyone is generally much better at listing their weaknesses. If asked to list 20 examples of 'I can't . . .', the list would be filled much quicker than the 'I am good at . . .' collection. (See page 47.)

In the area of career management, flipping the down-side up relates to gaining knowledge and understanding about the whole individual. We all have a shadow, a side that contains negative elements. What you must achieve is a situation where the positive elements flourish and the negative factors are not allowed to gain too much importance. In fact, everything should be viewed along a spectrum. There are good and bad sides to every aspect of your make-up.

Take, for instance, the word 'power' and consider some alternative words with the same meaning.

◄─────────────────── **POWER** ───────────────────►

Ability	Brawn	Command	Authority
Capability	Energy	Control	Licence
Capacity	Forcefulness	Dominance	Prerogative
Competence	Intensity	Dominion	Privilege
Faculty	Might	Influence	Right
Potential	Muscle	Mastery	Warrant
	Potency	Rule	
	Strength	Sovereignty	
	Vigour	Supremacy	
	Weight	Sway	

There is a range of options displayed on the spectrum. The words on the left convey positive meanings, while to the right the more sinister tones are revealed.

Your next activity is to acknowledge in your own life what your weaknesses and constraints are, while viewing everything from a perspective of reality.

In the quest for self-knowledge it is vital to know your weaknesses. It is, paradoxically, a strength because you can then understand your limitations and avoid situations which might make you vulnerable.

Certain weaknesses can be seen as strengths in themselves, depending upon the degree of perception of the individual. For example, I perceive my obsession with punctuality as a weakness because I waste so much time arriving at my destination too early. I also waste a great deal of negative emotional energy because I'm so cross with myself for wasting time, or that other people are keeping me waiting. I'm working on it, but I know it is a weakness. Other people, however, often perceive punctuality as a strength.

Some experts in the field of self assessment believe that weaknesses come from gaps in our skills and strengths. I believe this is true when applied to skills because skills can be learnt or acquired but you cannot simply learn or acquire a new strength. Strengths are part of our fundamental make-up, our inheritance from birth. When we consider weaknesses in the light of our strengths we need to think in another way. We need to consider the power of our strengths and that sometimes this force may be over used, resulting in our strengths becoming weaknesses because we play to one strength too much or use the strength in an inappropriate way or at the wrong time.

ACTION

The next exercise explores some of the negative attributes that you may have. Below is a list of negative traits which you may find familiar. Be honest with yourself and circle the ones that you really believe are part of your work pattern.

Weaknesses and negative traits

Workaholic
Laid back
Intrusive/busy body
Reckless
Obsessive
Stubborn
Self effacing
Driven/aggressive
Indecisive
Disregard danger
Blunt
Dogmatic
Intellectual snob
Illogical
Over cautious
Naive
Unrealistic
Inactive
Over analytical
Unimaginative

Pedantic
Too accommodating
Single minded
Self possessed
Self centred
Poor delegator
Frivolous
Emotional
Non political
Domineering
Impulsive
Wilful
Perfectionist
Righteous
Impractical

When you have finished this exercise and are content that you have not been too harsh on yourself, look at the lists of strengths and weaknesses below and opposite. Circle the strengths you have identified previously (Chapter 4) down the left hand column and then circle the weaknesses on the right that you have just identified. If there are any that correspond, this may indicate where you could be relying on a strength to such an extent it has become a weakness. If so, spend a little time reflecting upon this insight and explore the idea that maybe some of your major strengths could be getting in the way of your growth. Consider if it may be more beneficial to pay some attention to your lesser strengths which may help you to grow rather than continuing to do things in the same old manner.

Strengths	Weaknesses
Ambitious	Workaholic
Calm	Laid back
Caring	Intrusive/busy body
Courageous	Reckless
Dedicated	Obsessive
Determined	Stubborn

Diplomatic .... Self effacing
Energetic .... Driven/aggressive
Fair .... Indecisive
Fearless .... Disregard danger
Honest .... Blunt
Independent .... Dogmatic
Intelligent .... Intellectual snob
Intuitive .... Illogical
Level headed .... Over cautious
Open .... Naive
Optimistic .... Unrealistic
Patient .... Inactive
Perceptive .... Over analytical
Practical .... Unimaginative
Precise .... Pedantic
Rational .... Too accommodating
Resilient .... Single minded
Resourceful .... Self possessed
Self motivated .... Self centred
Self reliant .... Poor delegator
Sense of humour .... Frivolous
Sensitive .... Emotional
Sincere .... Non political
Sociable .... Domineering
Spontaneous .... Impulsive
Tenacious .... Wilful
Thorough .... Perfectionist
Trustworthy .... Righteous
Visionary .... Impractical

ACTION

List 10 facts that you don't like about yourself.

To gain full credibility for this list you need to apply the 'Reality Test'. Share your list with the two or three people you consulted for your skills audit. Record their feedback, especially when it is at variance with your own analysis.

Constraints

During the earlier exercises you have had the freedom to explore all the possibilities and all the various combinations which might apply to your situation. In reality very few people have this total freedom, especially when considering career options, for we all have a certain number of constraints which govern our choices.

Here are some examples.

Finance

It may be that your ideal requires capital which you don't have, or you may require too high an income to support your family to be able to choose the career which suits your values most closely. You have to be realistic about how much money you need to live on, and how much you are likely to earn from your chosen career.

It may be that helping society tops your list of values, but salaries in that area are very low and if you have children who are already half-way through private education or have special needs, or you don't want to sell the expensive house you live in, you are going to have to think again. Perhaps you could stay in your job but do social work in your spare time in order to satisfy your values.

Family

Anyone with a family has to take their needs into account. Your ideal career path might be to charter a boat and carry passengers around the Caribbean, but you can't do that if you have small children whom you want to educate in a traditional way, or ageing parents who are dependent upon you being around, or a partner who wants to do something quite different.

Location

It may be that you are not able to move away from where you currently live – or do not want to. This will automatically limit what you can do. If the sort of career you want only happens in London or New York, and you live in the wilds of Canada or Scotland, you are going to have to make some choices and compromises.

Skills

You may simply be unable to earn a living at your preferred profession because you are not sufficiently skilled. Not everyone can be a great painter or musician, nor can everyone be good at mending cars or nursing children. It may be that you would prefer to do your chosen job badly rather than not at all, but you may simply be unable to get the job you want or make a living at it – in which case you will once again have to find another way.

Retrenching industry

These days, with developments in technology happening so fast, and massive shifts in world economics taking place over decades rather than centuries, a great many industries are retrenching all the time, or disappearing altogether.

If you work in Europe or America, for instance, in an industry which is being eclipsed by rivals in the Third World, then you may find it hard to land the job you want or the working conditions which you feel you deserve in your chosen profession. In these cases you may have to look for other industries which use the same skills, but which are expanding rather than shrinking, or you may have to move to a different country, where your skills will be valued by an emerging industry. Once again you may have to choose between different values.

Qualifications and training

More and more jobs require specific qualifications, either in the form of educational attainments or professional exams. If you don't have the right ones for the career of your choice you have to decide whether you can afford to take the time to get them (it might mean taking two years unpaid leave in order to retrain). In some cases it may be too late; you cannot, for instance, decide to become a brain surgeon at 50 if you left school at 15 and have worked in the building industry ever since. There are, however, courses available in virtually every subject if you take the trouble to seek them out and are willing to devote the necessary time to studying.

Partner's job

Your partner may have a job which means that you can't move away from the area where you currently live, or you may need to fit your working hours round theirs, which closes certain options to you. If your values are wholly work orientated this could mean that your partnership may break up, but if you are family orientated as well, you will have to make some hard choices.

Children's education

This could limit you financially, or could limit how far away you are able to look for work if you don't want them to move schools. If you want to move to another country you have to think seriously about the impact this will have on their schooling – would you want them to join the local school, for instance, even if they weren't fluent in the language? Would you be willing to take them to whatever English-speaking schools there were in the neighbourhood, or would you be happy to send them to boarding school far away from where you are based?

Elderly parents

If parents are frail and in need of family nursing that is obviously going to limit you to jobs which do not require too much travel or too long hours. Even if they are in good health you may be reluctant to travel too far from them on a permanent basis, bearing in mind that you may only have them around for a limited time.

Illness

Your own health could be a major limiting factor. There may be medical reasons why you are unable to take too much stress, or some illness in your past may make you ineligible for a particular job. There may simply be reasons why you need to be physically stronger than you actually are in order to do the work required.

Handicaps

Any physical handicap is bound to limit the number of things you can do, whether it is you who is handicapped, or a member of your family.

Travel

For any number of reasons it may be impossible for you to travel enough to keep certain jobs.

ACTION

From your own knowledge of yourself, make a list of your constraints. Try to see if any of them can be overcome with thought or negotiation. Strong family ties, for instance, could be seen as a sign of stability and security by many employers.

Work out how you would talk about your constraints at an interview in order to show their positive sides.

Once you have worked out what your constraints and weaknesses are, you can then either attempt to work on them, improving or correcting them in some way, or you can make efforts to avoid situations which are likely to aggravate the problems.

Sometimes, with enough thought, a weakness can be turned into a strength. The fact that you find it hard to take instructions, for instance, will be a considerable weakness if you are working in a highly hierarchical corporation, but it could mean that you are a 'self-starter' and would therefore be good at setting up your own business.

Recognising reality

Once you have recognised your skills and values, and assessed their importance to you, you then have to set them against the reality of your situation, with the constraints involved and your personal weaknesses. Few people are lucky enough to realise all their ideals, to have all their values met at all stages of their careers. Sometimes you may have to take on a job which satisfies virtually none of your values in order to gain the necessary experience to do the job of your choice. Someone who wants to be a freelance journalist, for instance, because they like to be independent, to work alone, to work from home, to travel to interesting places and to have time freedom, may have to start out with a job on a local newspaper or trade magazine which offers none of these values, but which provides the necessary work experience.

There will always be some compromises, and the more realistic you are about what is possible, the closer you are likely to get to reaching your ideal situation in the long term. If you have wild dreams of achieving everything you want at no cost, you are likely to be left with nothing. Anyone who has a firm grasp of reality is more likely to succeed fully and achieve their objectives.

You may also have to choose between your values. For example, you might put money and status high on your list of values, and also want to be a nurse. Not many jobs satisfy all these criteria, so either you will have to forgo the money and status or, if you find that it impossible to do this, you may have to undertake some sort of voluntary nursing work in your spare time and give up the idea of making a full-time living at it, at least for the moment.

ACTION

Balancing work with fulfilment

Dr Bill Pfeiffer and Dr John Jones, two American psychologists, have developed a lifeplanning exercise to help individuals develop their lives.

It comes in three parts. In *Part 1* you need to answer the question 'Who am I?' They suggest writing down 20 adjectives that most accurately describe you at work, like ambitious, trustworthy or nonchalant. For *Part 2*, write down a similar list of adjectives for your relationships with your family and friends. In *Part 3* you describe yourself doing activities that are personally fulfilling or enhance your health.

They then suggest that you score each group of adjectives as being positive, negative or neutral. This can provide you with an awareness of your positive and negative traits in these three leading aspects of your life.

Then you should answer the question 'Where am I now?' in the same three areas – career, personal life (friends and family) and personal fulfilment.

For your career you should draw a graph or lifeline (see pages 48–9 and over), that shows the trend of the past, present and future. The future aspects of the lifeline may reflect either your hopes for where ideally you would like to go, or where you think you are most likely to end up (although you would rather not). Place an 'X' on the lifeline to show where you are now. Then write down a brief explanation of the career line you have drawn, highlighting high points and low points. Now you have a complete picture of where you have been, where you are at this point and where you are likely to go.

Repeat the process to create a lifeline for your personal relationships and again for your personal fulfilment, health and creativity.

Finally you ask yourself 'Where do I want to be?' List up to 10 ideal attainments in each of your three main life areas – again, career, personal life and personal fulfilment. Goals might include 'I

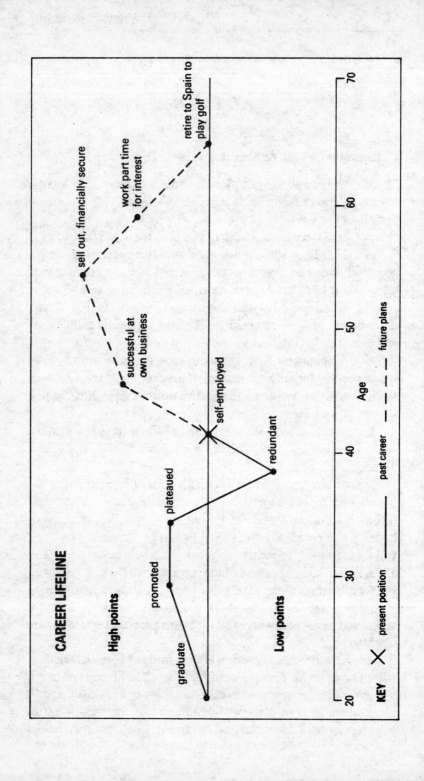

CAREER LIFELINE

High points

- graduate
- promoted
- plateaued
- successful at own business
- sell out, financially secure
- work part time for interest
- retire to Spain to play golf

self-employed

Low points

- redundant

Age

20 30 40 50 60 70

KEY

✕ present position

—— past career

- - - future plans

want to be self-employed', or 'I want to re-establish closeness with my partner' or 'I want to face my need for alcohol'.

Assign each ideal a priority value, using the following scale.

4 = very great importance

3 = great importance

2 = moderate importance

1 = little importance

Then combine all the ideals into one group and rank them again so that all the 4s are first, then the 3s and so on. The combined list shows the relative importance of specific goals, whether they involve your career, personal life or personal fulfilment.

Once you have completed the exercise you can begin lifeplanning by selecting the five highest-rated goals and writing down how you could achieve them, including the practical strategies you will have to adopt for each goal. None of this is easy, but it will help you to see solutions you had not considered before. Make sure you design specific strategies and objectives that can actually be implemented, rather than just vague ideas.

Analysing your present job

Having completed the exercises so far you should now have a good idea of what you want from life and what you are likely to be able to achieve. Now you need to look at your current job to see how it measures up to these expectations. Does it, for instance, provide you with the values which you consider important? Does it utilise your skills and strengths? Is it leading you in the direction in which you want to go?

ACTION

Start by looking at the positive factors of your job and listing them in order of priority. Use the following as a prompt list, but don't treat it as conclusive, since there may well be aspects of your job, not listed here, that give you great satisfaction.

Positive factors

- Does your job provide you with the recognition which you require for your self-esteem?

- Is it a friendly, professional and supportive work environment?

- Are you allowed to utilise your technical knowledge fully?

- Do you get good feedback and appreciation for the things that you achieve?

- Does the company produce a good quality product or service?

- Do you receive enough opportunities to use your management skills?

- Do you get chances to widen your knowledge and experience?

- Are objectives set and adhered to by those around and above you?

- Are you working with colleagues who you respect and from whom you can learn?

- Do you receive a good salary with benefits and status?

- Does the job provide you with sufficient challenges to keep you stimulated?

- Are the working hours sufficiently flexible to give you time freedom?

- Is your work valued and of value?

- Are there opportunities for further growth, development and promotion?

- Are you given the autonomy to organise your own workload?

- Does the job involve a variety of tasks in a variety of surroundings?

- Do you take an active role in client presentations or decision-making?

- Do you get opportunities to work as part of a team?

- Do you get to write reports?

- Are there opportunities for you to work with and develop junior staff?

Negative factors

Now repeat the exercise for the negative factors, some of which will simply be the reverse of the positive factors.

- Are you unable to organise your own workload?

- Are you not given enough responsibility?

- Are there too many budget restrictions?

- Do you have to work in isolation?

- Are you given no opportunity to participate in client contact?

- Are the time pressures too chaotic for comfort?

- Are you given no opportunities to travel?

- Are the company procedures too rigid and formal?

- Do the managers lack interest in their subordinates?

- Is there a lack of opportunity to gain management experience?

- Is there a lack of job enhancement?

- Is there an absence of challenge?

- Do you have a low salary or status, with few benefits to compensate?

- Are you always having to work behind the scenes?

- Are you given too much, or too little, management or administrative responsibility?
- Is your worth not recognised?
- Do your work tasks lack structure?
- Are there no clearly stated job tasks?
- Is there a lack of opportunity to learn something new?
- Is there no chance to use your skills fully?

Look closely at both the positive and negative lists of priorities, and think about any action which you can take either to add to the positive list or shorten the negative list.

Don't become over-ambitious and try to redesign your working life at this stage. Instead, start by doing things which are achievable and motivate you to continue improving.

External confirmation

You will have noticed that so far you have concentrated your search for information mainly on yourself. This has been deliberate in order to help you develop the inner self-confidence that you require to manage your career successfully. It can also be helpful, however, if you seek confirmation of your findings from other sources. However honest you may think you are being, everyone has delusions and misconceptions about themselves to some degree.

It may be that you are able to assess clearly what you think your values ought to be, for instance, but that may be different from what they really are. You may also have been telling yourself that you are bad at some particular skill for so long that it has become a self-fulfilling prophecy. If you have been denying something for long enough, the chances are that you could have started to believe your own denials.

A woman might, for instance, have been telling herself for years that money and status don't matter to her, to justify her decision to marry a low-paid worker and not to work herself. Or a man might have been telling himself that he is a 'bad leader' because he made a few mistakes at the beginning of his career and has never plucked up the courage to try again.

It is worth checking, therefore, that your picture of yourself is accurate. The chances are that most of it will be right, but you will benefit from having that confirmed. You may discover some revealing new things.

If you have not yet explored Reality Testing it may now be appropriate to return to page 68. It is often painful to find out what other people think of you, but it is always instructive, even if you believe they are wrong in their assessments. If your friends and relatives have reached certain conclusions about you, then potential employers may well receive the same impressions when you turn up for interviews. Also, current bosses might be labouring under misapprehensions that you are happier in your job than you actually are, or that you are discontented for the wrong reasons.

As well as knowing the truth about yourself, you also need to know the truth about how others see you. If they are wrong then you need to understand how they gained that impression, so that you can do something to counteract it.

Psychometric tests

One source of useful confirmatory evidence is to use psychometric testing. These tests can play a very important role in career terms, but as a consumer you need to find out certain things before you commit yourself. They must be administered and interpreted by people who are qualified, and they must be conducted according to the Code of Practice issued by the British Psychological Society (BPS) or the Institute of Personnel Development (IPD).

Some companies offer psychological testing as a vehicle for giving careers advice. From my experience this neglects the important ground work that an individual needs to cover before they can fully appreciate the results of any tests in relation to their career actions. If you are going to have someone else tell you what you should be doing with your life from the results of a test, you are handing over the control and responsibility for your career to them. It may sound an easy solution but it will not be an everlasting one.

Raymond paid a substantial amount of money to sit a number of psychometric tests in order to find out what career direction he ought to follow. He thought the resulting report was very comprehensive and it sounded like him, but after his one-to-one feedback session he felt he had moved no further on. He didn't fully understand the implications of what the results were saying and he felt like saying 'OK, but so what?'

When he experienced tests being used in conjunction with his own search for self-knowledge, however, it was much clearer, and the results acted as a very powerful confirmation tool and worked towards helping him to take ownership of his skills, strengths and achievements.

Many people are sceptical about these types of tests (I prefer to call them psychometric exercises), because there are no right or wrong answers, or highest scores. I believe they are one way of collecting information about you which should be pretty accurate, but at the end of the day *you* have to be the judge. None of them claim 100 per cent accuracy – generally it is around 80 per cent – so it is very important that you receive the feedback afterwards, in order that you can assess the true value of the results.

In a professionally organised career management or guidance session this always happens, and you receive the results automatically. But in a recruitment situation this may not always be the case, and you need to be aware of your rights. If, when you go for an interview, you are asked to sit some psychometric tests, always say 'Yes', but make sure you know if and when you will receive feedback. This is in accordance with the Institute of Personnel Development's (IPD) Code of Practice for the use of psychometric tests.

This is important, in case the results are saying something that is not true and you are given no chance to defend yourself or explain.

This happened to *Rose*, who scored very low on management attributes in a psychometric test. Her profile recorded that she was very self-conscious and mild. Rose challenged this during her feedback session, and provided examples to support her claims. After further questioning it was clear that she was experiencing a number of emotional problems at the time, which were affecting her inner confidence, and this was coming through on the test results. It was also clear that this was only a transient phase, but could prove difficult it she had to face tests during recruitment for a job.

We planned a campaign of action to cater for this problem if it arose, and with time the situation corrected itself and she was able to present a true picture of herself in future tests.

If, in career terms, you feel it would be beneficial to invest in some testing, always choose a qualified practitioner and sit a range of different tests.

But always do some individual analysis first, so that you can fully understand and appreciate the findings. The most beneficial way to utilise these tests is when they are used by a qualified and experienced career counsellor.

Below are some examples of tests which can be helpful for career management:

Saville and Holdsworth OPQ is a personality test that provides a profile of your personality under three headings: 1. Relationships with People, 2. Thinking Style, and 3. Feelings and emotions.

Myers-Briggs (MBTI) is based on the work of C. G. Jung and measures personality.

Belbin measures your preferred team style and indicates how you operate best within a team environment.

Watson-Glaser provides a critical thinking appraisal which indicates your level of intelligence against certain criteria predicted norms.

Test Systems Inc. DP is a decision-making indicator which maps out the way you prefer to reach decisions.

Thomas International PPA is a personality profile which shows your personality traits in three different setttings: 1. How you see yourself, 2. How you are viewed at work, and 3. How your personality reacts under acute pressure. This test has great value when used for career development discussions, but I have reservations when the test is used for recruitment.

The Herrmann Test gives a very interesting insight onto your preferred use of the left or right side of the brain. Analytical and logical thinkers tend to use the left side more, while intuitive, creative types use the right side. This type of insight can be extremely valuable when considering developmental issues, especially if you are in a highly technical job and facing decisions about moving into areas that involve more intuitive people management or teamwork skills; or if you are a gifted technical person wanting to become an entrepreneur and develop your own business.

16 PF was originally a clinical test, but has been refined for assessing 16 personality factors which relate to occupational applications.

There are also lots of free tests on the Internet. Worth trying are the Keirsey Temperament Sorter (www.keirsey.com) and Career Quest Pride (www.youthworks.ca/yw–top 10.htm).

Congratulations if you have undertaken all the **Actions** so far! You have successfully completed Phase 1 of the career management process. You may, at certain points of your career, have to revisit this phase for brief reassessment, but the serious bulk of the work has now been completed.

You can now identify your skills, values, strengths, weaknesses, constraints and reality. These are the building blocks in your career foundation. They are firmly cemented together by your achievements. After completing Phase 1 you should feel better about your self-worth, in fact you should have a much improved confidence level. If this is the case you have completed the actions to the right depth and are ready to move on. If you still feel uncertain, recap on any areas that are not clear. Please take time to attend to this now, since returning later for repair manoeuvres will cost you dear.

Remember ...

- Knowing and accepting your weaknesses is a great strength.

- Many down-sides should be flipped up.

- Keeping a realistic perspective will ensure success.

- Once you have built your foundation of self-knowledge it will always be there.

PHASE 2

CHAPTER 6

Exploring your options

You have now reached the second and most exciting phase of career management. The key to success here is to understand that it is a distillation phase which cannot be forced. It takes time and extensive effort.

By now you should understand more clearly your list of very valuable assets: your skills, your strengths, your achievements and your values. This information can be used to measure whatever opportunities are available to you. Now you are ready to move on to the next stage – exploring options and discovering what these opportunities might be.

For most people this is by far the most difficult part of the process. While the acquiring of self-knowledge is hard, most people find it interesting to discover more about themselves. Exploring your options involves research work which is every bit as arduous as anything you might do on a university course. You need to acquire as much information about the potential marketplace as if you were going to write a full-length book on the subject, and there are no short-cuts to discovering and understanding that information.

Many people falter at this stage in the career management process. Those who don't will succeed in attaining whatever goals they have set themselves, because they are the ones who are doing their preparation work and who will be in the right places at the right times for the right jobs – not by luck either, but by judgement. There is an old saying that hard work is the route to success, and that is certainly true of finding and choosing your best career path.

Also, there is a fascinating coincidental effect of action creating action. *Bill* had started on the process of career management and had reached this stage. He had completed Phase 1 and was beginning to feel the rumblings of his self-confidence returning. On Sunday he saw five advertisements in the *Sunday Times* that matched his skills. On Monday he received a call from a contact who wanted to discuss a proposal that was of mutual interest. Bill was quite taken aback, but it really demonstrated how action follows action.

From my experience it is extraordinary how many individuals will work themselves into the ground to get the right educational qualifications, and will work equally hard once they have found a job, but will skate superficially over the business of *choosing* the right job.

In search of knowledge

Phase 1 of the career management process is about collecting knowledge that is centred on you. Phase 2 involves accumulating knowledge about the outside world and being involved in a positive matching system.

What everyone needs, in order to make wise decisions and choices, is information. Just as it is unwise to buy a car or a house without studying the market, comparing prices and having the prospective purchase checked out by professionals, anyone who takes a job without being in possession of as much information as possible stands a good chance of making bad choices, and of failing to attain the goals they have set for themselves.

So many people tell me how they ignored the little niggly doubts they had at the back of their minds when negotiating a job move, only to find that six months into the job the little niggle had turned into a major problem.

Everyone at some time wonders what other type of job they could do. For many it is only ever an idle day-dream, but those with a driving urge to explore can discover exactly what is possible and what is impossible, and how to turn the possible into reality. If you are keenly motivated towards the goal of extending your option choices, the task will be easier and at times very exciting. Unfortunately there are no easy answers and no magical formula which will quickly bring success. The route is often long and frustrating, and at times progress is slow. At times like these you may need the help and support of others who understand what you are trying to achieve.

New ways of thinking

As we enter the new millennium the employment situation is extremely varied. Some sectors are experiencing growth and rapid change. Others are being hit by the fluctuating economic climate. The mixed messages of good and bad news do nothing to calm fears about career insecurity.

Given this difficult climate, many react with inertia, believing that they are powerless to achieve anything. There is a certain amount of truth in this view if you follow the traditional ways of career planning and job search, but what is required for the future is a new approach to the activity of searching for options.

The most successful key in this phase of exploration is being creative, thinking in ways that are different, not accepting that it has never been done like that before so it isn't worth trying. It is about pushing the boundaries back so that you can explore new ideas.

Understanding your brain

This is a complex task and one that it is not possible to achieve totally here, but I have discovered that by understanding certain of the brain's activities a little better, it becomes easier to use some of the techniques I will look at later in the book.

First, it helps to know that the brain does not work in a linear way. It does not follow direct lines or uniform, straight patterns. The brain works in a diverse manner. In fact, it goes all over the place!

Professor Bergstrom

The brain has two distinct sections: the cortex, which is the ordered knowledge store; and the brainstem, which produces impulses which regulate our consciousness. Professor Matti Bergstrom, a leading brain researcher from the University of Helsinki, believes that creative thought results when there is a clash between the two sections. We often refer to flashes of inspiration as 'brainwaves', and what Bergstrom maintains is that this activity is not a chance occurrence but that it happens as a result of a specific sequence of brain activities. He also maintains that you can control these with certain techniques.

These techniques encourage you to use your brain in more unusual ways. The idea is to move away from the years of training that encouraged linear thought processes, and to practise and encourage the sparring or clashing activity between the cortex and the brainstem. The more you foster this, the more creative your ideas will be. This is of vital importance to career management, but the process will also be beneficial to every aspect of your life.

Edward de Bono

One of the world's leading experts in this field is Dr Edward de Bono, whose concept of lateral thinking has promoted tools and techniques which encourage individuals to strive beyond the accepted patterns of thinking. He believes that it is vital to understand how your mind works if you want to increase your thinking power. Also, he advocates that deliberate, effective or creative thinking is a skill which can be acquired.

Creative thinking has little connection with intelligence, which can often be a block to new ideas, as can arrogance which leads an individual to believe that they have all the answers. According to de Bono, anyone with disciplined diligence can think. It is a deliberate act which can be turned on and off, not a subconscious activity achievable only by a lucky few.

To improve your thinking skills you need tools which challenge your brain in a confrontational way and methods that allow your brain to learn new patterns of thinking. The larger your repertoire of thinking patterns the more creative you will become in any activity you tackle. Career management is just one area where this mode of thinking is very appropriate.

De Bono has devised a number of tools to help you acquire and develop this improved thinking style.

PMI

PMI is the first simple tool. Generally your thought process is governed by prejudged conclusions which come from your past experience. These are the ruts of past thought, the linear process we know so well. PMI (plus, minus, interesting) points help us to break out of this conforming structure.

When facing any career issue, therefore, you need to consider PMI – plus points, minus points and interesting points of any issue.

Here is a very simple exercise to assist you to focus in a number of directions.

ACTION

Apply the PMI technique to the idea of learning a new language at evening class. List all the plus points, minus points and interesting points.

Spend no more than five minutes doing the exercise.

Look carefully at your responses. If you are anything like me your thought patterns will generally follow the minus path more readily than the plus one, thinking of any number of reasons why you should not take the classes. My plus column would quite likely contain no more than a few dream-like answers. The interesting column would certainly be exploring new ground, forcing me to change direction and focus on new areas.

APC

Another tool that de Bono advocates is APC (alternative possible choices). Often during your career you will remember times when you were faced with two difficult alternatives. De Bono believes that at this point you should abandon the dual contest and look for a third alternative.

CAF

CAF (consider all facts) is also extremely applicable to career management. This involves listing everything you can think of that is connected with the issue. Don't limit your thoughts to the present – remember the consequences of time. Every issue you face is affected by time, which, can be categorised into three distinct phases: short-term (1–5 years), medium-term (5–20 years) and long-term (20 plus years). In career terms you must have short, medium and long-term goals. If you are considering whether to study for an MBA, for example, your CAF list may start to look something like this:

Short-term *(1–5 years)*	*Medium-term* *(5–20 years)*	*Long-term* *(20 plus years)*
Cost	Promotion	Satisfaction
Time	Career change	Standard of living
Present job	Own business	Wider options
Qualifications	Location	
Suitability	Children	
	Partner's job	
	Quality of life	

Dense reading and listening skills

Linked with CAF is the wider need to research everything in detail. De Bono discusses dense reading and listening skills, which are often neglected in today's fast-pace world.

These skills require time to read and listen between the lines, to consider non-verbal messages and body communications. You miss so much when you speed-read or only half listen to a conversation. Although these time-saving skills have their place, they often block the creation of new thinking patterns.

Gut reaction

You will have your own view about the phenomenon of 'gut reaction'. Many people believe it is their guiding force, but de Bono feels that when emotions become involved they block the formation of new patterns. He advocates that emotional judgement, which is usually based on pre-structured thinking patterns, should be suspended until the final decision-making process. Then your gut reaction can add beneficial input to creative thinking.

Creative thinking is within your reach; nobody is barred from acquiring these skills. What is needed is the strict discipline to practise the tools which bombard the brain and force it out of traditional ruts. If you want to explore these ideas in more detail, Edward de Bono's *Thinking Course* (BBC Books) will give you a fuller picture, with tape and exercises which are applied to a wider setting.

Developments on the theme of lateral thinking

Professor Charles Handy has developed a similar idea which he applies specifically to career management. In *The Age of Unreason* he explores the concept of 'upside down thinking'.

Also, exponents of neuro-linguistic programming (NLP) explore the idea of 'Looking where you don't see'. NLP is a blend of the art and science of achieving excellence through studying how people from differing fields achieve outstanding success. By observation you can learn to improve your own effectiveness. By studying NLP techniques you can increase your own fields of communication. 'Looking where you don't see' is just one example.

If you wish to explore these techniques in more detail you can refer to *Introducing Neuro-Linguistic Programming* by Joseph O'Connor and John Seymore (see Book List).

Both these concepts are developments on the theme of de Bono's lateral thinking. The idea is that you should look at things from different angles, (such as upside down), and from perspectives which you normally wouldn't think of (where you don't see). It means looking behind the obvious façade to see how things really work. If you apply any of these disciplines to your research you will receive the right answers because you will be finding out how things really work, not how they seem to work. And you will be seeing what makes things happen, not just the things which are happening.

Whatever field you are in, the career ladder is growing more competitive all the time. This means that in order to succeed in finding the best career moves you need to have a strategy which is different from everyone else's, that goes deeper and more thoroughly into the way things are, and produces truly valuable information and knowledge.

ACTION

Try the concepts of 'Looking where you don't see' in everyday life. Next time you are in a queue or walking down a street, try looking above and below your normal line of vision, up to the roofs of the buildings which line the streets and down to the corners of the pavements. You will need to experience this awakening of your awareness to really understand how it works.

Normally, when passing down a high street, you see shop fronts and people on pavements. If you look upwards, however, you will see a mixture of buildings, some old and some new, some converted and some purpose-built, some shabby and some smart. You will see that some shops are obviously nothing more than the façades which open on to the street, while others occupy whole buildings. You will see that some streets are highly residential above ground level, while others are completely taken up by offices.

Suddenly you are getting a better idea of whether the area is prosperous or not, whether it has a resident community or is empty at night. Looking down side-streets and behind fences, through windows and at the litter in the streets, will give you more information about the area, and the people who live and work there. Are there trees? Are the trees full of birds?

Now apply the same logic to a company which you are planning to work for, or a newspaper article about an industry sector you are interested in moving into, or a situations vacant advertisement.

Reading behind the lines

Your attention may be attracted to an advert for a financial director, which is not appropriate to you, but the ad may be the third you have seen for that company in a week, which could mean that they are expanding and taking on people in all areas.

The style of the ad will also tell you if the company has a strong corporate identity, and whether they believe in looking after their staff. Do they talk about the benefits of working there or just boast about the size and pre-eminence of the company? Do they give any more information about themselves that you could look into or file away for later use?

Always look for a different angle and try to work out what is *not* being said in advertisements and articles that you read, as well as what is. Do not take everything at face value. Try de Bono's technique of dense reading.

The unspoken messages

When you go to a company for an interview you will get a much better idea of whether you will be comfortable working there by looking at less obvious things.

– Are the toilets clean and decently equipped?
– Was the building easy to find?
– Do they provide adequate parking facilities?
– Were you greeted in a friendly way by the receptionist or security people?
– Do the people you pass in the corridors look happy and friendly?
– Does everyone dress formally or is it a 'shirtsleeves' operation?
– Are the magazines in reception tatty old copies with security stamps all over them or are the daily papers laid out for everyone to see?
– How much attention is paid to the details?
– Are you made to feel valued or just one of the masses?

All these things will add to the official picture of the company which is put forward in public relations literature and by the people who are interviewing you. Do the two match or is there a conflict between the official story and the informal picture? If there is conflict, why? What does it mean? Would you fit into the framework?

Other methods of stimulating new ideas include brainstorming and mind-mapping, which are more techniques to bombard the brain.

Brainstorming

This is a creative exercise which uses free thought and word association. It can be a very useful technique to stimulate ideas and find innovative solutions to problems. It is usually thought of as a group activity, but the technique can be used by an individual. You can do the exercise alone and then show it to someone else, because you can gain real benefit from sharing and sparking off ideas with others.

The aim of brainstorming is to encourage a questioning approach and to lower barriers to creative thinking – the skill of relating things or ideas which were previously unrelated, stimulating chaos between the brainstem and the cortex. Most of these barriers will be self-imposed ruts – thinking patterns that we are used to looking for. You need to overcome your natural urge to conform and to evaluate things too quickly. It is all about challenging the obvious and overcoming your fear of considering wild ideas and exploring fantasy.

A brainstorming session on your own must be fun and quite spontaneous. You need to examine a variety of options, suspend your own judgement and write down anything that comes into your head. Working alone at this stage can overcome any embarrassment you could feel about including 'silly' ideas.

ACTION

Brainstorming warm-up

Jot down as many uses as you can think of for a paperclip. Fifteen is an excellent number. Three to six is more usual. Try this as a party game.

Career brainstorm

If you are faced with the question 'What alternative job could I do?', a brainstorming session may provide useful pointers for further research.

Take a large sheet of paper – a piece of wallpaper is ideal. Using a felt pen, write JOB in large letters in the centre of the paper. Now write down around it as many jobs titles as you can think of. Don't judge whether they could apply to you, just write whatever comes into your head. Take about 20 minutes over this exercise, by which time you should have added a good number of titles.

Pin your paper up somewhere visible, such as the kitchen, bathroom or loo, and leave a pen nearby so you can add any new ideas as you pass. You may want to ask for assistance at this stage from other members of the household, or friends. They will all have something positive to add.

The following is an example of an actual brainstorm:

PSYCHIATRIST PATHOLOGIST PHOTOGRAPHER COPYWRITER SALES MANAGER AIR HOSTESS PAINTER
TAXIDERMIST SPY GARDENER CORONER STUDENT DANCER HAIRDRESSER DIETICIAN
TEACHER GREENGROCER LIFEGUARD BARMAN SOLICITOR CONFECTIONER BEAUTICIAN
ASTRONAUT ANTIQUES DEALER NURSE ADVERTISER FATHER XMAS ROOFER BALLERINA
AGENT CARPENTER JEWELLER DENTIST SECRETARY ENGINEER LIBRARIAN SHELF STACKER
CLOWN PUBLISHER TRAFFIC WARDEN COMPUTER ANALYST LOLLIPOP PERSON TAXI DRIVER
PLUMBER EDITOR BURSAR WRITER FIREMAN DRY CLEANER SOCIAL WORKER VICAR
BRAIN SURGEON HEAD TEACHER CHEESE MAKER
CHIEF EXECUTIVE JUDGE ACCOUNTANT CHAUFFEUR BREWER MARKETEER CHECKOUT
ELECTRICIAN SOLDIER RADIOGRAPHER SILVERSMITH COACH/BUS FISHMONGER ASSISTANT
DRIVER BUTCHER CLERK
MIDWIFE ACTOR CLEANER RACING MANAGING DIRECTOR RECEPTIONIST BUILDER TUTOR
DOCTOR ARCHITECT NOTARY DRIVER SCIENTIST GOFER BRICKLAYER
REGISTRAR INTERIOR CHEF LECTURER PROFESSOR POSTMAN P.R. CONSULTANT
DESIGNER PRODUCTION FISHERMAN ESTATE AGENT CAR SALESMAN
ACTUARY SURGEON MANAGER PILOT FURNITURE LAWYER POP STAR COMPANY SECRETARY
OPTICIAN WAITRESS M.P. REPORTER FARMER MAKER DESIGNER
TUTOR TRAINER PURCHASING DRIVING INSTRUCTOR DEALER FLORIST SURVEYOR
FRAGRANCE CONSULTANT MANAGER PARK KEEPER LION TAMER ALCHEMIST INTERVIEWER
TELEPHONIST STALL HOLDER HOSTESS MILKMAN WEAVER PROSTITUTE PERSONAL
T.V. PRESENTER GUARD DOG HANDLER ROAD SWEEPER PHARMACIST ASTROLOGER ASSISTANT
MALE ARTIST TAX COLLECTOR CARPET LAYER DUSTMAN RABBI SPINNER
MODEL RAT CATCHER PRINTER DEBT COLLECTOR ORGANIST BANK CLERK PSYCHOLOGIST
PHARMACIST

JOB

ACTION

Read through the list of jobs found in the brainstorm example.

● How many of them did you not include in your own brainstorm?

● If you don't understand some of the job titles, here is where your research can start.

The whole aim of a brainstorm is to spark an idea for you, which will send you down a new avenue of exploration.

One example of how brainstorming can work involves *Linda*. Doubtful about its effectiveness, after completing the exercise she looked at the jobs she'd listed and reacted with, 'So what? I don't want to be a check-out assistant.' 'Why not?', was my reply. What followed was a dialogue about check-out assistants and how poorly they performed their tasks. Linda was a trainer and what emerged was a creative exploration of how her skills could be applied to help create training for check-out assistants.

For Linda this was only half the story because to follow this example through she had to explore another very important avenue, that of self-employment, because to really get this idea off the ground she had to consider the option of becoming a consultant. (See Chapter 7, *Going it Alone*.)

The activity of brainstorming opened up an avenue of exploration for Linda that she had never considered.

Mind-mapping

Mind-maps are a useful creative tool, originally developed by Tony Buzan. A mind-map is a way of presenting ideas in a non-linear fashion. It is similar to brainstorming in that it encourages lateral thinking and is non-judgemental. It differs from brainstorming in that its physical presentation is slightly more structured.

A brainstorm can be further developed by showing your sheet of paper to someone else, at a later date. That person then questions you in more depth about the words recorded on the sheet and adds their own ideas. This can be beneficial for seeking new ideas or helping a situation that has become either blocked or stagnant.

ACTION

Mind-mapping

Choose a piece of paper large enough (at least double the space you think you will need). Put your key word or words in a box or circle in the middle of the page and draw lines outward from the box for the main themes, and then further branches off these lines for sub-themes. See page 116 for an example of how you might begin a mind-map. On page 117 is a different, completed mind-map. Both examples are concerned with a career move, and the key words at the centre of the mind-maps are 'I want to be . . .'

Once your mind-map is complete you will see at a glance the connections between the different branches. These can be linked by colours to show the connection.

Mind-mapping is exciting, and more useful, if you use lots of colours, highlighting connections or separating one theme and all its branches from another.

Advantages

- You have all the issues on one sheet of paper, with all these connections indicated.

- You will have some surprises. The technique stimulates unexpected contributions. It reveals unexpected links.

- From the initial mind-map you can make a further refined mind-map, lists which prioritise and action plans.

- A mind-map can be as big or small as time allows, e.g. do it during a 10-minute tea break.

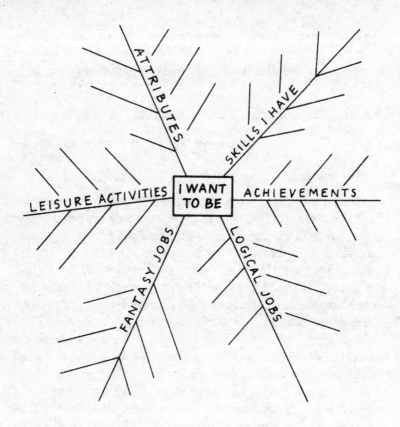

Applying creative thinking to yourself

Creative thinking can be applied to your own situation and ambitions to dramatic effect. You may, for instance, have your mind set on moving to a new company in order to further your career.

If, however, you start to look more closely into your own company, taking different angles and exploring new avenues, you may find that what you really want to do is move into a different department. Whereas before you had always assumed that every move had to be upwards, you might suddenly see that a sideways move could be more beneficial in the long run, or would suit your values better in the short term.

Alternatively, you might realise, by looking at your problems from different angles, that you would actually be more suited to being self-employed – an option which you had never considered before.

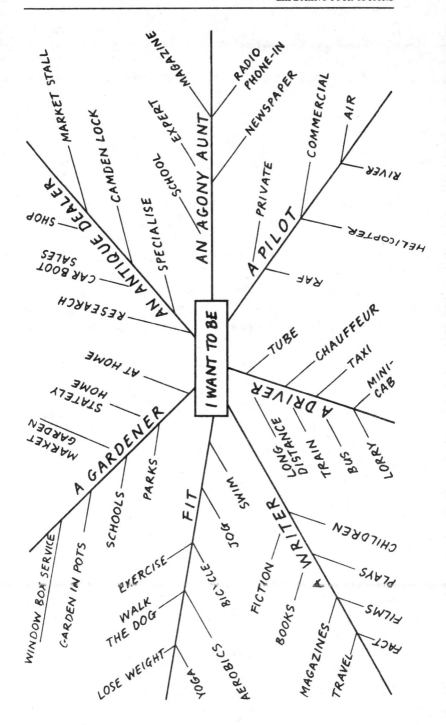

117

Gathering information

The key to gaining any information is research or 'sleuthing'. It divides into two main types:

- desk research;
- people research.

Desk research

This is a skill which some people take to easily, while some find it a chore. It means dense reading (see Edward de Bono's *Creative Thinking*) and exploring the written word. If you enjoy reading and have a naturally enquiring mind you will take to it immediately. If not, don't despair, it will just be a little harder to get going and you will need much more support from others during the difficult times. The key to success is that you must never give up until you have achieved your ultimate goal. You must be strictly disciplined in your actions.

If the concept of research is new to you, try to team up with someone who already has these skills or is naturally good at them. You will learn a lot from them and their support will be invaluable.

Your research should follow a pattern. First, you must identify the type of information you are seeking, then where to source it and, finally, how to retrieve it. Gathering printed information is quite simple, but if you are going to find out more than anyone else you will have to extend your search beyond the usual avenues.

ACTION

A visit to a business library or the business section of your local library, will be very beneficial. A chat to the librarian will show you how much they have developed in the field of technology. Much information is now available via on-line databases, but there are also numerous business directories whose existence you may be unaware of.

Sources of desk research

The Internet   This has become the widest and most creative source of research information. It can be a fantastic tool but be aware before you begin to search the net that this can be time consuming, especially if you are doing a 'free' or 'keyword' search rather than finding sites by using their addresses. Remember that sites are often international, so check locations of positions advertised carefully, and be sure to check the date on the site as not all are updated regularly.

A list of helpful website addresses is given on page 283, but remember that cyberspace changes at a rapid pace and although most sites will post a forwarding link if they move addresses, not all do so. Try a 'keyword' search, or check existing sites for links to related locations. And don't forget that jobs are often advertised on a company's home page, for instance BBC jobs can be found on the BBC website at *www.bbc.co.uk*. Finally, keep an eye out for website addresses on advertisements, on packaging, and at the end of articles. Most companies either have one now, or are in the process of setting one up. Even if they do not advertise jobs on the site, it is still a useful tool for finding out more about the company.

Daily newspapers   Most people will browse through these, particularly the business papers like the *Financial Times*, and serious ones like the *Telegraph*, *The Times*, the *Guardian* and the *Independent*. These are the papers which carry all the news about what companies are doing, which ones are expanding and which are cutting back.

There is also a lot of information to be gleaned from the more popular tabloids, although it may be disguised in stories about personalities. All of it will add to the general picture of an industry or a particular company. Don't forget evening papers.

Business directories   The following is a brief list of some business directories which are available, but your own investigations will reveal a further wealth of information. Try asking at your local library or careers service first. Job centres often have copies you can consult, too.

UK Kompass 98/99 (Kompass)

Key British Enterprise (Dune Bradsheet)

UK's 10,000 Largest Companies (ELC International)

Europe's 15,000 Largest Companies (ELC International)

The Times 1000 (Times Books)

The Personnel Manager's Yearbook (A.P. Information Services)

Kelly's Directory 1999 (Reed Information Services)

The Software User's Yearbook (Learned Information Europe)

The Computer User's Yearbook (Learned Information Europe)

Trade magazines These provide more specialist information on particular sectors, so if you have already identified which area you want to work in, there will be one or two magazines which you should read every week or month. If you want to get into marketing, for instance, you need to read *Marketing* and *Marketing Week*; if you want to get into publishing you need to read *The Bookseller*; if you want to work in the food industry you need to read *The Grocer*; for the building industry you need to read *Building*, and so on. Many contain appointments sections which carry jobs not advertised in the national press. Trade magazines can prove a real gold mine in your search; at the very least they can help you to understand your chosen field much better and gain a deeper understanding of the issues and challenges than you may get from other sources. Reading trade magazines can also ensure you sound up-to-date at interviews.

Beyond the obvious market leaders, however, there are often more specialist titles still. In the marketing field, for instance, there are magazines covering sales promotion, advertising, selling, direct mail, precision marketing, public relations, incentives, conferences corporate entertaining and other branches of the profession. All these will help to deepen your understanding of the marketplace and the companies which work within it, and will suggest ideas to you which you might have never thought of on your own.

Professional magazines   These are the magazines which pertain to your function or profession rather than to a particular industry sector, such as *Management Today, Director, Counselling, Accountancy Age* and *The Lawyer*. If, therefore, you are an accountant and you are interested in the oil industry you will need to study the media which covers both accountancy and oil.

To find all these magazines you either need to acquire a media directory (such as *BRAD, Willing's Press Guide*, or *Benn's Media Directory*) from your local library, or try to find an association or institute for your chosen industry or profession which has a library that you can use. Some can be ordered from newsagents; others are a little harder to track down.

Free magazines and newspapers   These are pushed through your door or handed to you in the street, and hold a lot of information about local companies and activities. The editorial may not be of a particularly high standard, most of it being provided by public relations people, but it will tell you what companies are planning.

Local papers   These are the traditional sources of information for any geographical area, and are mostly thicker and better written than the free sheets. Many carry separate business sections as well as appointments pages.

Company reports   Any larger company will send out annual reports to anyone who asks for them. However, some organisations have now started to charge for copies of annual reports. What hidden message does that give you?

Such reports, while designed to make the companies look as good as possible, have to be truthful and will give you a good idea of the plans and ambitions of the managements, and will also show how close they are to turning them into reality if you are able to read the figures as well as the words.

I have read an extensive number of annual reports from well-known companies. Something that struck me quite forcibly was their lack of information about employees. Only one had a reasonable insert about the staff, thanking them for their contributions to the success of the company.

Promotional literature Virtually all companies produce some sort of promotional literature, either for selling their products or services, or for informing the recruitment market about the opportunities which they have to offer. This can be a very good way of getting a 'feel' for a company and its product.

Career books These come in all shapes and sizes: sometimes produced by industry bodies such as associations and institutions, to help recruit the best people: sometimes written by external experts; and sometimes produced for the graduate recruitment market.

Industry reports These are written about some aspect of an industry. They are often produced for marketing purposes and will provide a variety of background information. These reports are generally lengthy documents and expensive to purchase, but by approaching the publisher or commissioning body, and asking to view the document as part of some career research you may get access to the information. Its value is that it can provide insights into the position of the industry, the market leaders, or new ideas which are being explored.

Reading skills

No one has time to sit down and read through all this material; there are simply too many words being written on every subject to make that possible. What you have to do is develop the skill of skimming and scanning, being able to flick through a book or magazine, picking up headlines, spotting important names and missing out the bits which are not directly relevant to your line of enquiry. You should cut out or photocopy any articles which relate directly to the subjects you are interested in, storing them in a filing system until another piece of information turns up which helps build a broader picture.

Once you have skimmed each document or paper, you need to read the appropriate material densely. This means developing the skills of reading between the lines, looking for the information that is not stated.

You need to be absorbing information all the time. The more facts and information you can amass, the greater your understanding will be. You will make a far greater impact at an interview if you can demonstrate that you have put time and effort into research. Any questions you ask are more likely to be relevant and productive.

The ultimate goal of all your research is to identify a direction that is likely to match your skills, and which would most suit your needs. At first glance that might seem to be a bewildering task. Once you begin to do your research, however, many of your ideas will begin to disqualify themselves, but the process of research will open your mind to new ideas and different ways of viewing your situation.

If you have gone deeply into finding out about an idea or direction and decide that, given all the evidence, you would like to follow it through, you stand a much better chance of success because you know so much more than the competition.

It is broadly true to assume that every change in an organisation's structure or trading position could provide an opportunity. You are initially, therefore, looking for any news of changes which might be creating opportunities which would be worthy of further investigation.

Here are some examples of things to look out for.

Acquisitions and mergers   If a company has just taken over another company in a different sector to itself, it may well be looking for people to help bring the two together or explain one to the other. While acquisitions and mergers can lead to redundancies, they can also create opportunities, since everyone involved is looking for ways to make the deal work and to move the newly-formed organisation forward.

Advertisements   If a company is investing in a large-scale media advertising campaign, that should mean that they are going to be stimulating demand for their product or service. That in turn can mean that they will need more people to satisfy the customer needs which the advertisements create.

Staff appointments   If companies are recruiting heavily in one area, the chances are that they are also going to need more staff in other areas to support their expansion. If, for instance, they are recruiting heavily in the marketing division, they are going to need people in personnel and accounts to handle the new staff and the business which they generate, and they may need to increase production to meet the demand which the new marketing people will be working to create. Similarly, if they are stepping up production, they are going to need more people to sell and distribute the goods they make.

Building programmes   It is safe to assume that if a company has built a brand-new factory or office block (a piece of information that you could find in a local paper), they are going to be expanding and recruiting. At the very least they are going to need people to clean the building and tend the gardens, but they may also need help with new telephone and computer systems, the running of staff canteens and all the rest of the infrastructure.

If a company has the confidence to erect a new building, the chances are that they are optimistic about the future and expect to be expanding.

Brand success   Any company with a brand which suddenly takes off is likely to be looking for ways to consolidate and build on that success for the future. As a result they are likely to be looking for people to help them do that.

Changes in company results   Good news in the financial results of a company are likely to be an indicator of the overall health of a company (although not always). Almost as important, good results will create an air of optimism and confidence within an organisation and this is likely to lead to expansion.

Contracts   Any announcement about a new or re-negotiated contract is going to demonstrate that a company will be in a secure frame of mind.

Decentralisation   If a company is planning to move responsibility out from head office to branches, it will inevitably mean that each of the branches will need to take on new people to handle the work. While some of these people will be transferred from head office, others will need to be recruited locally.

Distribution/reorganisation Likewise, a change in the distribution plans of a company will mean that levels of staffing around the country will change.

Expansion programmes Any announcement of an expansion programme is bound to mean that there will be opportunities. Your research will give you a competitive edge.

Export orders The winning of a major overseas order may not always be widely publicised, but is a good indication of the health of a company and alternative opportunities.

Funding operations Any company which is raising money to fund any sort of expansion is going to need people to run it, and will have the finance to pay for it. The financial press, therefore, provide a useful indicator of who has the confidence of the investors.

Inventions A new invention which has caught on and is receiving a lot of attention is likely to need developing before it can be marketed successfully. That means that as it goes through its product cycle a complete department may grow up around it, and anyone who gets in at the beginning is likely to be able to grow with the product.

Licensing agreements Any company which has won a licensing agreement from a manufacturer is going to need to build up a team of people quickly in order to fulfil their obligations and demonstrate that they are worthy of the job. Your experience could be valuable here.

Modernisation projects Again, this demonstrates a faith in the future and access to the necessary funds.

Other things which might get companies in the news could be new capital projects, office relocations, planning activities, product launches, promotional campaigns, the purchase of assets, new research and development programmes, staff resignations, technical developments and training programmes.

All these things add to the overall picture of a company's, or indeed an industry sector's, health, and provide you with information to help you to put together a case for your ideas. *Information is power and the more you have the better.*

People research

This kind of research is better known as 'networking' or 'contact development', and is something which many people find difficult to understand and often completely alien to their way of thinking. They equate it with the 'old school tie' syndrome which is distasteful to so many, but what it really means is talking to as many people as possible in order to gain information.

ACTION

As the word indicates, networking is something that grows, with each person you contact leading on to others. All you need to start networking is one other person, but most of us can come up with more than that.

For example you may work in finance and would like to broaden your experience by working in another area. You should make a list of everyone you know (aim for about 200 names). Now tick the names on the list who work in the area that interests you. Choose six of the ticked names belonging to people you know well enough to feel comfortable talking to on the phone. These are the people you should contact first. As you become more accustomed to this process of information gathering, and your confidence increases, you can start to contact people you don't know. Ideally you will have a contact name from someone in your existing network.

The most valuable source of research is the people you know and, as your network develops, the people that other people know. If you are good at this sort of activity the range is limitless. You will never run out of people to talk to.

The need to be focused

Most people are flattered to be asked their opinion or to talk on a subject which they are knowledgeable about. Even if they seem reluctant to give up much time at the beginning, once they have started talking they will often be hard to stop!

To get the most out of this type of contact you need to be focused on what you want to achieve from each meeting. This must be carefully planned beforehand, otherwise you will waste a lot of time talking about the things *they* want to talk about, not the things which *you* need to know. So you must have a clear idea of what you need and then express that need to the other person right at the beginning of the meeting, or maybe in a letter confirming the appointment. This preparation will also help you to present a professional image, which is very important. If the other person sees that you mean business they will have a better idea of how to treat your enquiry.

The information which you need from people could be in several forms. It might be that you need to find out how that person developed their career since they are now doing the sort of job you are interested in exploring. It might be that you wish to gain general background information on the industry that they are working in or specific information about their company. You might want to know the details about what a particular job entails, or you might want to find out more about the culture or style of a company.

You are not looking for the external veneer – that you can get from brochures – you want to know about the reality of the situation, so that you can make informed decisions, and pick up some clues about the best ways to make further contacts.

As you are talking you will find that ideas begin to spark in your mind which will relate what they are telling you to your own strengths, skills and values, and will give you ideas for further research, either at the desk or through another branch of the network which is growing before you.

After you have been to see someone, always write a thank you note, and remember that whoever they are they are now a member of your network. A lively network is one of the most valuable assets in developing and maintaining a successful career, and you need to keep tabs on everyone you come into contact with, since you never know when they will again be in a position to help you with information or, alternatively, when you might be able to provide some information which will assist them.

Always keep your network informed of what is happening, and remember that as it grows you will have to spend more time sharing *your* experience and knowledge with other people. That will mean being prepared to meet other people for networking chats. This need not be an onerous task since all the people you meet in this way are likely to become part of your network.

I see two or three people a month who are referred to me through networking, and over the years this has grown into a very interesting and unusual source of information.

Network contacts can come from a variety of sources, some of which are listed below.

Present business colleagues These people are always useful since you spend so much time with them, and have a great many opportunities to talk both formally and informally about the industry you are all in, and about any other interests which they might have. They will also be able to introduce you to other people, from customers to competitors, from suppliers to personal friends of theirs, all of whom will be able to continue the network and put more information into the jigsaw.

Former bosses If you left your former employers on good terms they will have as much to gain from having you in their network as the other way round. The biggest advantage in this situation is that you already have an established relationship.

Past colleagues These people will also be interested in hearing from you, since they will want to know what you have learnt since leaving the company where they worked with you. As you all move on through your careers you will always maintain that original bond, that will make you interested to hear news of one another and happy to help each other with advice and information.

Past subordinates who have progressed There are always going to be some people who will travel quicker up the ladder than others, but everyone remembers the people they worked for in the past, and they will always be happy to talk to you, if only to let you know how well they have done since leaving. If your relationship with them was good, they will be grateful for the breaks you gave them early on in their careers.

College lecturers and tutors   These people have a vested interest in knowing what is going on in the real world since it helps to give credibility to their teaching. They will also take some pride in your success. Because of their positions they get to know a great many people who are on their way up and will often be useful sources of further contacts.

Bank managers   Both your personal and company bank managers want to see you do well and they also like to know as much as possible about what you are up to, to ensure that you are not going to turn into a bad debt. They are also in the position of talking to a great many people, most of whom will be working and living in the same area as you, and they will have an equally strong interest in seeing that those people do well. If they can benefit either or both of you by putting you together, they will do so.

Friends from university, college or school   This is another area where you will be able to broaden your network into any number of different disciplines and sectors, since many of your friends will have taken totally different paths through life.

Society and club members   Again, these people probably come from different career sectors to you and will already feel friendly towards you because of your mutual links.

Professional associations and institutions   One of the main reasons for the existence of these sorts of organisations is to help practitioners in their industry, and they have a vested interest in being as helpful and useful as possible, since it strengthens their industry and makes people feel that they are lively and useful organisations.

Suppliers   There are also all the people who act as suppliers to your current company, which includes suppliers of raw material or equipment, builders, advertising agencies, recruitment consultants, public relations consultancies and management consultants. All these people are kindly disposed to you since you are a source of revenue to them, and all of them have a wide range of contacts, and so possess information which could be useful to you.

Friends, relatives and neighbours You should not underestimate this, the most important group of all. These are the people who are most accessible to you, and who are the most likely to be willing to pass you on to other people.

Any organisations with which you are associated, like chambers of commerce, trade or employer organisations, political parties, charities, parent-teacher associations or trade unions, are all made up of people from a variety of backgrounds who share mutual interests with you. They can all be highly responsive to networking.

The golden rule of networking is that you must be sure that each person leads to others. The ideal number is 3 new contacts from everyone you talk to. That way an initial 3 contacts become 9, which become 27, 81 and 243 within a very short time. Obviously, there is a limit to the number of people you will have time to see, and some of them you will be able to eliminate with just a telephone call, but it shows just how powerful a source of information people research can be if you understand the true meaning of the concept, work hard at it and always conduct yourself professionally.

Rob had worked hard searching for a job change for 12 months and had come a close second on a number of occasions. He had limited his search to headhunters and advertisements, believing that networking was not very healthy and that really, he didn't know anyone who would be of use or interest.

When he was introduced to the true meaning of networking, he slowly began to explore his own contacts, who were extremely diverse and good sources of valuable information. He worked at networking very hard and within six weeks he found a job which was completely in line with his own skills and values checklist. In fact he wrote his own job description and is now facing challenges that really utilise his potential fully.

In her book *Networking and Mentoring: A Woman's Guide* (men shouldn't be put off by the title), Dr Lily M. Segerman-Peck defines networking very simply: 'It means making contacts, and using those contacts for whatever purpose you need. For example, if you don't know something, ask someone who does.' Networking is as simple as that.

She goes on to explain, however, that just being in a network is not enough. Networking is active and dynamic. To use your networks fully you have to be 'go-getting'. That means that you must try to develop your contacts continually; attending meetings even if the topic is not of direct relevance to you, in order to meet people, and making sure you always have a supply of business cards to distribute. If business cards are not provided by your organisation, have your own printed. This is a wise investment and will indicate that you are professional in your approach to managing your career. It may mean sending Christmas cards to remind people that you exist, or asking around to find out who has the information and influence that you need.

'At all times,' says Dr Segerman-Peck, 'keep your eyes and ears open for anything that is useful, follow it up and use it, or store the information away for future use.'

Networking is a continual process. If you believe it is only relevant when looking for a new job, you will develop a weak and shallow network.

But remember that you need to develop a creative approach, something that is different and will catch the imagination of the recipient. Also, keep a check on your listening skills and go for de Bono's dense listening style (page 107), since it will add so much to your knowledge base.

Work experience and work shadowing

Work experience

Work experience is a term generally associated with students who are looking for holiday work within a sector in which they think

131

they would like to build their career. It is a good career management move since it allows them to sample an industry and a company without committing themselves to it.

It gives them the opportunity to ask a great many questions from the inside, and to see things which would never be revealed to them in the course of a formal interview, where everyone is on their best behaviour and the atmosphere is very false. In the course of work experience they will also be able to find out things about themselves, such as their abilities to fit into teams, accept the leadership of others and take initiatives.

In order to make the most of the chance, they need to be active. Many students just wait for someone else to take the initiative, but if they really want to gain the maximum from this valuable opportunity they must be continually exploring, and asking for information either through desk or people research. They must be willing to make moves to find things out for themselves. Employees are generally willing to talk but they are usually busy and often can't remember the type of information they wanted to know when they were leaving school, and anyway everything has changed so much since then.

More and more pupils are also now encouraged to get involved with work experience during their final year at school and the same rule of 'activity' applies to them.

Work shadowing

Work shadowing is a similar idea except that the student is attached to someone doing a real job within the company, and follows them around observing what they do. This way they do not get bogged down in the detail of some junior clerical role, getting given all the jobs which no one else wants to do, but they have the opportunity to see the company through the eyes of someone who has been there some time.

There is no reason, however, why these activities should be limited to the young. If you are thinking of changing fields or companies, you could approach someone and ask if you can shadow them.

That way you might, for instance, be able to find out what it feels like to work in the public sector when your own work experience has always been in private companies. Or you could find out about a job which has always sounded attractive to you, but which you have never fully understood, such as public relations or advertising. You might, for instance, have always worked in an advertising department of a client company and want to sample life in the agency sector. Or, alternatively, you might like the idea of being a company secretary, without having any clear idea what their duties are. A day or two spent with a company secretary would answer a great many of your questions.

You might be able to organise this through your own network, but if not there is no reason why you couldn't approach another department or company direct and ask them if they would have any objections to you doing it. This is certainly quite an unusual approach, but unless you ask you will not know if it is practical. Again, you will have to try some creative approaches.

Ask people you know if it would be possible to spend a day of your annual leave shadowing them. If you have a contact at a school or college (maybe through your children), a chat to the careers teacher may give you a helpful lead. Careers officers from your local Careers Service may also be able to help. This service is not just for school leavers and students – part of the service's statutory obligation is to provide a service for individuals who have started on their career path.

Some contacts will be very positive, others negative, but that just means you should go onto someone else. The more people you try the greater the chance of success, and you lose nothing if the response is no, but gain a wealth of information if it is yes.

When you have the opportunity to shadow someone at work you must prepare yourself thoroughly by doing desk research (pages 118–26) to acquaint yourself with basic facts and figures. What does it do? How is it structured? What is its turnover? What are its prospects for the future?

During the visit your antennae need to be highly tuned. Look and listen to everything that goes on around you and absorb the atmosphere. Don't make any judgements at the time, just collect data for future sifting and interpretation. At the end of the visit collate the desk research with the live information. Try some creative techniques at this point, such as mind-mapping (page 114) or the de Bono PMI exercise (page 106).

After exploring the creative angles you can then listen to your own gut reactions. By now you should have assimilated sufficient data to make some valid assumptions, and will be capable of setting objectives for moving your career forward. Remember that a decision not to act is as positive as a decision to act, as long as it is based on sound knowledge.

Unexpected results

Exploring your options is one of the most exciting phases of career management. Many of the techniques can be applied to other areas of your life, often with stimulating and unexpected results.

From my experience of career management, the ideas explored and unlocked in a creative way are extremely exciting and open up completely new vistas. *Jack* never realised how much his life was influenced by travel until he did a mind-mapping exercise. This led to certain action plans to explore further his present connections with the tourist industry and how he could add different dimensions to his present situation.

Creative thinking does not work in a predictable way. *Thomas*, after doing a mind-mapping exercise late one evening, awoke next morning from a dream in which he was arguing with a colleague he hadn't seen for years. Later, reflecting on the dream he recalled a remark the colleague had once made: 'You'd make a good magistrate'. He mulled over the idea and as his thoughts developed he came to the conclusion that it was definitely worth further consideration.

A word of warning, however: creative thinking can't be regimented or forced into a limited time frame but must be allowed to just happen. The brain needs time and space to explore. Results can be immediate, but generally the flash occurs when you least expect it. You must also have a certain amount of faith that, as a technique, creative thinking works.

If nothing else, the activity of creative thinking will result in some action because the mere deed of taking some action will bring about other actions. Action results in action – which is true, positive and powerful.

Remember . . .

- Applying creative thinking techniques to career management will give you a competitive edge.

- Everyone has the ability to be creative.

- The only blocks to creativity are intelligence and arrogance.

- The creative tools outlined in this chapter can apply to any aspect of your life.

CHAPTER 7

GOING IT ALONE

Have you got what it takes?

Many people hold the dream that working for themselves would solve all their problems. For some, self-employment is the best move they ever made, while others find that the reality is a terrible shock. Many are forced down this avenue because of the ever-changing patterns of work when in reality they are not well suited to it.

Charles Handy in *The Age of Unreason* writes about the portfolio career, a concept which is talked about widely as a pattern for future employment. The belief is that after working for a hectic but brief spell in a corporation, individuals will face burn-out or skill redundancy. This will require a career move which may result in a change of emphasis for them. Rather than one company buying your skills, you may have to sell them to a number of organisations.

What is often neglected in such a situation is the shift from your services being bought as a passive activity to you positively selling your skills. This is an activity for which many people are not trained, and nor are they suited to it in personality terms.

As part of any career exploration it is extremely important that you know and understand what is required to become self-employed. There are numerous books on the subject which give the nuts and bolts about accounting, legal advice, taxation, business planning, finance, marketing etc. (see book list), but before you reach this stage you need to explore why you are drawn to self-employment, and if you are really suited to this way of life.

Let's consider some of the factors for and against self-employment.

For
- Freedom to work in your own way
- Scope to work creatively
- No accountability
- Variety of tasks
- Freedom to work to your own time clock
- Your standards are achievable
- No company politics
- Less corporate stress
- Reduced bureaucratic structure

Against
- Responsibility for everything
- Having to take on tasks that may be beneath your status
- No colleague inter-action/ friendship
- Very lonely
- Always in charge, no deferring
- Often torn between priorities
- Extremely long hours
- Having to turn your hand to a variety of tasks
- Many factors beyond your control
- Loss of status

The most important factor here is self-knowledge. From the work you completed in Phase 1 of this book, you should now understand your key skills, strengths, values and needs. Do these really suit self-employment? Do you, in other words, have what it takes?

There is no formula that will guarantee successful self-employment, but there are a number of indicators which can help. It is certainly wise to be aware of these factors and to know whether or not you have them in your repertoire. If certain of these characteristics are missing or are weak, all is not lost. What you may need is to find them in somebody else with whom you can form a partnership or a working relationship, or maybe it is a skill you will have to buy in.

Being your own boss is generally considered to need some entrepreneurial flair, which means the ability to control effectively a commercial undertaking which involves risk effectively.

Occupational psychologists have spent many years researching the factors that contribute to entrepreneurial success, and with the aid of psychometric testing they can identify if you have the personality factors which would contribute to a positive self-employment profile.

Personality traits of an entrepreneur

Thomas International Management Systems Ltd have devised a personal profile analysis which can indicate your personality traits. From their research, David Lee Howarth, a director, believes that a successful entrepreneur will need to be some of the following:

driving	influential
competitive	persuasive
forceful	friendly
inquisitive	verbal
direct	communicative
self-starter	positive
assertive	demonstrative
mobile	firm
alert	persistent
active	stubborn
eager	strong-willed
restless	independent

ACTION

Here is a checklist of words that Thomas International use to describe a self-starter or entrepreneur. Which ones do you feel apply to you?

	Y	N		Y	N
Individualistic			Mobile		
Alert			Quick		
Social			Outgoing		
Talkative			Driving		
Enthusiastic			Optimistic		
Clever			Erratic		
Competitive			Influential		

	Y N		Y N
Egocentric	☐ ☐	Positive	☐ ☐
Impulsive	☐ ☐	Restless	☐ ☐
Independent	☐ ☐	Strong-willed	☐ ☐
Persuasive	☐ ☐	Decisive	☐ ☐
Demanding	☐ ☐	Self-assured	☐ ☐
Confident	☐ ☐	Friendly	☐ ☐
Inquisitive	☐ ☐	Assertive	☐ ☐
Venturesome	☐ ☐	Direct	☐ ☐

Now complete a reality test (page 68), and ask someone who knows you well to complete the same exercise for you.

Compare the results. There should be a very high percentage of ticks if you have the personality traits of an entrepreneur.

Personality traits of a consultant

One of the major sources of work for the self-employed is in the field of consultancy. A profile can also be drawn up for a consultant – although the word has many different meanings. To become a general business or technical consultant, Thomas International suggest it would be appropriate for you to be the following:

driving	compliant	competitive
careful	forceful	systematic
inquisitive	precise	direct
accurate	self-starter	perfectionist
assertive	logical	reserved
mobile	reflective	alert
suspicious	active	self-conscious
eager	probing	restless
serious	demonstrative	

139

ACTION

Here is a checklist of words that Thomas International use to describe a general business or technical consultant. Tick the words you believe apply to you. Then ask someone else to do a reality test (page 68).

	Y	N			Y	N
Self-starter			Direct			
Demanding			Assertive			
Forceful			Reserved			
Reflective			Logical			
Active			Mobile			
Alert			Eager for results			
Systematic			Precise			
Perfectionist			Inquisitive			
Probing			Serious			
Careful			Impatient			
Enquiring			Self-critical			
Cautious			Independent			
Blunt			Accurate			

Note, however, that if you wanted to be a marketing consultant, a profile more akin to an entrepreneur would be more appropriate.

Can you juggle your time?

One of the greatest traps of working alone, especially if you are working as an independent consultant, is that when you are doing the job you are bound to be neglecting your future planning and marketing. In other words, when you are busy working you can't be selling. The consequence of this is that when the job comes to an end you have to get back into the marketplace, so there may then be too long a gap before the money from your next job starts to come in. Erratic cash flow is almost certainly the single most frequent cause for self-employed people to come to grief.

Theorists say that the answer to this problem is not to commit yourself fully to a long contract and to ensure that marketing is an ongoing process. In theory, I agree, but in practice many people find that this is impractical, although they understand and accept the concept.

Can you stay in the limelight?

One activity which you must address is keeping your profile in the limelight. This also applies to anyone who is undertaking a successful career management process, but it is especially relevant for individuals who are self-employed. You need to have an organised campaign which includes attending meetings, talks, seminars, conferences etc., where you will meet individuals of like minds and other interested parties.

As these often take place outside office hours, it does not eat into your chargeable time, but it does seriously sap your energy levels, especially at the end of a hectic day. You must make an effort to remain in people's memories; to be around so that when they have a need, your name is top of the list.

Interim management

A recent development is the growth in organisations that specialise in executive leasing, interim management or temping for senior personnel. These services provide senior managers, with certain specific skills, on a temporary contract to companies who have an urgent or transient need. It is an easy and cost-effective way of resolving many problems that arise within organisations, especially as companies are becoming leaner and less able to accommodate sudden changes or crisis situations.

Nicky Cutts from Barton Interim Management believes that the freelance manager can provide an extremely valuable resource in the area of change management which could be resourced in a variety of ways:

- the in-house company change agent;

- the external consultant;

- the interim manager.

Change, by its very nature, is transient and is never situated in the same place. So the in-house specialist is an expensive resource and may not always be best suited to the particular situation or fully utilised at all times. Changes in the area of personnel are very different from new, high-technology development. An external consultant may be too far removed from the situation because he or she is never directly employed by the company.

The interim manager is only employed for the actual time worked, and when you consider that in any year on average, an employee is only available for work for 225 days out of 365, it soon becomes clear that a temporary manager is very cost-effective, as well as bringing new and often clearer perspectives to bear on changed situations.

But not everyone is suited to interim management. There are two initial views about whether an interim manager should be totally devoted to this type of work, or whether it is a useful activity to combine with other actions.

Nicky Cutts has very strong views that real interim managers have made a definite decision not to return to corporate life. 'I wish the "tweenies" would get re-employed and let us return to our core of specialist interim managers,' she says.

This view is shared by Robert Mark of Executive Interim Management, who believes that anyone wanting to follow this option of working must take a firm decision to follow this path, rather than try to straddle a number of alternatives. It is a real job which needs serious and firm commitment.

Others, especially outplacement consultants, suggest that executive leasing or interim management can be a beneficial source of employment opportunities. Some sectors, especially accounting and computing, have a tradition of working on short-term contracts and certain agencies such as Robert Half Accountemps specialise in this area. The best sources of leads for companies providing this service are trade or professional journals, where you will find advertisements which you can follow up, not particularly for a specific vacancy, but as a source of information such as address, telephone number and contact name.

David Searle, managing director of Intex, the longest-established executive leasing company in Britain, believes that a good indicator to success in this field is excellent business experience at the top, with a past salary indicator of not less than £50k.

Nicky Cutts believes that a good interim manager should be able to:

- stand on their own feet;
- take decisions quickly;
- operate alone.

They must be:

- self-motivated;
- hungry.

With less obvious, but equally important qualities such as being:

- a self-starter and finisher;
- over-qualified for the task in question;
- results orientated;
- a sales person.

Laurence Smith, managing director of Harrison Wills, an interim management provider, believes that becoming a self-employed independent executive requires many changes in attitude because there is a great deal of down-time which has to be coped with both by the individual and their partner. He strongly maintains that everyone entering the field must have the full support and commitment of their partner because it is a very lonely activity, involving great risks.

He stresses the need to be good at selling because statistics show that business from interim management agencies on average only provides 15 per cent of business, you need to generate 85 per cent yourself. He also says that interim management can only be successful if conducted as a full-time activity, but it can then provide a most satisfactory experience'.

Advice for consultants

In response to the growing question, 'What makes a good freelance or independent consultant?', Russam GMS Ltd conducted some major research in 1990 which found that there are key, recognisable elements to developing a successful independent consultancy practice, but much of the advice applies to running any type of independent business successfully.

1. Having a 'trade'. It is normal that excellence can usually only be achieved in a narrow range of activities. This 'trade' must be clearly defined and clearly recognisable by, and effectively communicated to, prospective clients.

2. Continuing effort should be made to retain and improve technical skills which have to be the basis of one's success and ability to command good fee rates.

3. One's physical appearance should be attractive and interpersonal behaviour should be of the highest standard.

4. The ability to approach business prospects effectively, the ability to sell, particularly face to face and good presentation techniques are important skills that require continuous development and practice.

5. Promotional materials should be simple, factual, beautifully presented, without being too glossy, and well supported by case study references.

6. Marketing should be well planned, comprehensive and continuous, even when you are very busy. The GMS research showed that everything works if done properly, and activities based on personal contacts work best.

7. Continuous efforts should be made to understand how the world of independent consultancy works because it is a fragmented, unstructured area where everyone involved in it is learning new things all the time. Nothing stands still, least of all opportunities.

8. Recognise that emotional stability and the dangers of loneliness need careful handling and, under the influence of effort and energy, situations will change from day to day.

In order to be successful, therefore, GMS drew the conclusion that skills and knowledge should be continuously developed in the following areas.

1. *Appearance skills*   Looking good is absolutely vital. Too many people do not make the best of themselves.

2. *Communication and presentation skills*   Never having had to sell anything to anyone often means that you cannot do it. The independent who cannot sell his or her work is doomed.

3. *Information technology*   The independent who does not have his or her own computer and is not able to perform basic functions on it will increasingly be seen as intellectually inert and out of date.

4. *Personal finance*   This is a highly complex area which even qualified accountants find tricky. It is silly not to arrange your financial affairs to best effect.

5. *Sales and marketing*   Knowing how and where to sell your professional products is almost as important as being able to do a good job once the assignment has been secured.

Selling styles

For many, selling is a distasteful idea, a task people find difficult and one that raises many problems for self-employed consultants. These attitudes generally seem to come from a lack of knowledge and understanding. Most people believe that there is one method of selling and this is the hard sales approach. This is an inaccurate perception because there are numerous selling styles, and there is sure to be one that will suit your personality and behaviour patterns.

One way to discover your own style is through behavioural exercises developed by the LIFO® (UK, Eire) Organisation (see Resources guide). The company is licensed in this country to train consultants to use a range of materials, including LIFO, that measure your behavioural styles. Their 'Styles of Selling' material is very helpful. It includes a self-report questionnaire with a supporting work book containing self-development exercises to enhance your strengths and give you a fuller understanding of how you interact with clients and which styles are most appropriate, where and when.

Informal and formal referral networks

Another, less formal, solution to generating work for consultants is the development of working networks. These are generally formulated on a basis of trust and understanding, with no legalised contracts. Often individual consultants working in the same field can recommend or pass work on if they are busy or not quite suited to the assignment in question. This informal networking can work very well, but there are pitfalls.

First, the area of trust and understanding is vital and must be clearly defined from the outset. Don't rely on a 'gentlemen's agreement', spell everything out, especially how and who should communicate to the client. The secret is that at no time should the client be confused.

One of the conflicts faced by consultants is being offered work which is not totally within their area of competence. The danger when they accept is that they don't deliver a completely successful result, and this can give consultants a bad reputation. However, with an informal network you get to do the work that is best suited to your expertise.

Certain professional associations provide a more formalised register of contacts. For example, the Institute of Personnel Development (IPD) has a consultancy service where practising consultants can apply for registration, providing they are corporate members, have one year's experience in consultancy, references from three clients and professional indemnity insurance.

Also the Association for Counselling at Work, part of the British Association for Counselling, has a *Referral Directory* which records members with their qualifications, training, experience, areas of specialisation and geographical situation. This is available to all members, but access is available through the membership secretary for anyone looking for a counsellor.

The Institute of Mechanical Engineers has a database of consultants and is in the process of compiling a directory for referral.

Many professional associations provide this type of service, either formally or informally, and that is why it is very important to develop your links professionally in this way, to ensure that you keep abreast of what's going on and that you are visible in your own professional arena.

Associates or networkers

Another avenue which is applicable to certain sectors is the employment of associate consultants or networkers when the volume of work in a company increases. The parameters for this type of employment will be different with each organisation. In some companies it is handled very professionally with rigorous training, updating and continuous communication with the individual, while others merely place an advertisement in the local paper, hold recruitment interviews in an hotel and, 'Bingo!', you have been engaged for a short-term contract as an employee of the company.

Generally, information about these types of assignments is by word of mouth within the sector concerned. You will only acquire the information through contacts or through a professional association or network, where you will meet people who know or can refer you to other contacts.

If this form of arrangement suits your particular situation and is practised in your specific work sector, make sure you look at the type of contract you may have to sign, as some have clauses that exclude you from working for other companies engaged in similar business. Make sure that you understand clearly what the contract is saying, otherwise you may find that you are hampered from earning a living in a particular field.

Writing your own business plan

It is vital that anyone who is thinking of working for themselves writes a business plan, whether you want to turn a hobby into a business or start your own limited company.

Even if you are contemplating being a self-employed or freelance consultant, a business plan is important. Many people are put off because they think it is a complicated or difficult document to compile, but this is not the case.

A business plan should have two objectives.

1. To help you clarify your ideas and think through some of the pitfalls right at the beginning.

2. To help you communicate your ideas to other people. This could be friends, family or colleagues, to gauge their reactions, or to professionals who may assist you with funding.

The main aim is to provide a clear outline of the business that you wish to start, and to demonstrate that you have undertaken some research to support your idea. The following is a simple outline of the type of information you should include.

The product

1. Define the product or service and the level of your expertise.

2. How do you know there is a demand for the product/service?

3. What is the competition?

4. What will distinguish your product/service from other similar businesses?

The costs

1. How much money is required to start the business?

2. What will the product/service cost?

3. How much income do you need each month?

4. What will it cost each month to run the business?

5. What income do you anticipate the business will be able to provide for you, and how much business must you do to produce it?

This section is very important, especially in the area of consultancy. You must cost in holidays, sickness and future development in order to give a true cost that will enable you to exist beyond the first assignment.

The marketing

1. Which group of clients is your product or service targeted towards?

2. How will you make people aware of your business?

3. How will you encourage people to buy your product or service?

Research has shown that companies who fail are often those that have not started with a proper business plan. Success is only achieved through detailed preparation, good planning and tight control.

Also investigate what help is available from government or educational sources. This area is fraught with bureaucratic red tape and finding the right information is often a nightmare, but help and financial assistance *is* available. You just need to be very persistent. In the Resource Section at the end of this book, you will find some useful addresses.

Going it alone will become an option open to more and more people as the world of work contracts, as companies become flatter, leaner and less encumbered by layers of management. It is vital that if you want to consider this option you need to know your own abilities, strengths, weaknesses etc. If you don't match up with a strong entrepreneurial profile there are other options available, so explore them all and find the one best suited to you.

If you really don't match up to the option of self-employment, be honest and accept that this is not for you. Be creative and look for other alternatives.

Remember . . .

- Consider being self-employed – are you suited?

- Find out about executive leasing and interim management. Is it suitable for you?

- Explore specialist registers.

- Create informal associations.

- Link up with associates and networks.

- Know your own selling style.

Transition from phase 2 to phase 3

Phase 2 in the career management model is a transition phase, that is full of uncertainty. The key to emerging from it successfully is to learn to live with the uncertainty for a while, because eventually clear action points will become obvious. The less you try to put structure around this phase and learn to go with the chaos, the more easily will the right objectives emerge.

PHASE 3

CHAPTER 8

ACTION PLANNING AND BASIC COMMUNICATION SKILLS

Returning to your foundations

In Phase 1 of the career management model you focused on finding out about yourself, your skills, strengths, values, weaknesses, constraints and reality. These are the foundation upon which you should build your career.

As a result of applying the techniques in Phase 2 you will have some clear objectives which need progressing. You will have to take some action to do this, and this action will have to be communicated in some way. This is what Phase 3 of the model deals with.

Warning When you move into Phase 3 it becomes obvious whether you have built a solid foundation or not. If you are clear about what are your assets and weaknesses then your confidence will be apparent, but if you glossed over Phase 1 your uncertainty will show through, and if you have built a false picture of yourself you will be giving out conflicting messages and your words will not match your actions. Your low self-worth will be communicated to others indirectly by the way you dress, your manner of speech and the way you write about yourself. It is therefore vital that you have completed the first two phases to your own satisfaction before advancing to Phase 3.

Action planning

Before exploring some of the communication techniques, let's make sure you understand what action planning is, and how it can be successfully achieved.

It would be all too easy to read through this book, nod wise agreement at some parts, disagree with others, put it aside with every intention of doing something about your career – and then forget all about it. All of us have pressing and immediate problems which distract us from making any long-term plans or changes. You need, therefore, to create an action plan for yourself which will ensure that you turn some of your good intentions into reality.

At this point in your career management process you need to understand the skill of positive action planning and setting objectives. It is vital if you are to achieve success and move forwards.

Setting objectives is a positive action and will give you the opportunity to measure your progress. In order to achieve measurable results, however, the objectives must be clear, precise and set within a time frame.

'I'll speak to some of my contacts' is not a good objective. It is too vague, is not measurable; it has no time frame and the success cannot be measured. 'Next week I will phone four contacts and arrange to meet them for a chat', is a much clearer objective which you can measure easily.

Start by setting yourself some guideline objectives. Don't set so many that they appear daunting or you will be put off trying to achieve them; just two or three would be enough to start with.

Here is an example: 'Next week I will practise listening skills for five minutes every day before lunch.'

Once you get into the habit you will be able to set new or updated objectives regularly.

Get SMART   Setting objectives is a positive action and one that can be used to measure progress. To achieve measurable results, objectives must be clear, precise and set within a time frame.

Remember:

Specific

Measurable

Achievable

Relevant

Timescaled

Overcoming avoidance strategies

Once you have started being actively involved with planning for the future, you may become blocked by negative barriers. You may not seem able to achieve objectives you have set yourself. People often mask this problem by using an avoidance strategy. This is very common when you find things difficult or uncomfortable.

When I am faced with a very difficult desk-bound task (like writing this book), I tend to get sidetracked by tasks such as cleaning the oven. Anything becomes more important than actually starting to write. Avoidance tactics can waste a great deal of time, so much that you never get round to the set objective.

It is important that you recognise avoidance tactics and when you are using them. Beware, you can use very powerful arguments to convince yourself that cleaning the oven is vitally important.

Force field analysis

Some obstacles are more difficult to overcome and you may find that a problem-solving technique is helpful to deal with them. Force field analysis is a very grand title, but it is a simple and useful tool for helping to overcome blocks.

First you need to state the problem clearly, then all the hindering or negative points, then all the facilitating or positive points. The objective is to work on decreasing the negatives and increasing the positives.

We will consider an example which many people, including me, find difficult, namely making telephone calls to people you don't know – better known as cold calling:

Goal Feeling comfortable when contacting someone I don't know by phone.

Negative factors
- Get tongue tied.
- Feel I'm intruding.
- Get blocked by secretary.
- Don't know what to say.
- Fear they may be rude.

- Feel embarrassed.

- Speak too quickly.

- Telephone slammed down on me.

Positive factors

- Good telephone manner.

- Use telephone a lot.

- Generally quite confident.

- Can usually talk to anyone.

- Always well organised.

The next stage is to work at the negative factors until they become less and less important, while developing the positive factors in order to achieve the goal.

Often, the activity of committing the analysis to paper helps to clarify the situation, and in my own case this exercise has certainly helped me to overcome some of my barriers to cold calling.

Basic communication skills

Before we consider the more obvious communication skills related to career management, you need to master some simple techniques which play a very important part in successful communication of any type, but which are particularly relevant to career management. Some of them you will immediately recognise because you use them every day. Others may be new but I suggest that even if you are familiar with them all it is good to recap and maybe check that you haven't slipped into any bad habits.

With these skills are some exercises which may also act as an introduction or help to recap.

The following are some basic skills:

active listening;
questioning;
empathy;

accepting;
reflecting or paraphrasing;
use of silence;
feedback;
assertiveness;
receptiveness.

Active listening

We all believe that we listen to others but, in reality, this is a very difficult skill to master, and most of the time it is poorly practised. Most people, when they look as if they are listening are actually only pausing before speaking again, or are thinking their private thoughts.

A small child, when told to eat her dinner, replied, 'How can I, because my mouth is full of words?' The wisdom of children is often *so* clear. How many times are our mouths not only full of words, but also our brains are jammed with thoughts? We are then expected to listen to someone else talking about something which is of interest to them.

The skill of listening, therefore, is often neglected, but is extremely valuable in so many situations. It is an asset which we should all pay more attention to developing because unless we listen we can't learn, and we can't understand what is going on in the minds of the people around us. If it was possible for each man to be an island then it wouldn't matter, but everything to do with work is about relationships with other people, and relationships require bridges of mutual understanding to be built.

ACTION

Try this listening exercise with a partner.

For between three and five minutes one of you talks while the other listens. Each person must adhere strictly to their role, concentrating on the action of listening, rather than the words that they are hearing.

The task of the listener is to concentrate on how it feels to listen; notice if you drift off, get embarrassed, focus on some things rather than others or become frustrated because you cannot enter the conversation yourself.

The talker must focus on talking, saying whatever comes into their mind and expressing something of what they are feeling. Notice if you are talking for the listener or whether you have blocked them out of your awareness and are talking for yourself. Are you looking for signs of approval or encouragement, or just charging ahead?

After five minutes change roles and repeat the exercise.

Now try introducing a third person to the group. The activity of this person is to be an observer, and to record the movements and interactions of the other two.

After another three to five minutes change roles and repeat the activity again.

At the end of the exercise, get together to draw up a checklist of positive listening skills, and briefly record your own feelings and observations about listening.

One very valuable tip, when it comes to using listening skills, is actively to stop what you are doing and clear your mind before you concentrate on the next conversation. One way is to change your seating position. If someone enters your office when you are seated at your desk and starts a conversation, get up and move to another seat if this is possible, as long as you both can be seated. The movement will help to clear your mind.

If this is not possible, actually say what is on your mind. 'Bob, can you just wait a second while I clear my mind – great, now I can give you my full attention.' This will improve the quality of your listening. It will also make the other person feel valued and this again will enhance the quality of the communication.

Open and closed questions

Closed questions are useful when you want concise and specific answers such as 'Yes', 'No' or 'Two dozen'.

Open questions encourage an individual to give more detail about the topic that has been introduced, providing the opportunity for explanation, opinions and examples to be added to a bland statement.

Open questions also encourage the speaker to guide the conversation, allowing for the development of confidence. They demonstrate that the recipient is listening and thinking about the speaker and what is being said.

Neither form of questioning is right or wrong. Each is appropriate for different situations.

'Do you like opera?' is a closed question, inviting a one-word answer.

'Why do you like opera?' is an open question which could lead the speaker into a detailed description of the pleasures it holds.

'Was your journey here today easy?' is a closed question.

'What happened on your journey today?' is open.

'Can you offer me a job?' is closed.

'What sort of role do you think I might be suited to?' is open.

Open questions generally begin with words like; how, what, when, where, or why.

- How do your managers communicate with their departments?

- What are your objectives for the next six months?

- When do you expect sales figures to improve?

- Why is your sales office open plan?

- Where do you want to be in 12 months' time?

Empathy

Empathy enables you to put yourself into the shoes of another person, to imagine how they feel, but at the same time to remain yourself. Empathy is not the same as sympathy, which is about saying how sorry you feel or agreeing with the other person's point of view. Empathy is about remaining non-judgemental and non-evaluative, about not taking sides but accepting the other person for what they are and what they are saying.

Imagine that you are listening to someone saying the following: 'I'm not getting on well with my job. I can't concentrate on what I'm doing and I am feeling really fed up with the project. I'm thinking about resigning.'

You might reply: 'I would like to hear more about the problem, if you would like to talk about it,' or 'Never mind, you know what's best for you,' or 'It would be unwise to resign without another job. You have worked hard at this project. I'm sure everything will get better if you just stick at it,' or 'Things are never easy all of the time. Just pull yourself together.'

None of the above answers would demonstrate that you had empathy with that person.

If, however, you said: 'You sound rather glum and depressed at the moment about your job, and concerned and anxious about your future,' you would be demonstrating a high level of empathy.

Read the following statement: 'I can't make up my mind whether I want this job. I don't feel confident, but my partner is pushing me hard to accept.'

You would be showing no empathy if you replied: 'I know exactly what it's like. I was in the same position last year. Men/women are all the same,' or 'Don't worry. Leave matters to settle for a few days and you will come to the right decision.'

You would be showing moderate empathy if you replied: 'Your partner seems to be making life very difficult for you. I wonder why?', or 'It sounds as though you really don't know what to do for the best.'

You would, however, be showing high empathy if you replied: 'It seems to me you are under a lot of pressure at the moment and feeling very uncertain. It sounds like a very uncomfortable position to be in.'

Acceptance

The objective here is to create an atmosphere of non-judgemental acceptance with another person. It does not mean that you have to agree with or accept their values or behaviour, but it does mean that you can accept them as valued individuals. They want to know whether or not you agree with them, whether you are on their side, and will you give their opinions a fair hearing?

Acceptance, or having a non-judgemental attitude, is extremely important in career management. Many career decisions are made because of snap judgements that are based on little information or prejudice which often has little grounding in fact. Edward de Bono believes that judgement kills creative thinking and that in order to develop this process judgement must be suspended.

The acceptance of others is largely dependent upon accepting ourselves. If a person continually thinks of themselves as being of low value, and is always running themselves down, this message will be quickly transmitted to others. It is the same with the tendency to apologise continually for your actions. So many people are totally unaware of this habit, but it gives a very negative picture.

Knowing and accepting oneself is a very important aspect of career management, because from this knowledge comes understanding and strength. Self-confident people have more time for other people because they can spend less time thinking and worrying about themselves.

Running yourself down is a misguided activity. It is considered to be an act of modesty, but what it is truly reflecting is a lack of confidence. The smallest negative reference, however brief, leaves the listener with an uncomfortable feeling. If they are very experienced communicators they use this feeling to dig deeper and reveal what is hidden behind the slight crack.

Russ was telling me about one of his very successful achievements as the financial director of a large communications group. The project had involved developing a team and the project leader had blossomed with the added responsibilities, but he eagerly interjected as an aside how 'She screwed it all up later' – nothing to do with Russ. If that was really the truth, why did he mention the fact? What this statement highlighted was his underlying lack of self-confidence which, when pressed with further questioning, quickly became apparent.

ACTION

Read the following three statements, and then the comments which follow them. Decide how each of the comments would make you feel if you had been the person making the original statements. Think about which *you* find to be the most accepting.

'I'm concerned about my appraisal interview which is due next week. I don't believe it will be good enough for the next promotion and I really want that job.'

a) Don't worry, you are always over-cautious; you'll be okay, the boss really likes you.

b) You have every cause for concern; you've certainly not worked as hard as me during the last six months.

c) Why do you think there should be a problem; has something been said to give you a clue?

'Should I go for this interview? The job sounds interesting but I don't know if I really want to move into that area.'

a) It's really a waste of time; you are well settled here and doing quite a good job; why upset the situation?

b) It's very difficult to know the right answer until you have explored all the facts and collected enough information to make a valid decision.

c) Of course you should go; it's a fantastic job with more money, plenty of expense-account lunches and just what you are looking for.

'My boss is very difficult to approach. I'm bored with my present job, but when I try to bring the subject up he's always too busy.'

a) Typical of him; he's always losing good staff.

b) Don't bother trying to talk to him; just look for another job – there are plenty around. When I'm bored, I just move on.

c) Have you tried giving him some advance warning that you want to talk to him about the future?

Reflection or paraphrasing

The effective use of reflection allows the speaker to feel that they are being understood correctly and accepted. The skill is to mirror what they are saying to you by using simple restatements, or paraphrasing the essence of what is being said. This skill is extremely valuable in any conversation about your career because it allows you to check that you really understand what is being said.

So many individuals fall into career traps because they misunderstand a chance remark which may have been said on the spur of the moment and with little thought, but because it is said by a superior it is given greater weight than perhaps was intended. The opposite can also happen, where a manager finds it difficult to address a tricky subject, so wraps it up in a throw-away line. Using reflection or paraphrasing can help you check what's really being said.

Here are some examples:

'I'm frightened about the prospect of changing my job. I realise that it is necessary for my career and the idea is sometimes a little exciting, but deep down it feels very scary.'

A reflecting reply would be: *'You are trying to weigh up the pros and cons of changing jobs.'*

'I'm worried about my father. He's not been well for a long time and now he seems to be getting depressed about his health.'

A paraphrased reply would be: *'It has been a long time since your father was in good health and this is worrying you.'*

'I am nearly 50, the children have all left home, I'm fed up with my work and wondering what I can do with the rest of my life.'

An accurate paraphrased reply would be: *'It feels like there is a big void in your life.'*

The exact paraphrase which you give to each statement would depend upon your perspective and on your understanding of what has been said. There are no right or wrong answers, and the above are merely illustrations.

Silence

Using the skill of silence is a very effective tool in communication. All too often you are afraid of silence, especially when you are nervous, you babble on and on, not knowing where the conversation is going.

The use of silence has three major advantages:

1. It allows you time to gather your thoughts and ideas.
2. It projects you as being confident and well prepared.
3. It allows you really to listen to the other person.

Silence can be linked with deep breathing. Not in an obvious manner, but if you are taking in a deep breath of air you cannot speak. It calms you down and helps to focus your mind on the really important matters under discussion.

ACTION

When you are not talking time seems endless. Practise using a watch with a second alarm or a kitchen timer. Become accustomed to being quiet for 10 seconds, 30 seconds and then 60 seconds.

Learn to recognise these lengths of silence and know which you find comfortable and which make you feel embarrassed, with an urgent need to jump in to fill the gap. As you become more aware of silence you should be able to lengthen the gaps.

Become more aware of the use of silence when you talk. Make a conscious effort to use this skill in a specific conversation you have with someone at work. Monitor how you feel, and if you have practised becoming aware of the length of a silence gap, you can continually extend it to your advantage.

Also, begin to recognise how other people use silence. One very useful way to monitor this is to watch people being interviewed on television. Judge how they use silence. Have they used it in a positive way to give themselves time to frame the answer or have they rushed in without space, often not even listening to the question?

Receiving feedback

During many of the communications concerned with career management it is vitally important that you are asking for feedback about yourself and about the impression which you make on others. Receiving feedback is one of the most important ways in which you can learn about yourself and monitor your progress continually.

You need to know if you would fit in to a certain situation. You need to know if there is anything about you which is sending out the wrong signals, so that you can do something to put it right. All the time you need to enhance your knowledge store about how you are seen and judged by others.

This is particularly true if you are thinking of moving into a completely new discipline or sector. Suppose, for instance, that you are thinking of becoming self-employed after a long career in a large, paternalistic company. You need to find out from people who have already done it, or who know a great deal about self-employment. Do they think you have the temperament for working alone, bringing in business, getting yourself started and motivating yourself to see projects through to the end? Will you be suited to the pressure of not having a salary to rely on or colleagues to share risks and responsibilities with?

You may not be the best person to judge your own abilities in this situation, and even if you do go against the advice which you receive, at least you will be making your decision with the maximum amount of information, and this will help you to take precautions and to make better judgements.

For some of us, asking for feedback is a very scary prospect, as we are frightened we might have to face up to something unpleasant. If, however, you are taking control of your career path, that means you are also taking control of yourself, and you can only do that if you accept yourself 'warts and all'. How other people see you is an important part of the equation.

You don't, of course, have to accept everything that people say to you as the absolute truth, and you may well get conflicting reactions from different people. This means that you will need to filter the information and use what you feel is useful.

If you find that a number of people are saying the same thing, however, and it is something which you started out by rejecting as being inaccurate or untrue, it would be unwise to go on ignoring what they are telling you.

It is always a strength to know and recognise your warts because you then have the chance to do something about putting them right. If you are unaware of how you convey yourself to others you may be at a permanent disadvantage. Encouraging people to give you feedback will help you to develop a more realistic and positive view of yourself. Once again I can't stress too strongly that knowledge is a powerful commodity, and the more knowledge you have about yourself the more confident you will become.

Non-verbal feedback

It is also important to understand the non-verbal communications which are going on during a conversation. What people are *not* saying is often as important as what they *are* saying, and sometimes it is obvious from their body language that they mean the exact opposite to the words they are speaking.

Non-verbal communication or body language is very powerful, but it is generally something you have little control over until you become more aware of the concept. Your body will always speak the truth while your words may not. If you are trying to convince your boss that you are ready for the next promotion, and deep down you are not certain, your eye contact will give you away. It is almost impossible to maintain eye contact if you are not convinced yourself about what you are saying.

This is just a brief look at a much wider topic, which alone could be the subject of a Ph.D. thesis. Body language is not restricted to the face alone; it involves the head, neck, shoulders, arms, hands, trunk, legs and feet. Every part of the body can convey messages about how you feel. The way you walk, stand, sit and dress also communicates messages which you need to be aware of.

A word of caution should be issued here. You can become over-analytical about this subject and begin to take it out of context. When I was studying to be a counsellor I did an in-depth study into body language and non-verbal communication and I would report back to my fellow students on the progress of my observations as I travelled to and from college on the tube. I became so involved in the subject that they were strongly concerned that I might be arrested for very unusual behaviour. Out of context body language can become distorted and be easily misinterpreted. So be careful to keep a balanced view if you want to learn more about the subject.

ACTION

Make a conscious effort to watch people more closely and see whether their words match their actions. Observe people on television when they are being interviewed (not when they are acting). Watch people in restaurants, pubs or while travelling on public transport. (Be careful – don't stare!)

Assertiveness

Few people are forthcoming with feedback, so it is your responsibility to ask if you genuinely want to know how you are progressing or coming across. Certain people will never be able to give feedback, so you need to understand this and not get put off if what you receive is unhelpful. Asking for feedback is your right, but often you don't feel comfortable about asking. You may need to be more assertive in requesting what you want.

Taking control of yourself is a way of describing assertiveness, a concept which is often confused with being aggressive. A good definition of assertive is 'being pleasantly direct', which means achieving what you want in a way that is mindful of other people's needs and feelings.

It is a crucial element in taking responsibility for yourself and your destiny. Being decisive, while at the same time being willing to listen to the opinions of others, understanding what they are saying and being flexible enough to find mutually agreeable solutions, is a very important component of successful communication as a two-way process.

The skill comes from being able to overcome emotions and feelings such as fear, anxiety, anger and frustration, in order to communicate your point of view effectively to others. To do this you need to be able to identify the goals which you want to achieve, and then articulate clearly the things you need in order to achieve them. It may require some advanced planning to work out what you want to say, the words you could use and the appropriate timing. Writing a short script is very useful. Whenever I have to conduct a difficult interview or conversation, I always employ this tactic because knowing that I have mustered all the facts on one piece of paper which is close at hand gives me great confidence. Afterwards I'm always amazed because I generally don't have to refer to the notes.

If you are not accustomed to asking for feedback, don't plunge in and ask a complete stranger on the first occasion. Ask someone who is not too close or someone who is not vitally important. That way if you fluff it you will not lose face or harm your reputation. Ask someone who communicates well and explain that you are exploring avenues to improve the feedback you receive. It is important at the beginning to experience positive feedback because this will build up your confidence to ask again.

In the end it comes down to developing self-confidence, a feeling of security and a healthy perspective on everything going on around you. These things generally come about as a result of increased self-knowledge and a clear self-image.

Assertiveness can go a long way beyond just getting feedback. From time to time, for instance, you are bound to come into conflict with someone, perhaps over a negotiation or because you are in a leadership position. If you become tongue-tied because you are overcome by emotion, you are unlikely to be effective in an argument. That means you will not achieve what you set out to achieve, and you may even go out of your way to avoid the conflict, allowing someone else to get their way when it isn't in your best interests. Whether you are negotiating with others, leading them or motivating them, you need to be able to communicate clearly, speaking honestly and directly.

The most common instance where assertiveness is needed is at meetings. It is all too easy for the non-assertive person to keep quiet and let others do the talking, the persuading and the deciding, fearing that if they speak up they will not be heard or may even be laughed at.

Being assertive is a valuable asset in career management, not just in the area of feedback but also in directly asking for what you want. Much of your success will be achieved when you ask for something you really want; suggest a way of doing something, perhaps in a different way; or when you say 'No, I can't take on that extra little chore'.

The following action will give you a little more insight into how assertive you are. If you want to explore further, the book list on page 275 gives suggestions for further reading, and many courses are run for assertiveness training. For example, local adult education centres generally run training courses in assertiveness, and these are usually not as expensive as those organised by private training companies. Try and persuade your employer to send you on a course, because the company will certainly share the benefits as well.

It is generally assumed that this type of training is more applicable to women, but both men and women can benefit from a better understanding of what individuals need and how this can be achieved in a proactive way.

ACTION

Read each of the following statements and make a note as to whether you think it is true or false.

T F

1. I often feel like telling people what I really think of them ☐☐

2. When I find myself in a new situation, I watch what other people do and then try to act in a similar fashion ☐☐

3. I enjoy doing things that others may regard as unconventional ☐☐

4. I think it is important to learn obedience and practise correct social behaviour ☐☐

	T	**F**

5. In general, I find that I dislike non-conformists

6. I prefer to listen to the opinions of others before I take a stand

7. I feel comfortable following instructions and doing what is expected of me

8. It often makes more sense to go along with 'the group' rather than trying to persuade them to my point of view

9. Confronting other people is extremely uncomfortable for me

10. I enjoy being seen as a person with strong opinions

If you answered 'True' to numbers 2, 4, 5, 6, 7, 8 or 9, award yourself one point for each. If you answered 'False' to numbers 1, 3 and 10, do the same. If your score comes to six or more, poor assertiveness may be a concern for you.

Receptiveness

Asking for feedback also means being receptive to what other people say. It is important that good feedback is nurtured, which means you can't afford to become defensive or attempt to justify your actions. Instead, you must be receptive to whatever people are telling you, remain quiet and listen to what is being said. You have asked for feedback so you must respect what is being communicated. You are not obliged to accept everything that is being said, but you should attempt to understand the other person's point of view.

Always ask for more information if you don't understand what is being said or if you disagree with any of it, e.g. 'That's extremely helpful, please tell me more.' Always be honest in your reaction, e.g. 'I'm surprised you see it that way, but you certainly have a point.' Always thank people for providing you with the feedback, even if you find it hard to take. At first it may be difficult, but as you become more accustomed to receiving this type of information, it will become easier.

Unless you encourage the free exchange of honest information, you will never learn to improve. To check on your own level of receptiveness, the following may give you some clues.

ACTION

Answer each of the following statements with a 'Yes' or 'No'. Try to be as honest as possible.

Y N

1. I get embarrassed when people point out mistakes ☐☐

2. I resent people telling me what they think of my shortcomings ☐☐

3. I regularly ask friends and associates whom I trust to comment on how I am doing ☐☐

4. I know how to offer constructive criticism to others in a sensitive way ☐☐

5. I like people who tell me their reactions to my activities because it will help me adapt my behaviour in the future ☐☐

If you answered 'Yes' to numbers 1 and 2 you may have an attitude barrier which could prevent people giving you feedback. 'Yes' answers to numbers 3 and 4 provide a more positive climate for the development of feedback. A 'Yes' answer to number 5 is what we should all be striving to achieve.

Skills are not easily acquired by reading the theory. They must be practised if you are going to gain confidence. Also, it is difficult to practise in everyday life because you don't receive feedback on your progress. Further reading or listening to audiotapes can help to increase your effectiveness in this area.

Remember . . .

- If your career foundation is not firmly constructed it will show.

- Planning your activities is the way forward.

- Basic communication skills are vital for future success.

- Be clear about what you want.

- Encourage feedback to learn about yourself and monitor your progress.

CHAPTER 9

PERSONAL PRESENTATION

Now that you have mastered the basic communication skills you can progress further into Phase 3 and maximise your communication skills in the following areas: non-verbal communication (i.e. personal presentation), verbal skills, and through the written word.

Non-verbal communication

In the first two minutes of any communication the other person has formed a judgement about you. The largest percentage of this impression will be based on what they see – not what you say. During those first two minutes the brain processes about 2,000 pieces of information, little of which is related to the spoken word.

According to Antony Marsh, of Acting for Industry, a consultancy in confidence building, interview skills and speechcraft, when you recall any interaction:

7–10 per cent of recall comes from the words;

20 per cent from body language;

30 per cent from emphasis or dynamic.

These figures highlight how little conscious attention we pay to this, the most powerful aspect of communication.

Ninety per cent of your body is covered by clothes at work, so you cannot ignore the powerful messages that clothes give. You cannot dress neutrally; every detail is giving a strong signal about how you feel and your attitudes about yourself, your job and people you work with. If you are well dressed you will convey the message that you care and value yourself and those around you. This is nothing to do with what you say but will provide some initial information for others to make decisions about you, your education, social class, financial standing, age, attractiveness, approachability and status, telling them whether you are likeable and trustworthy, and if they even want to do business with you. The fantastic computer of the brain has keyed in all this information in seconds and a judgement has been made.

Professional dressing

In career terms you must be aware of these powerful messages and how you can communicate the right meaning. Initially, you need to understand the importance of professional dressing in a business or work setting and matching this to you, your job and the company, to develop an appropriate style for you. This does not mean that you have to have an expandable chequebook, but it could involve some initial professional assistance from an image consultant, who would help you understand some of the basic rules, set you on the right road and eventually save you money because you will avoid panic buying.

Emma McPherson, a colour analyst and image consultant, believes that you should only buy something when it fits in totally with everything else in your wardrobe. This means that you never have to shop for that special occasion because your wardrobe should cater for every event in your lifestyle.

This does not only apply to women either. Men also need to pay just as much attention to their image because the same judgements are being made about them. Every time you select your clothes for work you demonstrate how you feel about yourself, and how much you value your contribution to the working day.

Many people dress the part of the victim because that is how they perceive themselves. Just look around, either at work or on your journey each morning. You can recognise the woman–victim with her crumpled, too-tight skirt, creased blouse and baggy cardigan, her hair badly cut and needing a wash, her shoes dirty and scuffed, no tights or stockings, no make-up and dangly earrings.

The victim–man is also recognisable. His suit is too small and is crumpled, his nylon shirt unironed, his tie stained and thin, his shoes needing repair, his pullover not matching, his hair unshapen and his anorak ripped.

The message is one of not caring either for themselves or for those around them. So, if you give out that message about yourself, why should anyone else bother?

Presenting yourself is no different from packaging a product. Many people have difficulty with this comparison because they believe that people should be above this commercialism, but unfortunately the psychology of human nature is influenced by what you see. Consider your reaction to a product that is well packaged and one that is not. Often there may be no difference between them, but generally you will never know because you will always be attracted to the better presentation.

Some people take an intellectual view about appearance, believing that this should have no influence on how the standard of their work is perceived or assessed. This view, unfortunately, can often clash with reality and a compromise may have to be reached.

Stuart, a very successful surveyor, dressed casually at work because he often had to visit construction sites. He was being considered as a partner of the firm, but some of the older, senior members felt that his dress did not present a professional image to clients, so he was passed over.

Monica was called in by her boss one morning and praised highly for the way her work had improved during the last six months, and how pleased everyone was in the team. Monica was rather mystified because she honestly felt that nothing had specifically changed in her attitude to work. She enjoyed her job and worked really hard. Then the penny dropped; about six months before she had visited an image consultant and invested in some professional clothes for work. This is what her boss had really noticed. Her presentation had improved, resulting in her being noticed. Three months later she was promoted.

According to Emma MacPherson, dressing professionally is more about authority than playing power games. It is the skill of making people feel safe, secure and confident in you. The message you need to transmit is 'Yes, I can do the job. I certainly know what I'm talking about.' Remember that authority is not arrogance any more than assertiveness is aggression.

Certain items of clothing carry high authority. If you consider some authority figures you will see that they are often dressed in uniform, and you can also learn a great deal from observing how military personnel dress.

Jacket
This represents armour. It keeps the emotions in and protects you in battle. Have you ever observed how vulnerable men look in their shirt-sleeves?

A belt
This is your ammunition store. Men wearing trousers with belt carriers and no belt are firing blanks!

Neck protection
Ties, necklaces, brooches, scarves, bows, stocks etc. are all symbolic protection for the jugular and will prevent you from looking vulnerable.

Jewellery and accessories
Men: cufflinks, tie-pins, silk pocket handkerchiefs, pocket or wrist watches.

Women: necklaces, earrings, brooches, watches and rings.

These are your badges of office which tell people whether you are a general or a private.

ACTION

Just for fun, see if your visual image reflects a picture of self-worth, self-assurance and a sense of purpose. It will also establish whether you seem to be under-dressed, well-dressed or possibly a little over-dressed.

Give yourself one point for each of the following you are wearing. Then check your overall look against the score.

FOR MEN

	Y	N
Clean-shaven		
Clean and tidy nails		
Dark grey or blue suit		
Leather briefcase		
Well-cut hairstyle		
Clean and tidy laced shoes		
Pocket handkerchief		
Socks to match suit		
Shirt with bold stripes, checks or contrasting colour		
Suit with unusual decoration, e.g. large checks or stripes		
Belt		
Chain		
Distinctive patterned tie		
Large gold watch		
Lapel or tie-pin		
Bracelet or decorative ring		
Wearing several contrasting colours		

Score one point for every 'Yes' answer

Below 8 points   You are under-dressed
8-12 points   You are well dressed. Congratulations!
Over 13 points   Perhaps you are a little over the top?

FOR WOMEN

	Y	N
Make-up	☐	☐
Nail polish	☐	☐
Jacket	☐	☐
Good, fashionable handbag	☐	☐
Hair ornament/ribbon/bow/scarf	☐	☐
Shoes with some decoration on them	☐	☐
Scarf/shawl	☐	☐
Tights/stockings that are decorative and match your outfit	☐	☐
Shirt/blouse that has some outstanding feature on it	☐	☐
Skirt/trousers that have something special or unusual about them, e.g. wrapover, lots of buttons, pleats etc.	☐	☐
Belt	☐	☐
Earrings	☐	☐
Necklace	☐	☐
Rings other than engagement or wedding rings	☐	☐
Dressy watch	☐	☐
Brooch/lapel pin	☐	☐
Bracelets, bangles	☐	☐
Wearing several colours other than in a scarf	☐	☐

Score one point for every 'Yes' answer

Below 10 points You are under-dressed.
10-13 points You are well dressed. Congratulations!
Over 14 points Perhaps you are a little over the top?

One of the most important keys to successful presentation is *quality*, because this shows the world what you are worth. Your watch represents the value you place on your time; your pen is what you sign your life away with. A plastic ballpoint in the board room is a quick giveaway to how much you value your signature. Your briefcase is your shield – a floppy, casual one won't protect you.

Authority dressing is nothing to do with double-breasted suits or large *Dynasty*-like shoulder pads. It is about transmitting the message that says 'I know who I am'.

To achieve successful authority dressing you should create your own look, which is an extension of your personality. It must be a true reflection of your inner self. If you pretend to be something different from the real you, the final result will be unconvincing, shifty and unattractive. When you know who you are, you should project a cohesive message.

A professional image is not achieved by being in the height of fashion. Ideally women should wear jackets and skirts and not trousers, even if they are permitted. Always look for quality and remember your badges of office and your accessories; they are all part of the whole picture.

Specific interview tips are given later in this chapter.

Actions speak volumes

You must be aware not only of what you say, and how you say it, but of the gestures that accompany your words. You will not give a confident presentation if you sit on the edge of your chair, wringing your hands. Your verbal messages must match your visual signals. Unfortunately, this is one area that many people neglect, giving themselves away with small, often non-important, gestures which conflict with their words.

Non-verbal communication or body language is a complete field of study in its own right, so I don't want to minimise its importance by attempting to give a quick solution. You want to look more deeply into the subject to gain a fuller understanding of it.

I find that non-verbal communication or body language is much influenced by your own inner self-confidence. If you have a clear understanding of your skills, strengths and values (which Phase 1 should have given you), and accept what you have achieved with these assets, you will be able to walk into a room, stand tall, look around with confidence, make good eye-contact and greet people in an open and warm manner.

This confident behaviour may not come overnight, but it can be successfully mastered. Some people believe that video training (receiving feedback via a television screen) is beneficial to learning about your own non-verbal mannerisms. I have reservations about the value of this type of training because it can create very artificial barriers. We are not making TV appearances in our general, day-to-day activities. I believe that feedback received from individuals you know, respect and trust is of greater value.

Nervousness is one of the most easily communicated emotions. Quite simply, you look nervous and the world knows. What you need to recognise is that nervousness gets the adrenalin to flow in the bloodstream, which heightens your awareness. This is a positive factor, but you must then learn to manage the situation to maximise the positive outcomes and not allow the feeling to turn into panic, nor to disclose it by your actions. A faltering start will raise doubts which will then be difficult to reverse. A simple gesture may transmit very strong messages which make the recipient feel uncomfortable and insecure.

Antony Marsh, an actor and communications expert, works with individuals to harness their nervous energies into positive reactions. He has refined some helpful techniques used by actors. They are just as effective for calming meeting or pre-interview nerves and harnessing all that nervous energy:

● **Hear the fanfare**   Re-live your most successful moment – when you were a winner and felt wonderful. Select some appropriate music to set it to and listen to the music and relive the success before any presentation, meeting or interview.

● **Walk in to win**   As you walk into the room, imagine you are taller than you are and that you are climbing five steps or a ramp. You are going to be given a prize, your music is playing – SMILE! Imagine the audience is cheering and clapping – tell yourself you are a winner!

● **Shooting the shake**   Remember the film *High Noon* and the shoot-out between the sheriff and the bad guy? It is always the

Baddie who draws first, but the Goodie is the first to shoot – and lives to tell the tale. When shaking hands, watch for the first twitch of movement from the other person's right arm. Only then start your move, but get there first and have your hand out ready before they do. This wins points for assertiveness and confidence.

• **Quelling the quease**   Before any important meeting visit the cloakroom and follow this simple routine. Clench all your muscles inward towards your diaphragm fast, as if punched hard in the solar plexus. Unclench. Take a deep breath, and hold for three seconds, let it out in a rush, take a normal breath and sigh.

Spoken communication

Spoken interaction is generally considered to be the most important vehicle of communication in career management. Nobody is ever appointed to a position without at least one interview, whether it is an internal promotion or a new role. From what has been discussed so far in this chapter it should now be clear that communication is achieved via various channels.

Generally, when you think about your career, interviews seem to be the most important element in the process. In no way do I wish to detract from this, but rather to expand the understanding and context of interviews. In the career management setting, conversations based around your situation, progress, options etc., happen on a regular basis. At this moment you may not consider each interaction to be an interview. What I hope you will begin to understand is that many of the hints, skills, techniques and knowledge that apply to the interview are also valid in the wider context of any career management discussion.

For the sake of clarity I will deal with the interview from the job search perspective because at some time you will have to face a recruitment interview, but I will continue to stress that the information included in this section has a much wider application.

Interviews

Ninety-nine per cent of firms use interviews as part of their recruitment strategy, even though it has been shown to be a very inaccurate indicator of a candidate's potential, particularly when they are conducted in an unstructured manner.

However poor an indicator, interviews are quite predictable because interviewers generally ask much the same sorts of questions and are interested in finding out the same sorts of things, no matter what the job is. And because the interview is predictable it can be planned for.

A recent survey of top personnel executives ranked the following, in order of priority, as the most influential factors affecting a successful job offer:

1. how hard you work;
2. your educational and technical background;
3. the qualifications you have for the position;
4. your personality – how you present yourself during the interview;
5. your experience;
6. your background and references;
7. your intelligence and capacity to learn;
8. your future prospects;
9. the enthusiasm you show towards the organisation and the job;
10. how you get on with other employees.

There are three key elements to any interview. First there is your *attitude*, secondly, the amount of *preparation* and thirdly, the effectiveness of your *performance*.

Attitudes

In the typical interview one person (the interviewer) is attempting to be friendly but in command, while the other (the interviewee) is attempting to appear in command while trembling with nerves. If you are going to manage your career then your attitude towards interviews must be different. It should be seen as an interaction, not an interrogation. You should be using the meeting to gain information for yourself, just as the interviewer is finding out about your abilities.

If you fully support the concept of taking responsibility for your own career the interview must become a two-way process. This should free up the interview situation, allowing you to meet the interviewer as an equal who commands respect.

Your attitude towards yourself is extremely important in the interview. If you are feeling insecure or uncertain this will be quickly transmitted to the interviewer by non-verbal communication or body language, as we have already discovered. You must develop positive attitudes about your skills and achievements. These are the foundations of your own career management. If you are clear about your own worth and value, you will communicate this unconsciously to the interviewer and release some of the negative tension which can adversely affect your behaviour.

Preparation

The importance of preparation cannot be stressed enough because it brings with it knowledge, which in turn cultivates the confidence that is a valuable asset at any interview. All too often people attending interviews do no preparation at all, and the fact is obvious to a competent interviewer almost immediately.

Taking the trouble to find out about the company, the interviewer, the product range, the competition and the market, produces two important advantages. First, it gives you confidence and makes you appear knowledgeable, Secondly, it compliments the interviewer who feels good that you have shown some initiative and made an effort.

A word of warning should be given here. Be mindful of how you use this information you have researched. A personnel director of a major bank has reported that he was tired of being told by young graduates about the bank's financial situation. Research alone is not enough – you must know *when* it is appropriate to use the information. Reading a copy of the company accounts on the way to the interview is no answer.

Sources of preparation research are very similar to those you used for your option choice research (in Chapter 6). It should include both desk research and active networking with your contacts, which will be a particularly valuable source for the 'non-quotable' insights.

Preparation starts from the moment you receive the letter or phone call inviting you to attend an interview. Swing into action immediately. If you have been contacted by letter call the company to accept the interview date and time.

Use this opportunity to start information gathering. What is the job title of the interviewer? Will the interview be one to one, sequential or panel? How much time should you allow? Is there any information you could have about the company?

Also try to gain the secretary's name and attempt to recruit an ally. Secretaries can hold quite powerful positions when it comes to interviews, since they often notice many of the details that may be passed over by the interviewer.

If the date and time are not suitable try to negotiate new ones, but be flexible. If you are invited to an interview and given a free choice of dates, don't appear to have a completely empty diary – remember, demand creates demand.

Self-preparation

As you are now aware, most interviewers make up their minds within the first two minutes of an interview – so it is vital that you make a good first impression. An awful lot hinges on appearance and that magic word – 'chemistry'.

During those crucial first few moments be very aware of how you feel and your initial reaction, because it is almost certain that your feelings will match closely those of the interviewer. Those first few moments will set the tone for what is to follow. If the first reaction is good and the interviewer feels you will fit in, the rest of the meeting will be constructed around those positive reactions and he or she will proceed to ask easy questions, ones which you can answer well, reinforcing their initial reaction and confirming that you are the right person for the job.

If the reverse happens, however, then you are in for a rough ride. Questions will be tough, the atmosphere hostile and your reaction will again confirm the interviewer's first reaction; you won't fit into the team or company ethos, you are not the right person.

Appearances and personal presentation were discussed earlier in this chapter; but there are a few extra points to consider where interviews are concerned. The key is to dress appropriately to match the situation. A pin-striped suit would not be acceptable on a building site – to make an extreme example – nor would a loudly coloured shirt fit in the board room of a firm of solicitors. Choose an outfit which is middle of the road so that you avoid offending anyone.

The following tips may help as a guide.

- Be comfortable in whatever you wear.

- Have a co-ordinated outfit with complementary colours and patterns.

- Know that the outfit enhances your appearance. If you are uncertain about this, perhaps an investment in some image consultancy would be to your advantage.

- No club, regimental or school tie, badge or insignia.

- Pay close attention to hygiene, hair, make-up, jewellery, perfume or after-shave – there should be no strong smells.

- Spend as much as you can afford on quality clothes and accessories.

- Never smoke.

- Ensure that everything is clean, neat and tidy.

- Pay attention to the complete image – raincoat, briefcase, news-paper, handbag, gloves, scarf etc.

Arriving in plenty of time is essential, but do not be too early. Always check your travel arrangements carefully, allowing extra time for mishaps or train cancellations. Ensure that you have the right address and find out if expenses are paid. Is parking available and which spaces are kept for visitors? You won't be very popular if you take the chairman's parking space.

Enter the building a little early and find the toilet so that you can check your appearance. Then sit, if possible, in the reception area for a while, collecting your thoughts and assessing the atmosphere of the company. How do people behave and react as they pass through this generally busy area? You can pick up some interesting impressions from listening to conversations and to the way the receptionist answers the phone.

Try to avoid becoming too cluttered, especially when you are first met at reception. Nobody can give a good first impression when scrambling up from a deep-seated sofa holding a coffee cup, raincoat, newspaper, briefcase, umbrella and handbag, while at the same time trying to return the all-important firm handshake.

Check that your handshake is firm and positive by practising beforehand with someone who will give you feedback.

Questions

Interviews are all about questions, the ones you have to answer successfully and the ones you want answered about the company, job, boss etc. Let's look at the first category, questions you will have to answer, which generally follow a basic pattern.

First, there are the silent questions which are answered without words.

Appearance   From the moment you arrive, silent questions are being answered concerning how you will fit within the existing team, your health or pension risk, or safety hazards. This is the opening phase when not much is said, but clothes, physical make-up, bearing and speech are all being assessed.

Then there are the spoken categories, based around the following.

Attainment   What standards have you reached in education, qualifications, training and experience? What evidence is there to support your claims?

Intelligence   This refers to your intellect at a general level and what capacity you might have for further growth. How shrewd or mature are you? Do you have realistic aims and the ability to grasp concepts? (This aspect can be more accurately assessed by tests.)

Special talents   What are your marketable assets and what examples do you have to illustrate your achievements?

Interests   These provide a wider view of you as a person. Are you totally immersed in intellectual pursuits or is there a balance with physical activities, creative outlets and socialising?

Personality   What type of disposition do you have and how will this fit into the existing framework? (Again, this aspect can be more accurately assessed by tests.)

Circumstances   This will cover economic, social, cultural and family background, financial responsibilities and mobility and how these will affect your future prospects.

ACTION

The most successful way to cope with these questions is by
preparation. Below you will find some of the most common interview questions. Read through them carefully and write down your
own answers. The action of writing will help to commit the
information to memory. Keep the answers safe, and the night
before any interview read through them to refresh your memory,
but don't learn them parrot-fashion because this will give the
interviewer a false impression.

Remember that honesty is always important. Your details may
have been checked. The interviewer could have spoken to someone
from their network about you and discovering any lies will destroy
your credibility entirely. Always be candid in your answers and
distinguish between questions calling for facts and ones asking for
an opinion. The latter are more difficult, but keep in mind that
honesty will work best in the long term and answer to your best
advantage. Never speak ill of anyone or any action. You do not
know how people are connected and 'bad-mouthing' a past employer creates a very poor impression.

Interview questions
The following questions give you the opportunity to sell yourself:

1. What are the reasons for your success?

2. What is your energy level like? Describe a typical day?

3. Why do you want to work here?

4. What kind of experience do you have for this job?

5. Are you willing to go where the company sends you?

6. What did you like/dislike about your last job?

7. How do you feel about your progress so far?

8. How long would you stay with the company?

9. Have you achieved the best results you are capable of
   achieving?

10. How long would it take for you to make a mark within this organisation?

11. How do you see your career developing in the next five years?

12. What are your qualifications?

13. What is your greatest achievement?

14. Can you work under pressure?

15. What do you do to relax?

16. What is your greatest strength?

17. Why does the job interest you?

18. What salary are you looking for?

19. What did you earn in your last job?

20. What are you looking for in your next job?

21. Why should I hire you?

22. Describe a difficult situation you've had to deal with.

23. What have you learned from jobs you have held?

24. What will your referees say about you?

25. What type of decisions were you involved in making in your last job?

26. Why were you dismissed?

27. What was the most time consuming part of your last job?

28. How has your present job prepared you to take greater responsibility?

The following questions and statements have traps hidden within them:

1. I'm not sure you are suitable for this job.

2. Highlight your weak points.

3. Wouldn't you feel happier working for another company?

4. What kind of decisions are most difficult for you?

5. Why have you been out of work so long?

6. Why aren't you earning a larger salary at your age?

7. Why have you changed jobs so often?

8. Why did you leave your last job?

9. What interests you least about this job?

10. What do you believe to be a good attendance record?

11. What is your general impression of your last company?

12. How did you handle some of the problems in your last job?

13. List some of the minuses of your last job.

14. What type of people do you find it difficult to work with?

15. How have you successfully worked with a difficult colleague?

16. How did you get your last job?

17. Which skill did you find most difficult to master?

The following questions are designed to reveal the 'real' you:

1. How do you take direction?

2. Would you like your boss's job?

3. What do you think of your present boss?

4. Tell me about an occasion when your work was criticised.

5. Give me an example of an initiative you have taken.

6. When did you disagree with your boss?

7. How do you think your boss could have improved his or her performance?

8. What things did you dislike about your boss's management style?

9. How well did your boss rate your job performance?

10. How interested are you in sport?

11. What personal characteristics are necessary for success in your field?

12. Do you work better alone or within a group?

13. Tell me a story.

14. What have you learnt from your previous jobs?

15. How would you define co-operation?

16. What difficulties do you have tolerating people with different backgrounds and interests to yours?

17. Tell me about yourself.

You should also be prepared for the awkward question designed to reduce you to a stuttering wreck, such as a request to empty your pockets or handbag, 'because I think what's inside is such a good guide to a person's character'.

One certain question is, 'Do you have any questions that you want answered?' This is your opportunity to right the balance and show the extent of your knowledge. You should have planned a number of questions such as the following.

– What is the most important aspect of the job?
– How will my performance be measured?
– What facilities are there for further training?
– What responsibilities will I have?
– What happened to the previous holder of the job?
– What are the promotion prospects?
– What measurement techniques are used to evaluate progress?
– What are the main problem areas connected with the job?
– What are the organisation's future plans? Rapid growth? Consolidation? Decline?
– How is the company structured?
– What are the lines of communication?
– How are objectives set? What input would I have to this activity?

Always double-check the answers to these questions with your own research. The interviewee is always encouraged to be honest but, unfortunately, an interviewer is not bound by the same ethics. He or she is also selling the company and may be painting rather a rosy picture. Never turn a deaf ear to the little nagging voice in the back of your mind. Be brave and face the niggling doubts, because these are what turn into big reality issues when you are firmly into the job.

Salary

The question of salary should be avoided at all costs until common ground has been established with the interviewer wanting you and you wanting the job.

From that position negotiations can develop. Salary packages are never fixed, there is always room for manoeuvre, but only if you hold a strong bargaining position. Disclosing your present salary does not put you in a strong position.

If this question is raised at the opening stage of the interview try deflecting it with, 'At this stage of the interview I am more interested in the job content/promotion prospects/experience than salary.' Most importantly you need to hold your ground without angering the interviewer.

Before entering into any negotiations about salary you must do some important preparation. First, price your existing salary package. Most people know their annual gross salary, some are aware of their net monthly income, but few are fully aware of the true value of their salary package.

This can be a difficult exercise, but if you wish to maintain financial growth with a job change, it is essential that you do it. It also helps you to target the right job when answering job adverts, and headhunters also need this information. When you are doing this calculation you need to know the cost of your car/health insurance/pension/bonus subscriptions/lunches/travel/loans and other perks or benefits paid for by the company each year, and add the total to your annual salary. This will give you your true salary indicator.

Secondly, you must do some research to find out what is the going rate for your job. Advertisements can help to some extent, but many do not disclose salary. Your network may be a good source of information. Headhunters and recruitment consultants may also have this type of information. Professional institutes may conduct salary polls within the industry sector and publish the information. The best policy is continually to keep yourself up to date with salary trends in your industry.

The right time to discuss salary is at the end of the interview process, when a job offer is a reality. Aim high in your negotiations because you can always come down. Even if a salary is quoted, ask for at least 10 per cent more. If you have convinced the interviewer that you can do the job, you can probably get him or her to offer you more than the original figure, but always remember the reality factors.

When discussing salary, always be clear about all the items included in the overall package, because certain of these benefits can make a significant difference to your net salary. Also check when the next review is due and whether you will be included. Try to get a review after six months. After all if they are willing to offer you the job knowing little about you, they should give you a rise if they are satisfied after six months' work.

Red or green lights
Towards the end of an interview you may be asked one of the following questions.

- Do you really think you have enough experience?
- Do you think you are ready to cope with additional responsibility?
- Are you mature enough to handle the challenge?

You may be put off by this line of questioning, thinking that you have failed, but that is not the case. This type of question is a signal that the interviewer thinks you are the right person and is just checking his or her decision before making the final offer. So always respond in a positive way to these 'green light' questions.

Interview style
Interview style is very important and needs to be given careful consideration, both in the style of communication expressed through body language and in levels of rapport.

The level of rapport must be somewhere between 'cosily warm' and 'lukewarm'. It should obviously not go down to 'cool' or 'sufferance' levels, nor should the temperature rise to 'hot', which is more suitable for seduction than career management!

Your body language will tell a lot, so here are some of the signs and what they will say to the other party.

Inhibited   Saying little. Speaking very softly. Allowing interruptions. Meek tone of voice. Downcast eyes. 'Handwringing'. Sitting beneath others.

Assertive/responsive   Smiling. Relaxed tone of voice. Eye contact. Open gestures. Balanced posture. Being on an equal level.

Directionless/reckless   Uncoordinated gestures. Strident tone of voice. Avoiding eye contact. Losing track. Falling asleep. Yawning. Restlessness.

Aggressive   Forceful gestures. Harsh tone of voice. Interrupting. Ignoring responses. Speaking too much. Staring. Standing over others.

Developing your own interview style is as important as it is for your career summary and letter-writing techniques. The best way to develop and enhance your style is first by role play, perhaps working up to a videoed session as you become more confident and practised. Here, professional help can be valuable but there is really no better way of developing your own style than experiencing the real thing. Attending an interview is the best learning ground, especially if you evaluate your behaviour and, wherever possible, ask for feedback from the interviewer.

One of the dangers during an interview is in becoming too relaxed. This can weaken your barriers and an experienced interviewer can learn more than you would normally want to disclose.

Maintain your interview skills

It is good practice in career management terms to keep your interview techniques well tuned. To admit that you have not had an interview for 20 years is admitting that you have totally neglected your own career management and abdicated responsibility to another party. Keeping your interview skills up to date goes hand in hand with managing your own career and, if you do nothing else, attending an interview every year is good practice.

Improving and developing your network of contacts will automatically improve and enhance your interview techniques. The reason for this is that while networking you generally meet people in an informal situation with no real interview pressures, but you are having to put over a positive and constructive view of yourself. At the beginning this is not easy, especially if the concept of network development is new to you or even alien. But gradually, as you become more practised, you will develop and improve your interview style so that when you are next faced with a career interview you will be prepared, relaxed and confident.

Assessing the interviewer

From the moment you meet, the interviewer is sizing you up through observation and silent questioning. You must be doing the same thing, and asking yourself the following sorts of questions.

– Do the interviewer's clothes match the status?

– What messages are being transmitted by his or her appearance?

– Does the interviewer appear confident?

– Does he or she have a good handshake? Are his or her hands dry or damp?

– Is the office organised or untidy?

– What indications are there of work methods or style?

– How do other employees react in the presence of the interviewer?

– How does the interviewer use space?

– Are there any territorial signs (e.g. their position and distance in relation to you)? An interviewer who sits behind a large desk displays signs of insecurity. If he or she moves in front of the desk to conduct the interview, this indicates their confidence, and that you are being considered on equal terms.

– Are there signs of power dressing or power furnishings? Remember the difference between power and authority.

– Is eye contact maintained?

– How are interruptions handled?

– Are there any signs of personal interests like photographs, diplomas or executive toys?

– What evidence is there of reading matter such as books, newspapers and magazines? Do they look used or merely purchased for show?

Much of this information will be absorbed subconsciously and you will need to retrieve it soon after the interview. Also, the more aware you are of the importance of this type of information, the more you can train yourself to be alert to non-verbal communication.

Assessing the interviewer and asking your own interview questions should be closely linked to your work values. These are two of the most important opportunities to gain the facts you need to decide whether or not this role will satisfy your needs. Link these closely with your values exercise.

Silence and checking progress

This important aspect of an interview is often neglected because people are frightened of silence. They believe that every second during an interview should be packed with verbiage, resulting in a continual stream of often unmemorable chatter.

Use silence to reflect on the question you have just been asked and collect your thoughts. Don't immediately respond with the first idea that flashes into your mind. This can result in you heading down a track which you can't even remember starting out on.

Always keep your answers brief, using questions to check and monitor whether the interviewer has understood or gained enough detail about a specific subject. Watch the interviewer's eye contact closely; if their eyes are wandering they have lost interest. Assess their body language to judge whether they are interested in what you are saying. Ask the interviewer a question from time to time, but never dominate or take control of the interview.

Interview debrief

During any interview the communication rate will be fast, furious and at many levels. By the time you leave you are holding a vast amount of information, much of which will evaporate from your memory with the speed of light. You must capture as much of this detail as you can. Your own private debriefing session will be valuable and the following checklist may help.

1. What was my immediate impression during the first few minutes?

2. Was my personal presentation good?

3. Was I fully prepared?

4. Was I relaxed? (Hopefully not so relaxed as to let down your guard.)

5. Did my confidence and enthusiasm show?

6. Were my answers short, to the point and directly answering the questions?

7. Were there any questions which I didn't answer well?

8. Did I take notice of all the surrounding detail?

9. Did the interview flow, producing an interchange of information?

10. Was silence used to advantage?

11. What is the next stage?

12. Is a follow-up letter required?

Only send a letter after an interview if there is a valid reason for it. Perhaps you want to stress a certain point or make something clear which you feel may have been misunderstood or neglected.

The goal

Most career moves are only secured after a number of interviews, so learn to pace yourself. Don't give an academy award-winning performance at the first interview, leaving little to say at follow-up meetings.

Don't play hard to get at any time during the interview process either; interviewers will not take kindly to candidates 'stringing them along'. Nor should you give the impression that you are playing one employer off against another, especially at the offer stage. When you do finally reach this goal, ask to see the offer in writing. This will give you time to consider it in detail and measure it to your own criteria.

Never succumb to pressure at this point. Accepting a career move is a very important decision, requiring time and space. If you are being pressured, attempt to find out the underlying reason why. Everyone should be given at least 48 hours free decision-making time, and should always be able to go back for more information if certain points are unclear.

If you are rejected at the final interview stage, always try to get some feedback about the reasons. This may not be easy because most interviewers will be embarrassed about having to deal with the unpleasant truth, but after all the effort and preparation you put in you are entitled to discover why you didn't succeed. If you can make the initial contact in a non-threatening manner, this exercise is usually valuable.

If you have developed a good rapport with the interviewer you can turn this conversation into a networking opportunity.

Interviews should be interesting challenges, not doleful experiences, and once you have fine-tuned your interview techniques keep them polished. Don't wait for another 20 years, because your network will quickly die if it is neglected.

Telephone techniques

The telephone can either be an asset for career management or it can be the bane of your existence. It all depends on your individual attitude. The telephone, however, is undeniably a part of business life and if used well it can be helpful, but you need to start with a positive attitude.

The telephone can be used in a number of ways for career management, most obviously for confirming arrangements and meetings. Its use can also be extended to include research and information gathering.

Telephone interviews

Recently the telephone has been used more and more for interviewing. This can be the formal telephone interview, a technique which started in America. It starts with prior arrangements being made by the interviewer for you to set aside a certain length of time to answer a range of pre-set questions. Usually there are only a limited range of answers available and this forces a rigid structure to the exercise which often frustrates the interviewee.

If you are faced with this type of interview, prepare your material well, sit in a comfortable setting where you will not be interrupted, stay relaxed and think before you answer the questions. Talk slowly. The conversation is often recorded so you may wish to check whether or not this is the case beforehand. Another frustrating element in this type of interview is the lack of feedback, both verbal and non-verbal. The interviewers are generally not permitted to comment on your answers. They work from prepared scripts and record the answers as they go along in order to ensure that a uniform standard is achieved, so that candidates can be compared with one another.

The informal, pre-interview chat is a more common use of the phone. This may occur when the interviewer is uncertain about whether or not to short-list you and can delegate the task to a secretary or junior colleague. For you this call could be very important, making the difference between winning a face-to-face meeting or being rejected out of hand.

Answering machines
Many people curse the phone and, even more, its close cousin the answering machine, but the latter can play a very constructive part in career management. It is a valuable investment, particularly if it has a 'page home' device which allows you to check on incoming calls while you are out.

Not only does an answering machine make you contactable at all times, it also allows you to take messages at times when you might wish to relax. You may receive calls quite late in the evening, especially from headhunters and recruitment consultants. They may wish to conduct a short, interview-style conversation which could prove embarrassing if you have 'switched off' for the day and have had a couple of drinks. You need to be thinking clearly if you are going to be answering skilfully-worded questions, some of which may have been designed deliberately to catch you off guard.

Record a short and concise message, remember to switch on the machine either when leaving the house or at the start of the evening, then you can return all calls in a prepared manner. Some machines have a conversation record facility which can be useful to analyse your own techniques and provide feedback.

Improve your telephone style

Many people, even senior managers, have a poor telephone style and it is generally due to three major mistakes.

1 Not listening   We are all guilty of this during normal conversations and the fault is exaggerated when using the phone. We hear only what we expect to hear and this can lead to mistakes. We often have preconceived views and only want to hear what is in tune with our thinking. Our listening can be very judgemental, which means we listen only long enough to hear what we have judged is right.

We are all guilty of engaging in other tasks while listening to a caller, signing letters, skimming through a report, not giving full attention to the conversation. This is a dangerous fault. If a phone call is important, it warrants your full attention.

2 Poor synchronisation   When you are engaged in a face-to-face conversation you have access to a fount of extra information such as facial expressions and body language. On the phone you are limited to words and voice tone alone. To use the telephone successfully you therefore need to be more sensitive to the other person's voice.

3 No structure   A phone call can often leave you muddled and confused when you finish. You have received a torrent of information but, because it lacked structure, you cannot make sense of what was said afterwards. Giving a telephone conversation structure is one of the most important ingredients in achieving a successful technique.

Preparation is all important. Be clear about the objective you wish to achieve. Identify the person you wish to contact and check their name. Don't waste time talking to anyone else.

Write down a script or word plan, especially if you are nervous about using the telephone. Have the area adjacent to the phone organised with pen, paper, contact cards, diary, career summary, appropriate correspondence and anything else you are likely to need.

The time of day you make your call can be very important in getting through to the right person. Early morning or towards the end of the day can often be successful, because the screening secretary may not be around, especially if you have the number for a direct line.

The structure of a call should follow the mnemonic: AIDA

Attention A telephone call is usually unannounced, which makes it an intrusive medium. You must therefore gain the listener's attention immediately. The most successful way of achieving this is by having a referral name or some personal information. If this is not possible, be clear in your introduction and purpose for calling.

Interest This must be maintained and can be helped by using open questions which require explanatory responses and cannot be answered simply with yes or no. At this point you could meet objections and counter them with a benefit.

Desire This leads on from interest and if at this point it is obvious that you will not achieve the next stage do not close the door, e.g. 'Yes, Mr Watts, I understand you are very busy but do you mind if I keep in touch?'

Action This means that you are in sight of achieving your objective. Remain positive and keep taking the lead. If the objective is to gain an appointment be ready with suggestions. It's always easier to arrange meetings a couple of weeks in advance. 'Would Tuesday or Thursday suit you better?' 'Thursday is fine, is 3 p.m. all right?'

Busy executives are usually shielded by secretaries or PAs. You need to understand that they are paid to screen calls and save their boss from unnecessary hassle. You need to gain the support of this person and convince them that the boss will want to talk to you. It is not always easy but polite persistence often pays off.

Voice style
Your voice is the only indicator that the listener has of what you are like, so always speak clearly, slowly, and with a confident and friendly manner. Choose a simple and precise vocabulary to limit the loss of understanding due to the lack of non-verbal feedback. Also avoid negative words, such as 'problem', 'trouble', 'doubt', 'perhaps', 'maybe', 'never'.

Everyone should listen to a recording of their telephone style because some people have a very abrupt manner. This can be

...if you are a successful senior executive, but very off-...g if you are attempting to achieve a networking meeting.

The smile technique

Always talk through a smile, since your voice will automatically become warmer and more pleasant. Be relaxed, so before you start check your body posture and if you feel tense engage in some deep-breathing exercises. Some people prefer to make calls standing up, since this gives them a more relaxed and positive feeling. Try different ways until you find the most comfortable for you, but avoid using the 'hands-off' style of telephone as it distorts your voice.

Use active listening throughout the call. Avoid interrupting, but let the other person know you are attentive by interjecting, 'I see, hmm, I see, yes, quite'. When you are doing something active explain this to the listener. 'I am just reaching for my diary'. This way they can visualise what is happening and will remain in contact with your train of thought.

Learn to use pauses effectively. When nervous, people tend to gabble. If you have a tendency to do this, train yourself to speak more slowly and pause to allow the listener time to absorb what you have said. Never be uncertain about asking the person to repeat something that you didn't catch.

ACTION

Try preparing answers for the following situations. You could try using them in a role-play situation or record them to assess your techniques.

1. A secretary answers the phone; you want her to put you through to her boss. The following are her words, how would you respond to each question or statement?

   'Hello.'

   'Who's calling?'

   'May I ask what it's about?'

'He's in a meeting. Could you tell me why you wish to speak to him?'

'Give me your number. He'll call you back.'

2. You are speaking to a managing director to whom a contact has referred you. The following are his words, how would you respond to them?

'Hello.'

'Could you tell me briefly about your experience?'

'What is the purpose of this call?'

'Yes, that's interesting, but I'm afraid I'm very busy at the moment.'

3. How would you deal with the following responses?

'Which company are you from?'

'Who do you represent?'

'Does he know you?'

'How did you get this number/extension?'

'Who referred you?'

'She is very busy.'

'Can I [the secretary] be of assistance?'

'Could you call later?'

'I am holding all calls.'

'It is not convenient.'

'He does not accept unsolicited calls.'

'Could you write first, enclosing your CV.'

'He is not in.'

'She is in a meeting.'

'He is on holiday.'

'She is at lunch.'

'He is not at his desk.'

'She is not available.'

'Why are you calling?'

'What is the purpose of your call?'

'What do you want?'

'How can he help you?'

Always remember that you are responsible for your own career management, so don't fall into the trap of sharing that burden and leaving your number with a stranger. The chances are that your call will not be returned.

One final point, remember to organise your family. If you have children and they are old enough, train them to take accurate messages. If children are very young it may be more appropriate to use the answering machine.

Remember . . .

- First impressions make the most impact.

- How you look is initially more important than what you say.

- Be aware of what your clothes and accessories are saying about you.

- Make sure your gestures match your words and meanings.

- Good interview techniques are useful in all career management situations.

- An interview is an interaction, not an interrogation.

- Preparation is the most important element to an interview.

- Be prepared to sell yourself.

- Don't be frightened of silence.

- Debrief yourself after an interview.

- The telephone can be an asset for career management – if you use it effectively.

CHAPTER **10**

WRITTEN
COMMUNICATION SKILLS

Written communication skills are very important in career management. They are often the skills that open doors to meetings. Also, they provide the link in people's minds with which they can remember you, not as a crashing bore who is to be shunned but a timely reminder that your skills and talents are around.

I become more and more astonished at how poor people's memories are, or perhaps how single-tracked individuals become, fixed to remember details in a limited contextual setting. So, unless you or your particular need happens to meet with the other person's track of interest, you need to know how to remain fixed in people's memory banks until the appropriate moment.

Letter writing

It is always assumed that everyone who can write grammatically will be able to construct an effective letter. This may be true when you are acting out the role of marketing director, chief engineer or financial controller for your company, or personnel assistant for your boss, but not necessarily when you are writing on your own behalf. When you are speaking with your professional hat on you have a clearly defined, impersonal function, which is identified and given credibility by your job title.

You have the backing of your company, complete with letter head, and all its implied status. In many cases you will also have the help of a secretary or PA when it comes to choosing your words and putting them on paper in a professional and effective manner.

When it comes to writing letters about yourself the situation changes radically, and most people compose letters of this type to a very low standard. In many cases the higher up an organisation a person is, the worse their letter-writing skills become – possibly because they have more support staff or because no one has the authority to tell them how bad they are. Above all, people simply lack experience because they so seldom have to write or talk about themselves in any detail.

Once again we come back to the problem of modesty. People are very reticent to write positively about themselves for fear of sounding like boastful, unsympathetic characters. Again, modesty must be defeated because people will initially take you at your own evaluation of yourself. If you dismiss your achievements or apologise for them, and take no trouble to make your letter tempting to read, then there is no reason why the recipient should bother to go any further with the matter.

Letter writing is one of the most valuable skills in career management. Its importance cannot be stressed too highly, but it is an area which is sorely neglected by most of us. So often a letter is the first contact you have with someone, and they will consequently be making a great many initial assumptions about you from the style and content of what you write, just as they will at an initial meeting from the way you dress and talk. First impressions are immediately being formed the moment your letter drops on to the recipient's desk, even before they open the envelope.

Good letters are a valuable method of communication and a way of keeping you uppermost in a person's mind. The danger is that if they are produced badly you will remain in the recipient's memory only as a crashing bore or a nuisance, if you remain in his or her memory at all. Poor letters are usually ditched without a further thought.

General guidelines

Paper and envelopes
The paper you use must be of good quality, A4, at least 80 gram in weight and preferably 100 gram, with matching long envelopes. Avoid envelopes with windows or using labels, because these can look like a mailshot.

You really are looking to present a very personal and individual image as well as a professional one. The paper used should match that of the career summary, for example. Colour is very much a matter of choice; grey, blue or cream are all acceptable, but white is always the safest bet. The envelope should be as neatly typed or written as the contents, and should carry the correct postage, not a hotch-potch of old stamps which look as if they came from the bottom of your stationery drawer.

Typing
A typewritten page is always more professional and, with so many people having keyboard skills, more acceptable. If your handwriting is outstanding it may be a plus in the eye of the reader, provided it is easy to read, but remember that this will add to the time factor. If you have access to a word-processor you can produce tailored letters very quickly.

Handwritten correspondence
Prompt, hand-written replies posted immediately after a meeting, can be extremely effective and very personal, but only if the writing is legible.

Graphology
The analysis of handwriting is a technique used by a number of companies as part of their recruitment practice. If, at any point, you are specifically requested to write something by hand, always comply and be aware that this could be used for analysis.

If this is the case, don't panic! Don't take a crash course in calligraphy (the art of handwriting), and don't get someone else to write for you. Just write as you normally would. Graphology analysis does not depend upon being able to read what has been written.

If you are interested in finding out more, then ask if a graphologist will be used, and read up on the subject.

Contact
Never send a letter addressed to 'Dear Sirs', always research the correct name and title. A quick phone call to ensure that you have

the spelling and gender right is always worth while, since people always notice an error in their own name.

Signature
A wild signature may denote character, but is often difficult to decipher. Always print your full name under your signature.

Content
The general rule is to be clear, concise and to the point, generally not exceeding one page.

Printed notepaper
This is expensive but may be a good investment. Computer graphics can provide a cheaper solution which you can design yourself with many wordprocessing software packages.

Different types of letters

There are a number of different types of letter that can be very effective in career management, and being clear about the different categories can help you decide when to use each type of letter.

Direct target letters
Direct targets will emerge from your research. You will gradually be able to identify the person who you are interested in talking to. The aim of the first letter will usually be to achieve a meeting, at which you will be able to find out more details.

This type of letter provides great scope for creativity, but remember that brevity is the most important ingredient. The moment you start to bore the reader you run the risk of having the letter binned. Who wants to give up valuable time to meet people who sound boring in their letters?

There are no hard-and-fast rules about what to write because, as with a career summary, you must adopt your own style in order to demonstrate your own personality. It might, however, be worth considering a few guidelines.

An ideal letter would probably consist of three paragraphs.

1. The link or the reason for writing. Getting straight to the point.

2. The presentation of your case.

3. The action or outcome you wish to achieve.

Always try to ensure that you are sending your letter to a decision maker, not to someone whose job it is to filter the letters. It may be that the decision maker will pass your letter on to the 'filter', but at least you have had a chance of catching their attention first.

It requires careful research to find exactly the right person, but the more effort you put in, the more likely it is that your letter will reach its target and achieve the desired goal.

Letters to recruitment consultants
Executive search companies (headhunters) and recruitment consultancies, like to know what is happening in the marketplace, but they are only interested in a small percentage of the people available.

If you have the appropriate skills and background, therefore, you should be writing to these firms, even though the odds of them having something specific for you are low. Most of these firms have databases of candidate information and your details can be inputted ready for the moment when some appropriate vacancy appears.

The key is to ensure that your letter, as far as possible, has your information categorised in a usable format, and this could be an area where you could do with some professional help. Few headhunters will reveal the secrets of their computer or coding systems, so you have to provide your information in a format which will assist the process if possible.

A letter to a consultant must include the type of position you are seeking. If you are vague they cannot neatly place you in a pigeonhole and you will therefore not find a place in the system.

You must state the remuneration package you require, and this is the only time you should mention money in a career management letter. Once again the headhunters need signposts as to the sort of positions that would suit you and that you would be interested in. Money is an important category for them, and if you neglect to include these figures the letter will almost certainly be discarded.

You must state the job location or parameters that you would be willing to consider. Make sure that if you put 'no ties' you mean it. Search consultants become extremely frustrated with candidates who, at the final hurdle, refuse to move to a distant location for family reasons. Have these sorts of issues clearly decided in your mind (or, better still, committed to paper as one of your constraints), before you start writing these letters.

The letter you write to a consultant should be accompanied by a career summary, and the content of the letter should not repeat anything that has been included in the career summary, but should add extra information which will tempt them to read on, and will demonstrate that it is a specific and individual response.

Remember that executive search consultants do not have a ready supply of job vacancies. They react to their clients' needs. Also, the top league of headhunters are only searching for the top calibre to recruit, usually at the lower end of the age profile. So, as a rough guide, if you are below 40 years old, earning over £75,000, you may be of interest. If you are a 50 year old earning £20,000, you are wasting time and energy writing to headhunters in the top league.

If you want to learn more about executive search read *How to be Headhunted* by Yvonne Sarch (Century Business Books).

Networking letters

Letters play an important part in developing and fostering your network of contacts. People can see that if you have taken the time and trouble to write to them you do genuinely value their advice.

You might use a letter for the first approach, although a telephone call is more likely to elicit a positive response if you are able to get to the right person. It is much easier to ignore a letter than someone talking on the other end of the line, and much easier to say 'no' in a letter.

If you have made the initial contact by phone you should then write to confirm any arrangements, making clear the objective you have for the meeting and thanking them for their time. Another thank you letter would then be in order after the meeting.

Generally, if approached in the right way, people are extremely helpful and willing to spare valuable time to discuss career issues.

Follow-up letters

Follow-up letters are a very useful way of ensuring that you remain in the memory of someone you wish to influence, whether it is a contact in your network or a valuable source of information.

The letter might be to say thank you for the meeting, advice or contacts. It might be to keep someone up to date on your progress, or to report back on the outcome of a referral meeting. It might be to emphasise a specific point after an interview or to ask for further referrals if you have been unsuccessful at the final interview stage.

Remember that you must always have a valid reason for writing a follow-up letter. If you just write for the sake of it, or because you believe it is the 'done thing', you run the risk of falling into the 'crashing bore' or 'shunned nuisance' categories.

Don't dismiss the idea of writing follow-up letters. If someone has given freely of their time this should be acknowledged. Also, giving information about final outcomes is good, so that people acquire knowledge for their own networks.

This is fundamental to having a professional attitude towards career management, and especially to areas of contact development. Unless everyone adheres to these standards, the activity will not develop as a positive and valuable asset to career management.

Replies to advertisements
Whenever you reply in writing to a recruitment advertisement, you must always include a covering letter with your career summary or application form. The letter must be brief, stating where you saw the advert, on which date, and adding any extra information that is relevant to that particular job and which is not covered in the summary or application form. The objective of the letter is to make your application specific and individual.

A letter of application can also be used either when you don't have a CV or career summary, or when the document you do have is inappropriate for the particular position. It may be easier to write out a letter of application than to rewrite your career summary.

Take from the advert the relevant items which they are asking for and match them with examples of your own experience. Use bullet points, lists, columns and any other layout techniques which will make the text easier to follow, focusing the eye and picking out the relevant facts (in fact you should use many of the techniques which apply to the layout of a career summary).

ACTION

Find an advertisement that interests you and suits your skills, and then write a covering letter to accompany your career summary.
Now check the following.

Is it clear?

Is it concise?

Is it appropriate?

If you can answer 'yes' to these questions, place the letter in an envelope addressed to yourself and post it (second class). When you receive the letter, note very carefully how you react when you first open the envelope. Read it through, checking your impressions all the time. Turn to your letter-writing checklist (below), and see if you wish to make any changes to your letter.

Letter-writing checklist

Here are some pointers which may help you improve your letter-writing skills.

1. Does it create a good impression?

2. Can it be easily read?

3. Will it photocopy clearly? (Black ink photocopies better than blue.)

4. Are spelling, grammar and syntax correct?

5. Are you proud of the letter?

6. Does it match the style of your career summary?

7. Is it addressed to a specific person whose name is spelt correctly and whose job title and gender are correct?

8. Does it draw attention to your specific skills in relation to the reason for writing?

9. Is the language positive and direct?

10. Does it offer additional information which is of interest to the reader?

11. Does it ask for an action on the part of the reader?

Application forms

For many jobs the standard procedure is to be asked to fill in an application form. For many of us, however, who have had diverse and varied careers, they can be very restrictive documents. Their design seldom allows for much individuality, and can often place rigid and uniform constraints on you.

The application form is particularly prevalent in the public sector and in large, bureaucratic companies, and every job searcher must be aware of the nuances which are associated with it.

Always treat the form with respect. Someone will have lavished a great deal of time and effort on its design and will want you to adhere to the instructions, however banal they may seem to the outsider.

Always read the questions carefully to make sure you are providing the information they are asking for.

Answer all the questions. If a question is not applicable to you then indicate this by writing 'N/A', to show that you have not simply missed it out. Never make the judgement that any question is irrelevant. This annoys personnel staff and creates a negative feeling for the reader of the form.

There is often a question about salary, which is always difficult, but it is better to give your salary range and not be tempted to leave it blank. This gives you some manoeuvrability when it comes to negotiating.

When you receive the form, start by taking a photocopy of it and work on the rough copy first. This will help you to avoid mistakes and repetitions.

When you fill in the final form, always use black ink or biro because they will usually want to make copies.

Before completing the form, gather together all the relevant information such as the advertisement, the job specification, company literature and your details. Analyse it all to ensure that there is a good match between your skills, knowledge and experience and the needs of the company. Then you can start to fill in the form in a concise, well-organised and positive way. Using bullet points, headings and lists, similar to the layout of a career summary, this will help to make the finished result clear and easy to read.

When the form is complete, write a brief covering letter, stating which position you are applying for and, if it is in reply to an advertisement, where you saw the advert.

If your career summary is concise this could also be included.

Use a large envelope in which to post the documents in order to avoid folding them too much. This will improve the image of the application when it is opened. C5 envelopes are best suited for application forms and career summaries.

The CV, resumé or career summary

There are as many opinions about this subject as there are documents in circulation. For anyone managing their own career this is a vitally important piece of paper and it requires time and effort to get it right.

First, let's get the terminology clear:

A CV (short for curriculum vitae) is a chronological record of employment;

a resumé (an American term) highlights or gives a summary of a career;

a career summary is my preference as a title for such a document in a career management context.

The title CV is strongly linked to the idea of searching for another job, and in this situation most people are furtive about the document. They creep around outside office hours to get access to the computer when nobody is around, or they bribe their secretary to secrecy with champagne or flowers. This is not the way a career summary should be viewed, and for that reason I promote a different name.

The objective of your career summary, then, is to provide a clear, concise picture of you in terms of your assets, skills, strengths and achievements. It is a document that should be regularly updated and frequently used within your present organisation. It is not something that should signal feelings of frustration or discontent, but a communication tool which can be used during an appraisal; after a networking chat; as an *aide-mémoire*; as an update to ensure that your own progress is being monitored; as an information document for someone who is not certain about what you do or has no idea what you have done in the past.

There is no single correct formula for writing a successful career summary. Each person is unique and has a different story to tell, so each document should be individual. It should not be a copy or a clone, or written in the style of anyone else.

It is very important, right from the beginning, to be clear that only one person can write a career summary, and that is the owner of the document. No one should be so busy that they have to give the task to someone else. If anyone else attempts the job you are abdicating responsibility, which is one of the first don'ts in successful career management.

By writing your own summary you are claiming total ownership of everything that appears in it, and you will be able to feel completely confident about what has been written. If you don't do this you can get into serious problems when you have to live up to the written word. If anyone suspects the slightest gap between what appears on paper and the reality that is presented, you will lose face and immediately damage your chances of success. There are no short cuts to writing this document. If you seek professional help, remember that their role is to provide guidance and expertise about current trends in the marketplace, and to act as a sounding board and interpreter for what you are attempting to say. It is not their job to write it for you.

The first test of a good career summary is that you are confident and proud of the document, and happy to show it to everyone.

Objectives

A career summary is primarily for use within an organisation as an important communication tool, but it has a dual function when considering situations outside.

The objective of a career summary, when used in a job search, will be different for different groups. A headhunter uses it to impress a client who is paying a fee and requiring a great deal of detail about an individual.

Headhunters always complain that CVs never contain enough detail, and this is where I believe the conflict of objectives comes into play. Their client is paying for a detailed search for an individual. My argument is that this detail should not be gained from a piece of paper, but from a face-to-face interview and other avenues of research. If an executive search consultant is interested enough in the career summary in front of him or her, and wants more information, the document has done its job successfully.

If you ever receive a phone call from a headhunter asking for a more detailed CV, don't fall into the trap of doing the job for which they are handsomely paid. Instead, you should negotiate for an interview so that you can present the extra information in a more valuable way, personally.

The objective of your career summary in career management is to provide a clear and concise picture of you as a whole person with a number of different assets. It should be non-threatening, and as you actively develop your career path it will become a familiar document to people who know you.

The objective for the job-searcher is twofold: a) to secure an interview; and b) to act as a prompt script during the interview, especially if the interviewer lacks experience. The skilled job-searcher, with a good career summary, can guide the interview in a positive way.

A junior personnel officer will see it as an initial filtering tool, especially if the advertisement has been too general and has attracted an avalanche of replies.

The question of length

The longest CV I've ever encountered was 48 pages, with an 8-page addendum that would be supplied on request. The shortest was five points scribbled on the back of an envelope.

The correct length is entirely up to you but, before making the decision, consider the recipient. Whether they are personnel staff, a contact, recruitment consultants or the chairperson of a blue-chip organisation, they are busy people who may receive numerous documents of this nature every day.

I would also suggest that an overly long document can indicate a certain degree of insecurity. If it is difficult for you to accept that your career can be condensed into highlights, this can raise questions about your real worth. You should therefore look closely at what you have achieved, not simply draw up a list of responsibilities or technical jargon.

It would be a pity if the most wonderful CV was never read simply because no one had the time to plough through all the pages. So try to put yourself in the place of the recipient; if it is received in response to an advertisement it may be one of hundreds, and even if it is a direct approach it will still be just one item in a whole in-tray of correspondence.

On the whole, I would recommend brevity – one page is ideal, two pages acceptable and anything more verging on the danger of giving away too much information, and falling into the trap of allowing a paper decision to be made, or worse still the receiver never finding the time to read the material.

Ask around to gain some views and feedback on the subject, although you may find that your enquiries open up floodgates because, for some, this is an emotive subject. Listen to everything that is said, but be selective. Learn from the experience of others and begin to formulate your own views. Always be prepared to be flexible at this early stage of drafting your career summary.

Presentation and style

The presentation and style of the document is extremely important, and should reflect your individual flair. People with computer keyboard skills, knowledge of computer graphics or desktop publishing have an advantage here. If you do have these skills, mention them in the career summary, so that it is clear that you have achieved the finished look of your document by your own efforts.

If you have to use the design and printing services of someone else, you begin to tread on dangerous ground, just like having your CV written for you. You must have your own style and not be attracted to plush, ritzy presentation for its own sake. Personnel staff tend not to like 'professionally manufactured' documents, and are quite likely to extract them and bin them without even reading the contents. Some recruiters even believe that they can spot the origin of a CV at a glance, meaning that they know the individual styles of the various outplacement companies. These prejudices do exist and you need to be aware of them.

Some people advocate the use of coloured paper, while others recommend fancy folders. My experience shows that good, clear quality, with no gimmicks, always wins.

If you are in a business like advertising then perhaps a clever gimmick would be appropriate, but you must consider your market. Anything being prepared for the City will have to follow the life-long traditions of that sector. A public relations agency might allow you greater scope for creativity, but don't lose sight of the objective that the document must be easy to read.

If you analyse how busy people read, often using the skim-and-scan technique, you will see that they will be glancing quickly through your document, picking up the general sense, before going back to read in more detail if they are interested. The skilful use of layout, space, headings, lists, bullet points, capitals, emboldening etc., all help the reader to focus on the important gems.

A general tip; don't underline and embolden together, since one counteracts the other.

Photographs

Photographs of yourself are generally more appropriate for the American market than the European one, and if you do use them they *must* be excellent. It also helps if you are photogenic, which most people aren't. You must invest in a good, professional photographer – four snaps from a slot machine will not do.

A dubious 'mug shot' immediately creates barriers of prejudice and puts you at a disadvantage. Why create a negative atmosphere before you have started? What you should be aiming to do is achieve a pleasing invitation to read on and find out more.

The CV as a marketing document?

Some people like a CV to sales and marketing literature; others dismiss this analogy as too slick and pushy. I believe that you can learn a great deal from examining professional sales literature, because a successful career summary ultimately achieves the same result.

The true essence of the job market is that on the one hand, you have the employer, who wants to buy skills and expertise, while on the other, you have the skills to sell – a very simple transaction it would seem. Of course, it isn't simple, but if you keep this idea in mind, writing your career summary will be less complicated.

> Know what you have to sell.
> Analyse what your buyer wants.

A clear and concise view of your achievements and skills is essential, because an employer needs staff to run a business, and these staff must be assets and provide value. The employer is thus looking for evidence of success and achievements, not a history lesson about the applicant or a list of their responsibilities.

If you are a sales manager or personal assistant for example, people generally have some idea about what the job entails, so a litany of responsibilities only tells the reader what he or she already knows. What is of real interest is what you have done with those responsibilities, and how you have used them to move something forward.

Many people write their career summary as a direct copy of a job spec. This is a bad mistake and should be avoided. Use the job spec. to elicit your responsibilities and then analyse what you have achieved. Here are some examples.

'Responsible for leading a team' should read, 'Headed a team of six to produce the PR campaign for the successful launch of new consumer magazine'.

'Responsible for budgeting and financial control' should read, 'Managed a budget of £1.7m with the assistance of two staff'.

'Responsible for training a sales force' should read, 'Designed and introduced a nationwide customer care training programme for a sales force of 300'.

Knowing what your assets are

The key to success is knowing what your assets are, and this can only come from rigorous skills analysis. Once this information has been collected, with some excellent examples, writing can begin. (If in doubt return to Chapter 4.)

Honesty must pay

It is vital to be honest at all times. All the information must be correct because facts are often checked by prospective employers and headhunters who want to validate details, especially qualifications. Also, you never know who knows whom in the world of successful networks. Unofficial telephone calls are made between contacts and personnel directors of their acquaintance or your name might well be mentioned during a conversation. A small 'white lie' is never worth the risk, because if found out you lose credibility and this will jeopardise all your hard work.

Exactly what should be in your career summary will depend upon which stage of your career you are at. This is an area where a professional adviser might be able to help, since they know what the trends are.

The format you choose is completely up to you. A CV is usually a conventional, chronological list of jobs, generally with a description of the activities. Consider, however, who is likely to be reading the document. If you are applying for a position of personnel manager and the applications go to the personnel director, he or she will be only too aware of what is included in the job. This applies to most jobs, so what is of real interest is what you have done as an individual. The resumé or career summary therefore allows far greater freedom for you to present yourself in a more interesting way.

The essentials

The following information must always be included.

Full name Give names you generally use.

Address

Telephone number Office number if this is appropriate, or home. An answerphone is a valuable asset and reference to this should be included.

Qualifications   Gained after leaving school. Standards attained with the name of the institution plus dates is all that is required.

Education   Secondary level only. Details must be brief, and if you have higher achievements you generally do not need to include the lower examinations, e.g. if you have A levels it is less important to record O levels or GCSEs. The number of examination passes is usually enough, unless there is an unusual or relevant subject such as Japanese or computer technology. The general rule is that the higher you progress the less important are early exam results.

Membership   These can include professional and social organisations.

Interests   These are very important because they give an all-round, balanced picture, but be specific. If reading is a hobby say what type of books, e.g. Len Deighton or natural history. Attempt to list items that are interesting and get away from the general boring list. Use your imagination.

Age   Date of birth can be a vaguer mask for the older individual, but do not attempt to leave out this information.

Job record   In any career documents, this section forms the bulk of the material, and all too often it becomes a boring list of information that the reader already knows. Recording the duties of a marketing manager will not make for original reading. What the reader wants is a clear pattern of your work record with job title, company names and dates (year only is generally enough at this point), plus some relevant pointers. The present job is of most importance and the longer your career the less important are the earlier positions. If you choose the resumé or career summary formula, this section can be quite brief, recording only the valuable pieces of information. The key information that should be gained from the job record is progression.

The next batch of information may or may not be relevant, depending upon your individual circumstances. This is where professional guidance can be of particular benefit, with someone objectively telling you what is or is not appropriate.

Nationality   For certain applications it may be appropriate, but it does raise the question of race discrimination. Prejudice is a very complicated issue and recruitment is rife with individual bias, so this question must be given careful consideration.

Marital status   This is a difficult question which must be viewed from each individual angle. Professional counselling can help in this delicate area.

Military service   Will depend on age.

Health   The date and result of the last health check can be useful if everything was OK.

Languages   This information is becoming more and more important. Always record the standard attained, e.g. 'conversational French' or 'business German', but always be prepared to demonstrate this at the interview. If it is an asset, make the most of it.

Training   It is good to demonstrate that you have been active in advancing your standards, so highlight a few examples that will be of interest.

The next section includes the information that, in my experience, is most important to any successful career document.

Achievements   Many people's first reaction to this word is 'I don't have any,' and this is where professional career guidance is beneficial. What an employer really wants to know is your worth, not in financial terms, but in actual examples of what you have done. The value of this type of information is that if you have achieved something for one company you are likely to be able to repeat the success somewhere else. Many people fall into the trap of underselling themselves on paper and at interview. Achievements given must be true, concise and factual.

Skills   This is another area that is often neglected. This type of information is especially important if you are considering a move from one sector or discipline to another. Today, we hear a great deal about transferable skills and how important they will become in the future. Unfortunately, this is a very difficult concept for people to grasp, especially recruiters, who tend to think within confined parameters. They are not renowned for their creative thinking. Also, you have to overcome prejudice. Everyone, for instance, has preconceived views about civil servants, accountants, teachers and administrators. They all think they know exactly what the jobs entail and believe there could never be any valuable overlap. Someone who has been a civil servant, for instance, might be considered unable to function in the private sector – a sad misconception. Skills are generic and can, to a certain extent, help to break down this area of prejudices, but it is not easy. This is another area where professional advice can prove valuable.

Experience   Breadth of experience is a valuable asset and needs to be carefully highlighted. The full impact of this is often lost within a normal list of job titles.

Companies   In certain sectors, such as retailing or fast-moving consumer goods (fmcg), a blue-chip company or brand name is very important and should occupy a prominent position.

References

This information should not be included with a CV or career summary. References are generally taken up at the later stages, when an offer is being discussed.

Starting to write

It is now time to start writing your own document. It will take a number of drafts before you get it right and the techniques of 'cut and paste' are very useful – as is a word-processor.

If you are working without professional help, show a draft to someone who knows you well and whose opinion you respect. Remember that they will have their pet likes and dislikes, but listen to their comments and act on them if you think they are appropriate.

Always be prepared to make minor alterations and amendments, even to the finished document. If you are not controlling the final printing yourself, make sure you order reasonably short print-runs, so that you aren't left with hundreds of copies.

ACTION

Always send yourself a copy of your summary, using a second-class stamp to give yourself some space from the tortuous memories of writing. When you receive it, record the impressions you have when you are opening the envelope. You should have feelings of pride; if not it may mean going back to the drawing board.

Remember that you should be proud of your career summary, keen to let anyone read it and use it often as a document to help communication. It will assist you during appraisal interviews or career development meetings.

Remember . . .

- Good written communications skills will open doors for you.
- Find ways to fix yourself in people's memories.
- Overcome your natural modesty.
- Prepare a career summary openly and use it to help communication generally.
- Write in your own style, using your own words.
- Make texts clear and easy to follow.
- Treat application forms with respect.
- A career summary is a selling and marketing document.
- Know what your assets are.
- Be honest at all times.

PHASE 4

CHAPTER 11

CAREER MONITORING

Phase 4 of the career management model is the most valuable phase, but, in my experience, it is also the most neglected. If you have worked through Phases 1 to 3 you will have invested a great deal of time and effort in *You*. It is now vitally important to monitor and maintain your progress. Chapters 11 and 12 tell you why, and how.

A continuous process

Most people believe that once they have achieved a position which they like, or have managed to get into the company of their choice, they can then sit back and let their career look after itself. That is never the case, however. Career management is a continuous process, which you must be aware of and practise throughout your working life. And even in retirement many of the principles can still apply.

This means that you must continue to keep your tools and techniques sharp, even during periods when you might believe you won't be needing them again. You will also have to add new skills and tools to your repertoire, to ensure that you continue to develop and grow, and do not slip back into old ways and bad habits. If you allow your guard to drop, and you stop planning and asking 'what if' questions, you will be forced to take drastic, and possibly painful action at a later date when a crisis strikes, or you relinquish control of your future to others.

Career management isn't something which you just 'do' for a year while you are enthusiastic or a crisis is brewing, and then forget about until the next emergency. It has to be a continuous process.

If you owned an expensive, rare painting it would be unwise to just let it hang over the mantelpiece. You would need to keep the insurance up to date, and therefore the valuation, and from time to time check on its condition. It may require a controlled atmosphere. If you ignored these jobs and the picture was damaged or stolen you would be left with nothing.

Similarly, there are certain jobs that must be tackled on a regular basis to monitor your career. If these are neglected the consequences can be just as devastating as the loss of a valuable possession.

Monitoring actions

Every six months you need to take stock of where you are, reminding yourself of your goals and ensuring that they haven't changed, and that you are still on course. Re-examine your skills to ensure they are keeping pace with changes in your sector. Check your values and decide if you are still being true to them. Do they still fit with your company's values?

Every year you must ensure that you do something to move your career forward. It might mean reading a book or attending a development course, whatever it is it must be career orientated and not function orientated. That means taking a course that will make you better at something, or will increase your personal knowledge, not something which will simply make you more efficient at the job you are doing now.

This means broadening your outlook and having vision beyond the normal confines. On certain occasions you may need to include a functional action, but generally this commitment should be beyond the immediate requirements of the present job. Career management is about forward thinking.

Most companies will be receptive to suggestions for training schemes for employees if they feel that they are valid, and if you 'sell' the idea to them effectively. But even if they don't it is now possible to 'do-it-yourself'. Training and Enterprise Councils in Britain have set up training initiatives based on a mixture of loans, awards and personal contributions.

'Pay as you learn' is an increasingly popular idea with many people advocating the idea of everyone having their own 'personalised' training account – a three-way partnership between the employer, employee and government.

My hope is that once the concept of career management is more generally accepted, negotiations between individuals and employers over salary packages will include a stated sum for career investment, with clauses relating to the percentage of company financing and the percentage of individual commitment, with a sliding scale depending upon whether you leave the company within a set number of years.

For example the T.D.A. Consulting Group has launched a career investment charter for all employees. A percentage of funding is agreed for each individual and a joint partnership is formalised which balances a commitment from all sides. One example is that all administrative staff were given the opportunity to have personal colour and image analysis. The company's contribution was financial, while the individuals gave their time as the workshops were organised on Saturdays.

At the beginning of each year you need to ask yourself how much you plan to invest in your career, because your success will be directly related to the amount of time, effort or money that you are going to spend on career management. Most people are still caught up in the demands and targets of their organisations, having little time left to assess their own views and values, but you can no longer afford to do that. You must be clear in your mind about what is best for you, and you must let your employer know how you feel.

Avoidance behaviour

This requirement to monitor your career may sound easy, but it isn't. First, we are all blighted by old habits which are hard to break. For example, when external pressures build up the first thing to be neglected is *you*.

Having too much else on to devote time to yourself is not a valid excuse. If you owned that priceless painting you would not ignore the notification that the insurance was overdue, because ignoring such information could result in a very expensive catastrophe. The same applies to ignoring career maintenance and monitoring signals.

Part of recognising how hard it is to pay attention to *you* is to highlight and acknowledge your own avoidance behaviour – excuses you use to stop you getting down to the job in question.

- 'No time' is always the classic block and this can raise two very important issues:

  1 *Time management*   How effective are you in using time to the maximum advantage? This is closely linked to what I call . . .

  2 *Time posing*   How much time is it politically expedient to spend in the office?

  Time management is an individual issue which can be improved by training. Time posing is linked to company culture and values, and is, thankfully, being dispelled more and more because enlightened managements are looking for quality not quantity. Working a 14-hour day does not mean you are producing more. Someone who works 8 hours effectively must be better value.

- Fear of failure can block many good intentions, especially if you have a tendency to be a perfectionist. This block also has a lot to do with company cultural issues. 'Change', the dreaded word, is all about taking risks, which means that some will result in success but a certain proportion will result in failure. It is how this failure is viewed within an organisation which is so important.

  If failure is perceived as disastrous, resulting in punishment for the individual, then risk and change will be minimal. Failure must be accepted as a fact of life, the most important rider being that you learn from your mistakes. Fear of failure can be reduced if you believe that it is OK to fail and that mistakes can produce very successful learning experiences.

- Another fear is linked to the unknown and not wanting to explore into new areas because you are unaware of the ground rules. Try to overcome this barrier by research. Get to know the unknown in whichever way is appropriate. Even the smallest piece of information can help to displace the fear. Often it can be a pleasant surprise to find that the unknown is not such an awesome place after all.

- Other responsibilities which are greater than the responsibility you currently have. This is a matter of valuing your needs against those of outside forces. This is another very difficult choice, but at the end of the day true responsibility starts with yourself and at certain junctures you and your career have to take priority if you are committed to the concept of career management. This does not mean adopting a selfish stance, but it does require commitment at least twice every year when *you* come first.

- It is easier not to change. Old habits are comfortable and change means taking risks which are uncomfortable. We all accept this, but change is a fact of working life. Do you want to wait until it is imposed upon you from outside or do you want to be in control of the change process? The choice is totally up to you. Everyone has free choice over this matter, but you must face reality before you start to whinge about what happens when situations are out of control.

- Using avoidance tactics. We all have a long list of activities which we do rather than tackle the real issue. Start to recognise this behaviour and confront yourself. Ask yourself, is the avoidance tactic a matter of urgent importance? If the answer is no then get down to the action you are trying to avoid.

ACTION

Part of recognising your own delaying tactics is to build strategies or plans that give you support. The first step is to identify how you flag up the 6-monthly action points. If you are a diary person mark your 6 and 12-month diary dates now.

Two interesting psychological time scales in career terms are January and September. January marks the new year and it is also the most active recruitment time. It is a good time to take stock and commit to new objectives. September is important because generally we have had a break during the summer months which gives an opportunity for relaxation and thinking, which automatically leads us to wonder about the future.

So if you can't think of any better time scales to use, January and September are suggestions, but April and November are just as good if that will suit you better. What is most important is to choose your time scale now and commit it to your diary.

Honouring your commitment

The next stage is to make sure that you honour your commitment. This can be achieved in a number of ways. Through my experience of working as a career consultant I have been interested in developing the concept of group interaction within this field. The reasons for this are varied, but one important aspect is that of self-help within a group.

Self-help

The value of this activity has long been recognised in a variety of settings and from my own experience, when applied to career management, it can be equally successful.

My reasons for wanting to explore and encourage this concept in career management have two main themes. First, it is about recognising and using the full potential of others. We all have a lot to give but often cannot find the opportunity to fully maximise these abilities. Helping others offers great opportunities to grow yourself. Also, a group of people working to pursue a common goal develop strong bonds which can take advantage of other people's networks. Secondly, there is a straight economic factor linked to self-help since it does not generally cost the individual anything, and the group purchase of professional services helps everyone.

If you are interested in forming a self-help career management group it may require some creative thinking, but you have one major advantage; all professional people are interested in their own careers and this interest is growing.

A good place to start looking is within your own professional body or institute. The officials of these groups have often identified that their membership is requesting this type of guidance and they are often willing to arrange for experts in the field to speak to a group. I have given a number of talks to professional bodies about career management, always to packed audiences. From this initial start it is easy to form smaller self-help groups that can address many of the topics covered in this book.

If you belong to a professional body, why not suggest to the events organiser a talk on career management. From this event it may be possible to identify 4-6 people willing to work together using the suggestions in this book.

Mentoring

Mentoring has its origins in Greek mythology, when Odysseus entrusted his son into the care of Mentor before leaving on a long journey. The benefits and value of mentoring have really always been around in our culture. The apprentice–master craftsman relationship has encapsulated many of the mentoring qualities. But it did not really come into prominence in management circles until the 1980s in the United States.

Formal mentoring

There are two distinct forms of mentoring. The first is the formal mentoring scheme which was set up by organisations such as IBM, the NHS, BP or the Brewers' Society to help the development of younger employees, either new recruits, management trainees, graduate trainees, high-fliers, MBA students or craftsmen. These types of schemes develop relationships within an organisation to enhance the calibre of future management. It also strengthens management's commitment to training and self-development, if they can see at close quarters the value for an individual.

The benefits of formal mentoring are being closely monitored in Britain. The Industrial Society/ITEM Group Survey in 1989 showed that some of the most important benefits are in the area of self-development, improved motivation, communication and interpersonal relationships, which help to prepare young employees for the rigours of leadership. If you want to go into mentoring in more detail *Everyone Needs a Mentor* by David Clutterbuck (IPM) makes a good reference point.

For the purposes of career management I wish to follow in more detail the path of *informal* mentoring, because I believe it is more appropriate for career management.

Informal mentoring

A mentor is generally someone older and wiser than yourself who is in a position to advise you, and to give you actual help and assistance in your career. The idea is to get someone powerful on your side, someone who will help to build your confidence in yourself and your skills, and someone who is able to give you a perspective to issues beyond your experience.

In her book *Networking and Mentoring – A Woman's Guide* (Piatkus) Dr Lily M. Segerman-Peck lists the things that mentors can do for mentees.

They can help them see:

- where they are;
- what options for the future are open to them;
- which options they want to pursue;
- what routes they have to travel to get there;
- what milestones they must pass on the way;
- what knowledge, facilities, equipment and experiences they need to get there.

In a formal mentoring situation the relationship is often arranged by another party. There is a certain amount of debate as to whether there should be free or structured choice in choosing a mentor. I believe that the choice of mentor should be freely within the control of the mentee.

In most cases, however, the most successful mentor/mentee relationships are formed when the latter has chosen to approach the former. It is vital that there is a feeling of mutual respect and that both sides feel that they will get something out of the relationship. This aspect is often overlooked, assuming that the mentee is the only one that develops from the relationship. Experience of mentoring schemes has highlighted how much the mentor has grown as well. To have someone 'allotted' to you could be as much a chore as a pleasure for both sides of the relationship.

It may be that you already have a mentor, without having thought about the relationship in those terms. You may have approached someone and asked for their help with a decision which you have to make, or their advice about a situation in which you have found yourself. You may have discovered that they give useful, impartial advice, and that you like each other, so the relationship has developed.

If this is the case you may like to make this relationship more structured by acknowledging the type of relationship it is, giving it a name and setting some parameters. But don't frighten the mentor away by using grand titles if you think it inappropriate. What you must remember is that if the relationship is working for you, it is fine.

If your mentor is also a successful person, on the way up, they may well take you with them. They will make sure that the right people get to hear about you and that your name is considered for promotion when appropriate. Having a champion is always invaluable, since they can speak for you in influential places. Other people will be happy to listen to them since everyone is looking for clues which will lead them to picking the right people for the right jobs.

Your mentor, especially if the relationship is within an organisation, may have a vested interest in pushing you forward because they know that you are loyal, hardworking and effective. They may gain politically if they can place people who are loyal to them, and who think along the same lines, in positions of influence, Often, when a managing director is poached from one company to another, he or she brings their team with them. That is because they know they can rely on these people. They have built relationships in the past and they don't have to get to know a new set of people or explain the way they like to work.

Attitudes towards mentoring can be very close to those of networking, which relies on going to people and asking them for information. Some people feel that it is wrong, that they should do everything themselves, without any help. But how can you learn without teachers? How can you do business without contacts? How can you function as a human being without forming relationships with other people?

Choosing a mentor

Since it is inevitable that you are going to form relationships with other people in the course of your career, it is better that they are people you choose, whom you like and who are going to be most useful to you in achieving your ambitions.

In their book *The Managerial Woman* (Pan Books), Margaret Hennig and Anne Jardim list the questions you should ask yourself when choosing a mentor.

- Where am I now?
- What is my present level of knowledge, skill and competence?
- Who are the people I know?
- What positions do they hold?
- What can they help me with?
- What can they teach me?
- What information do they have that I need?
- Whom do they know who can help me?

A good mentor is someone who is a good teacher, or who is good at helping you to learn. They will also advise and counsel. If they have a wide network of contacts that will also be helpful, and they must be willing to share those contacts with you and share their experiences. Someone who feels in any way threatened by you will not make a good mentor.

It is generally accepted that anyone with whom you have a supervisory connection will not make a successful mentoring relationship because there will be conflicts of interest from time to time, and this will hamper the impartial ideals of true mentoring.

A mentor needs to be intelligent, which will probably mean that they have qualifications, and an ability to think through and analyse situations dispassionately. They need to have empathy in order to appreciate what you might be going through at any particular stage of your career, and they need to be good listeners.

Most importantly they need to have had a variety of experience. Qualifications may be a good initial guide, but experience is what you are really seeking, linked with their eagerness to share it.

It is vital that they are also discreet, since you must be able to be completely honest with them, without fear that what you say will get back to people in authority. The issues of confidentiality and hidden agendas are the main drawbacks of a formal mentoring scheme, but as long as mentees fully understand and accept the implications of these two issues, they should not prove to be obstacles. A mentor must also command respect and be trustworthy.

They need to be perceptive, and have a commitment to developing people. That will mean that they will probably be patient, direct and enthusiastic by nature.

Not many people can fulfil all these criteria, which is why you may need to have more than one mentor. As you expand your network you will find people who have different things to offer. You might, for instance, find somebody in your company who has had experience of the department to which you have just been transferred, and can guide you through the office politics, introduce you to the right people, and give you practical survival tips. Someone else may have had your specific job before you, and someone else may work for a company to which you supply products, or which supplies you.

Some senior executives hire non-executive directors, management consultants or advertising agencies because they want people who will have the courage to tell them when they have got something wrong. They look for people they can trust, with broader or different experience to themselves, who can bring new perspectives and experiences to bear on their problems.

Mentors should be able to do the same for you. They should be able to speak the truth, even if it hurts, and show you things from a different angle, rather in the way that your parents and teachers did when you were a child.

They must be part of the action. It was once believed that employees about to retire could be used in a mentoring role, but this did not prove successful because their mind-set was moving out of the organisation and they were often a step removed from the issues of younger employees. This can also be the case if the mentor is too senior in rank and status, because the reality gap will also be too great.

Informal mentoring means looking for someone, usually outside your organisation, who you respect, trust and feel comfortable enough with to develop a relationship. Meetings should be regular and you both must understand the time commitment required. Set objectives so that you can monitor your progress.

Unfortunately, as yet there is no register of willing mentors, so it's down to you to search. Again, professional bodies can be a starting point, but finding the correct mentoring partner is not easy. One of the most valuable sources is through your network of contacts. If, at the moment, your own network is small or inactive, don't panic! As you expand and develop your contacts you will meet more people, and while you keep in mind your needs the right choice will emerge. Just remember that if you work at it, it will happen.

Role-models

Having a mentor is an active, two-way relationship. Having a role-model is a more distant and one-way relationship, and can be with someone we don't know very well. Much of our learning during early childhood has been through watching and copying role-models. This is a very powerful method of learning, particularly in career terms. It is also one that is often neglected.

Unfortunately role-models for men are becoming less and less obvious within organisations as layers of management are being stripped out and new career structures are being created as a result of flatter organisational structures. New role-models are beginning to emerge, but you may have to look very hard to find one who suits your particular needs.

Women have a different problem, which is a lack of role-models at senior levels. Many successful career women emulate male attitudes and behaviour at the top. In my own case the female role-models available to me during my career have mainly taught me how I *don't* want to be.

Nevertheless, role-models are important and can certainly help you learn many difficult lessons, especially in undefined areas such as cultural attitudes, ritual and company politics. Watching people is the best way to help identify who would make a suitable example for you. Ask silent, open questions to help you explore the rationale that may lie behind their actions. Occasionally you may have the opportunity to verify your opinions, but this is not essential. The relationship is usually passive. What you need to do is look, listen and assimilate a wealth of information. Experience is a great teacher, but you don't have to experience everything for yourself; you can learn a great deal from observing others and taking from their success or failure what is appropriate to you.

Remember . . .

- Career management is an ongoing process – it never ends.
- Review your situation every six months.
- Make an investment in your career every year.
- Recognise your excuses for what they are.
- Take risks and welcome change.
- Consider forming a self-help group.
- Look for a mentor and role-models.

CHAPTER 12

CAREER AND SELF MAINTENANCE

Career monitoring is about checking that your career objectives are kept in view and not submerged by external demands. Career maintenance, the final part of Phase 4 of the career management model, is about looking forward so you can avoid the head-in-the-sand posture or the knee-jerk reaction to a career crisis.

Career maintenance is just like car maintenance or a positive preventative healthcare regime. It will ensure that you will be prepared for what ever occurs along your career path, and be ready to grasp opportunities.

Your professional image

Your professional image is your statement to the world about how much you value yourself. It is your own individual price tag. Does your price tag say:

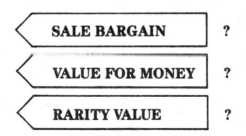

It may be that during the earlier stages of career management you realised the need to do something about your image, perhaps because you discovered from feedback that you were giving people the wrong messages through the clothes you were wearing, or at an interview you may have realised that you needed to work on your presentation skills.

It is surprising how many people will dress really smartly to attend an interview, but once they have the job they will let all their standards drop. It is as if getting the job was all that mattered and from then on they never need to progress or make any sort of impression on anyone. This is a mistake for anyone who wants to progress or improve, since people will always judge you by your own valuation of yourself.

You need regularly to reassess your image in the same way as your values, skills and goals once you are into the maintenance phase, since the requirements of your new position may mean that you need to make adjustments or, if you are very wrapped up in your job, you may have allowed yourself to slip back into old habits, impeding your chances of moving on successfully at a later date.

It's worth stressing again that whatever your job or position, it is always beneficial to promote yourself in a positive light. You constantly need to be asking yourself what the outside world is understanding about you from the way you dress and behave. Someone who feels that they are a victim of others, for instance, will dress and behave in that way, causing people to see them in that light and so make their situation worse.

In many cases it is simply a question of behaving in a professional manner, wearing the 'uniform' which is expected for that job, whether it is a suit or a white coat, a tie or a donkey jacket.

Your profile

Your profile is an important component of career management, and needs regular attention. Each person must consider how they view their profile in terms of their career. Many may believe this is only appropriate for the high-flier, but to manage a successful career everyone needs to consider this aspect.

It will not necessarily mean getting extensive media coverage, although that is generally a help for those who need it. In some cases it may relate to the profile of your team or department. Profile is about what information people have about you. If they know nothing about you you can never progress.

Raising your profile might involve something as simple as paying more attention to your personal appearance, considering what it is saying about you, not only your clothes, but your posture and body language as well. If you are giving people messages that say 'I'm going shopping', 'I've just popped in from the disco', 'I am available', 'I'm relaxing for the weekend', they will not take you seriously in career terms.

Your profile at work is very closely linked to how you act in given situations. Are you noticed? Your presentation skills are very important in this area, not just to secure a job, but also to ensure that you develop within it.

Importance of good communication skills

There are skills which you can learn that will help you to put yourself across to others, and to effect their impression of you. You should be aware of all the avenues of communication which are likely to be opening up to you as you progress through your career, and you should prepare yourself for them as they approach. Standing up to talk at meetings, for instance, both large and small, making presentations to clients and potential clients, and training situations are all likely to arise with greater frequency as you progress through your career. Very few people are naturally good at this sort of thing, but with attention the appropriate skills can be mastered.

Spoken communication

It might be that you can polish your skills to an acceptable level by reading a few books, watching other people and then practising. It is likely, however, that you will need to have some formal training at some stage. Most senior managers who speak in public a great deal in the course of their work will have constant coaching on their general style. Most successful people take the art of presentation and spoken communication very seriously indeed.

Everyone needs to be able to communicate verbally in order to talk to their bosses, their subordinates and their colleagues. They have to talk to their customers and suppliers, investors and the media. The ones that succeed are the ones who can get their messages across clearly and memorably, and can also project their personalities.

In his book, *High Impact Business Presentations* (published by Business Books), Lee Bowman, chairman of the Kingstree Group, puts forward the theory that all spoken communication is selling in one way or another. 'It may not be a product that you are selling, it may just be a point of view or an idea,' he says, 'but often the most powerful way to put it across is with the spoken word.'

He then goes on to show readers how they can use their voices to 'take control' of communications. If you write something down for somebody, he or she then has the choice of reading it or not. You have no way of reinforcing the message, or of adjusting the emphasis of the second sentence to match the reactions to the opening words. You probably won't even be in the room when it is read, and even if you are it is unlikely you will be able to judge how the reader is reacting to your words. If you are speaking, however, you can gauge from the response whether or not you are getting through, and you can adjust your message and your delivery accordingly.

Antony Marsh, from Acting for Industry, uses many stagecraft skills to help people improve their communication skills at various levels, from the career interview to the large public speech.

It is often in the smaller, less formal environment that people demonstrate their lack of communication skills. The speech which is carefully written, rehearsed and then delivered at the annual conference may go well, but the surprise question at a meeting which has you stumbling for the right answer may give people a more accurate insight into your real communications abilities. Antony maintains that preparation is the key, even to the smallest occasion.

Written communication

The importance of spoken communications cannot be underestimated, but at the same time anyone working within a business environment must also be able to communicate effectively in writing, simply because of the demands of most jobs. As with listening skills, people often assume that they can write effectively, simply because they were good at English at school and write good letters. There are in fact many different written communications skills which need to be mastered in the corporate environment.

Report writing, for instance, is a highly specialised skill, and someone who has studied how to do it, either with self-teaching or on a course, is likely to reap the benefits.

Making your name known

This is what most people mean when they talk about raising their profile – getting 'better known'. This certainly is a major part of it, but you can also contribute to your reputation by the way you look and the other 'image' techniques which we have already discussed. Someone who has got their image right, after all, will be noticed by other people, and is therefore more likely to be given opportunities, than someone who melts into the background or gives off 'victim' signals.

Image, of course, is only the outer dressing, and to make an impact on a larger scale you need to demonstrate your actual abilities, gain the respect of the people who matter to you, and make known your desire to progress and achieve certain goals. This is where assertiveness, which we discussed earlier, becomes very important in achieving what you want. Can you ask for it? If you feel uncertain in this area there are many short courses available which are well worth the investment.

Raising your profile may mean simply making your name better known within your own company, or it could be extended to take in your industry sector or the wider world. Sir John Harvey Jones, for instance, started out by being well known within ICI. Once he became chairman he became well known within the business world, and when he retired from ICI and began appearing on television he became famous to a general audience. Few people take the pursuit of fame as far as that, but the principle of gradually expanding your profile as your career progresses can apply to anyone.

In his book *Hype! – The Essential Guide to Marketing Yourself* (Business Books), Andrew Crofts claims that if you are well known you 'will be offered better jobs, win more business, earn more money and increase your sphere of influence'.

He claims that there are two fundamental rules to becoming well known.

Firstly, you must do a good job. Whether you are working as a cog in a giant company, or are a star of a television show, make sure that you are supremely skilful at what you do, because otherwise you are going to be found out.

Next, you have to let people know just how good you are. If no one knows you are a genius, then you might as well not make the effort to be one, because you will never be given opportunities which will stretch you and use all your capabilities . . . so, work hard, let people see the results of that hard work, and don't let them forget it.

Few of us believe we are geniuses, but all of us are good at something, and most of us are good at more things than either we realise or admit. This brings you back to recognising and developing your skills. It also requires, however, that you are able to communicate those skills effectively, either through spoken or written communications. Being a brilliant engineer is not enough; you have to be able to explain what you are doing to other people, so that they will recognise your brilliance and give you credit. The same goes for being a good organiser, a good secretary or a good leader.

Inside your organisation

If you are aiming to make your name better known within your own organisation, there are a number of things you can do.

You could, for instance, talk about the work you are doing and how it fits into the company's strategies, either to individuals who you think will be interested, or to groups of people. That might mean holding a meeting of other department heads, or it might mean standing up at the company's annual conference and explaining what you have been doing. It might mean reporting to the board of directors or briefing a consultancy of some sort.

It may be that talking in this way is part of your job, but if you do it with too great a degree of modesty and diffidence, other people will accept your efforts at your evaluation, and assume that what you are achieving is no big deal. You need to seek out creative opportunities to talk, and then have your presentation fully prepared in your head, if not down on paper, so that you sound fluent, confident and in charge of everything that is going on.

Equally, you could promote your efforts by writing about what you are doing, perhaps in the company magazine, or in a report which you can then circulate to people who you feel are relevant to your cause. If, for instance, you are trying to get a new social club built for the staff, you could do some research into the needs, the costs and the potential benefits for the company, perhaps even going as far as suggesting potential sites for it and necessary levels of staffing.

That research could then be presented to the board of directors, circulated to the finance and personnel departments, and anyone else who might have some input. You might not succeed in getting the facility built exactly as you would wish, but at least you have made people aware of the need, of your concern, of your willingness to make an effort, and of the possibilities which are open to them. The alternative would be to go on complaining to all and sundry that 'no one cares about staff' and 'the old social club is a disgrace', and leave it up to someone else to act.

Anything which you feel is wrong, or could be done better, may offer you an opportunity to show your administrative, organisational or leadership abilities. There may be company politics involved which make it harder for you to be completely open in your suggestions, but the successful negotiation of difficult political situations will also help to demonstrate to other people that you are an able and determined operator.

It doesn't have to be a completely self-centred exercise. By making sure that people hear about your work, you will also help your team and your colleagues (as long as you aren't unfairly claiming personal credit for achievements which were a team effort). People like to work for someone, or with someone who they feel is strong and able, and who is not afraid to stick their neck out. If you have a high profile within your company, provided they do not feel personally threatened by you, people around you will usually be proud of this and will respond well.

It is a question of taking initiatives and letting people know that you are taking them. It requires you to be open about what you want to achieve and what you are doing about it. It often means joining committees and special working groups, taking positions of responsibility on matters to do with your work and to do with the good of the company. It means being assertive and taking action. It does not mean being aggressive, bullying, pushy or whinging.

Within your profession or industry

It may be of more benefit to you, and to your employer, for you to raise your profile outside the company, within your industry sector or profession.

It might be useful, for instance, if you are a finance director, for your name to be well known within the banking and investment community. From your point of view it will help you to develop your network of contacts.

From your employer's point of view it will help when the company wants to raise money or talk to the financial community about something. Your reputation will then reflect on your employer. If your name is known you will always find it easier to get access to people who will be helpful to you and to your company.

The same applies at virtually all levels. A famous lawyer will find clients queuing up because they have heard or read about him or her; just as a famous chef will find it easier to get backing for a new restaurant and to persuade customers to come; a well-known management consultant will find it easier to win clients and persuade them to listen to advice than someone they have never heard of; a salesperson who is well known for his or her views will find it easier to make appointments.

It is all about building a reputation for yourself, so that people know what it is you do and assume that you are good at it. If they also think you are likely to be an interesting person that will increase the likelihood of them wanting to meet you and do business with you.

In order to get your name known at this wider level you will need to do many of the same things that you would inside the organisation. You need to speak at meetings, seminars and conferences, write reports, publish articles in trade papers, publish books and perhaps even become a source of quotes in the media when there is a news story about your industry.

All this assumes that you have developed your speaking and writing skills, and your self-confidence, to a level where they will be useful to editors, producers, seminar organisers and all the other people who need a constant stream of authorities to talk and write on specific subjects.

In the public arena

In some cases (such as that of the famous chef), it is worth going on to become well known to the general public, since that will raise your value in the eyes of many of the people you work with, or would like to work with, and may have a spin-off for your business. Richard Branson, for instance, has a higher profile in Britain than most chairpersons of large companies would like, but it helps him to launch new projects to the public and keep the name of Virgin in the public mind.

If you have had your own television series, or have written a best-selling book on your subject, people will be interested to meet you, and this curiosity value will assist you with your networking, and will also raise your value in career terms.

Few people decide to take the pursuit of fame this far unless they are in a business which is selling its products directly to the public, such as retailing, showbusiness, book publishing and catering. But many businesses in other areas have found that having a chief executive or founder with a high profile, whether they be hair-dressers or footballers, actors or self-made millionaires, helps them to compete.

Making yourself an expert

In order to build a reputation and persuade the media to use your words and promote your name, you must specialise, finding something which defines you as an individual and will make you different from the thousands of other people who do the same job as you.

The first step, therefore, is to decide where your specialisation should lie. Is it, for instance, in the way you train your sales force? Or the method you use for ensuring your cash flow remains positive? Or the new department which you have set up from scratch? Or the office move which you have just completed so successfully?

This brings you back to analysing your skills. What is it that you do well, and which you might be able to talk or write about in a way that would be useful to other people? What have you done recently which you are proud of, and from which you think other people could learn?

Take, for instance, the example of the office move. If you have successfully moved a few hundred people from New York to Chicago, or from London to Derby, you will have learnt a great deal which would be useful to other companies planning to do the same thing. By writing or talking about your experiences you are giving the relevant trade media genuinely useful material, and at the same time you are telling the outside world how clever your organisation was to do things this way (and, incidentally, how clever *you* were). You are also letting the world know your organisation's new address and any other corporate messages which you have chosen to include, like the ability to adapt to change, or the way in which lower overheads will mean that you can become more cost-effective.

Once you have established yourself as an expert in one specialised area, and you have managed to get to know some editors and have won their trust, you can then widen your horizons and begin to talk and write about other issues which are relevant to you, and to the people you are wanting to reach.

If you work in personnel, for instance, you might start with a specialisation in recruiting from ethnic minorities. From there you could move on to write about the whole spectrum of human resource problems. As you progress through your career you will be learning more and more things that will be of use to others, and that means that you can use your knowledge to make sure your name is well known to increasingly wider audiences.

Selling yourself to editors

In order to persuade editors to buy and publish your words (or in some cases just to publish them), you have to convince them: a) that you know what you are talking about; b) that it is a subject which will be of interest to their readers; and c) that you are able to write.

As well as needing well-written articles by experts, the editors also need 'industry sources', i.e. people they can contact for comments on stories; people who can be relied on to say something intelligent, interesting and, hopefully, different.

Anyone who is very successful in their job will eventually build up a reputation within their industry, and will become known by the media which covers that industry. The problem is that by the time you have reached the top of your profession you may not have as much need for the publicity as you had on the way up. You may even have to start avoiding it because of pressures on your time. To make publicity work to your advantage, and help raise your profile, you need to draw yourself and your expertise to the attention of the editors while you are on the way up, not merely to confirm it once you have got there.

The first thing you need to come up with, therefore, is a list of ideas you can suggest to editors which might make either feature or news stories. (Public relations people do it all the time in the form of press releases, but that is too impersonal an approach.) You can't have too many ideas, and there only have to be relatively small differences in angle between them. This is where some creative thinking can be extremely useful.

The golden rule is to think. 'What do I know that would be useful for others to know?' You also need to think what it is about your job, your company or your industry which is of most interest to people who know nothing about the subject. When you tell people what you do at a dinner party or in the pub, what sort of questions do they ask?

Then produce a hit-list of journals you would like to appear in, study them until you feel confident that you understand the sort of material they like to use and start suggesting your ideas to them (keeping a careful record of who you have suggested what to, so that you don't go back to them more than once with the same idea).

You will have to be careful about 'puffery', which means giving obvious and unsubtle publicity within an article for a company or service, beyond what is necessary to explain and illustrate the arguments being made. There is a very fine dividing line between when it is and isn't acceptable, and it basically comes down to common sense and good taste. If you are writing an article about a case study, you are obviously going to mention the companies involved in the job. If, however, you are writing a general article about the double glazing industry it would be unacceptable to keep saying 'At Bloggs and Co. Double Glazing we always . . .'.

When you do have an article published, make sure that you send copies to people who you want to know about it. Don't rely on them seeing it themselves. There is no reason why you shouldn't be openly proud of what you have done and keen to show others. False modesty is foolish and might lead people to underestimate your achievement – if you're not pleased and impressed, why on earth should they be?

Book publishing

The same principles apply with the writing of books, although here the success of the whole project will rest on whether enough people can be persuaded to buy the finished product. In a magazine your article is only one of the reasons someone would buy or read it – and the chances are they are not paying for the privilege anyway, having received the publication on a controlled circulation or borrowed it from someone else.

To have had a book published on your subject will add enormously to your credibility within your industry, and publishers always need good ideas from writers who are able to execute them. You must convince them that you are capable of coming up with the goods, that there is a market for what you are writing and that no one else has got there first. If someone else has already got there, how will your book be different?

Radio and television

Being asked to talk on radio and television is another way of raising your profile, but it is unlikely that the broadcasters will discover you unless you put yourself forward. They may, however, follow up a book or article which you have written and drawn to their attention, and they may respond to an idea which you have suggested to them.

If you are going to be putting yourself forward to these electronic media, you will need to ensure that your spoken communications skills are sufficiently good. If you are already experienced at live presentations you are half-way there, but it might be worth undertaking some media training as well, to ensure that you are able to put your points of view across with maximum effect.

There are, therefore, a wide range of ways in which you can raise your profile, and most of them take a long time to bring to fruition. No one is going to believe you are an expert in something until you have spent a few years doing it, or have had some conspicuous success. It is therefore something that you should be working on throughout your career, using each achievement as a stepping-stone to the next.

If you make a successful contact with an editor while you are in one job, keep that contact going even when you move to a new job, and use the fact that you have been published in one magazine to convince other magazine or book publishers to consider your material. Each achievement will add to your credibility, build your reputation and spread your name a little further afield.

Raising your profile takes time, so don't be discouraged. Have a number of ideas bubbling along together. They won't all succeed, so when one thing doesn't work out other things are still progressing. When you are successful it is amazing how many ripples one small article can make and how long the time lag can be.

Taking care of yourself

You are a rare and very valuable person. You are responsible for many things within your career and outside your work. These responsibilities can mount up, especially when things get tough and the one area that suffers is the care that you take of yourself. Because you are such a valuable asset, you need to understand that you must treat yourself correctly and not abuse your own strengths and assets because if these fail your whole career could be in danger.

Commitment to career growth at the present moment may

not be your wisest course of action. Adding extra pressure may be the one thing that you do not need. Everyone's lifestyle seems to be becoming more hectic with less time to think and reflect on what is happening. To develop your career in the right direction for you, you need some space to think and reflect, we all need this to really appreciate the type of life quality we are experiencing. A poor quality of life is not the best environment to foster growth and development. In fact it will be counter productive to your aims.

Admitting that you are neglecting to look after yourself is often a difficult thing to face, especially for women who are brain-washed into the role of having to look after others, and into thinking that to consider your own needs is selfish. The following exercise may help you to reflect on this issue.

ACTION

Are you too committed to your work?
Answer yes or no to the following questions.

Y N

- Is your work a very important part of your life?
- Do you demand high standards of work?
- Are things always black or white, never grey?
- Do you fear failure?
- Do you always want to win?
- Are you quick to criticise others?
- Is it vital that you are always right?
- Do you get bored easily?
- Are you often exhausted at the end of the day?
- Do you work long hours and weekends?
- Is your pace of work fast, always on the run?

	Y	N
• Do you feel guilty when you try to relax?	☐	☐
• Do you read work material in your spare time?	☐	☐
• Do you make lists to help plan your day?	☐	☐
• Do you feel different from those around you?	☐	☐
• Do you neglect to take long holidays?	☐	☐
• When on holiday do you phone the office?	☐	☐
• Are you often filled with a feeling of panic?	☐	☐
• Do you avoid planning for old age?	☐	☐
• Do you avoid personal decision making?	☐	☐
• Do you forget family occasions?	☐	☐
• Do you get angry if things don't go your way?	☐	☐
• Do you live only for the moment?	☐	☐
• Do you work to strict self imposed deadlines?	☐	☐
• Are you impulsive?	☐	☐
• Are you up-set by negative feedback?	☐	☐
• Does being interrupted annoy you?	☐	☐
• Do you easily forget what people say?	☐	☐
• Do you face conflict head-on?	☐	☐

More than 20 'Yes' answers will need some serious reflection.
You are too focused on your work with no space, time or room
for you. In fact you have a very low value of yourself and this
will need to be addressed urgently. You must take more care of
yourself right away.

The following suggestions may give you some ideas on how to
improve your own self-care.

Time to switch off

If you are working in a very pressured way this will take a great
deal of energy which needs to be replenished on a regular basis.
Your daily pattern needs to take account of this so that you can
maintain this high level of demand and work more efficiently.
Most people who have hectic and pressured lives do not always
work to their full potential and in the most economic way.
Much energy is wasted in negative activities. Time to switch off
from your work focus is vital. This can be achieved in some of
the following ways:

Relaxation   This can be organised like yoga, meditation or
massage or by using less organised techniques such as breathing
exercises to calm you or a relaxation tape to induce deep and
quality sleep.

Hobbies   These can be so valuable in giving you some space to
use your brain in another way. This will benefit your work by
extending your brain power which will give you a wider scope,
especially if you need to think in a more creative way. The type
of hobby or interest does not matter as long as it is very different
from your work. If your work is sedentary or desk bound, a
hobby that is physical will help to address the balance. Work
that uses a lot of cerebral energy could be balanced by something practical.

Friends   Busy and heavy business schedules often freeze out
friends. You cancel dinner party invitations at the last minute
or if you do accept you may end up leaving too early or committing the worst mistake of falling asleep over your coffee. Gradually you find that your friends distance themselves because
they don't feel that you are interested or interesting any more.
Friends are a very important element of a balanced life and they
need time. Contact with friends can be an excellent opportunity
for relaxation especially if you are not very good at some of the
more organised or 'trendy' techniques. But they need time and
attention.

Family   The demands of a family and a business can cause
endless conflicts, especially for women. The wife and mother

never seems to be able to get it right. You are never there at the right time for children. Your partner may never feel that they are as important as your business when a crisis looms. You may not believe that everyone plays their part or pulls their weight. One strategy that may help is to define clear times to spend with your partner or children. Make a date for a special meal or an evening in with a video.

For women, much of the conflict in this area is caused by a woman's own guilt for not being perfect. You need to have a realistic view about what you can achieve and how best your talents can be employed. From an early age in my business career I made a decision that although I was very talented at house cleaning, washing, ironing etc., it was not the best use of my skills. I did not get deep fulfilment from endless cleaning and cooking. So I have always paid someone else to do these jobs within the home and have never wasted any guilt about my decision.

Time alone   Time to yourself is usually the first thing that goes in a busy schedule. The demands of your career and a family squeeze out time for you either to pamper yourself in a long relaxing bath or to pay attention to your looks. It is vitally important that you spend some time alone to think and cater for your own needs. This time must be seen as valuable and important so that you never give it away to the demands of someone else. This way of thinking is not selfish but self-centered, which is what you need to become if you really want to achieve your full potential within your career.

Health

Your health is crucially important in today's stress-filled world. You may feel very fit at present but are you storing up problems for the future? The stress of being responsible for so much is a great burden to carry so you must be aware of the things you may be doing which could damage your health long term.

Time to switch off will have some very positive effects on your general health but there are some additional factors that you will need to watch.

Exercise   Busy working days with long meetings and

extended hours often rule out time for exercise. Ideally you should spend at least three hours every week in some form of exercise. If you are not used to physical activity try something gentle at first. Try to build the exercise into your work pattern so that it naturally becomes part of your day. The biggest bonus to exercise is that it gives you more energy when you apply yourself over a length of time.

Health checks   Ensure that you take advantage of regular health checks to monitor problems that may become serious in later years. Never give the excuse that you are too busy to attend because this only demonstrates a very low valuation of yourself.

Diet   Many people are unhappy about their diet in some way. Business entertaining and travel can be difficult but with a plan of campaign it can be made easier. Set yourself some simple rules and reward yourself from time to time when you have stuck to the rules for a reasonable length of time. Under-eating can be as much of a problem as over-eating. Irregular eating habits can be the cause of many problems. Plan ahead, take food with you to the office or meeting and try not to be caught out in a situation where you are tempted to eat your downfall food.

Alcohol/cigarettes/drugs   We all have our own views about these substances. For some they may not be an issue but for many, a large drink at the end of the day can be a great reward, or a cigarette with a cup of coffee wards off hunger pangs or provides a brief spell of peace and quiet. Fine, but just be aware of the affect these substances could be having on your health and be sure that they are not becoming a crutch that is sapping your energy.

Remember . . .

- Re-assess your image regularly.
- Keep your communication and interview skills well polished.
- Update your career record as necessary.
- Raise your profile, both inside and outside the organisation.
- Become an expert in your field.

BRAINPOWER FOR THE FUTURE

Everyone is searching for something new. Many organisations are investing millions in new techniques to manage staff, to find the answer to how they should behave in the next century. Unfortunately few have found the true answer. Really it is quite simple, as great ideas often are, and within the reach of everyone. Chapter 13 will help you find the new way of working for your future.

The answer lies in how we utilise the most important organ in our body, our brain. Sadly it is the most under used part of our body and we must learn to make better use of this fantastic power-house. Your future success depends upon increasing your brainpower.

From the earlier chapters you will have gained a wealth of information about yourself and how you have used your skills, strengths and weaknesses to achieve success. It does not matter how small or how large your achievements have been, what matters is that you recognise that you have these assets which will help you to achieve success in this new area of development.

Brainpower

To fully understand how you should develop you need to see that you will have to acquire some new skills connected with how you think and how you use your brain. You have infinitely more brainpower than you are likely to use and at present you are only utilising a fraction of your most powerful organ. Inside your skull you have a machine that is often compared to a massive computer but unfortunately this is the only computer that is delivered without any instructions. Nobody tells you how to use your brain. We leave it all to nurture and experience. We take it for granted that our brain has worked OK for years so we believe that it will continue. Although there is a dangerous myth that as we age the brain becomes less efficient, research has shown that this is not true. Our brain becomes inefficient through lack of use, not old age.

In order to utilise more of your brainpower you need to understand how your brain works in more detail. Scientists in recent years have discovered that our brains are actually split into two separate halves that are joined together by connection fibres. They operate quite independently of each other and have very different styles of working. One half is called the Right Brain which is responsible for vision, imagination and insight, while the Left Brain is concerned with logical thought and language.

Traditionally Western culture has applauded the attributes of the Left Brain. In school we are praised if we can read, write and accomplish mathematical problems. In society we look up to accountants, scientists, engineers and lawyers. We are less enthusiastic about the attributes of the Right Brain. Artistic and creative subjects at school are not really encouraged, if they are taught at all. Students who wish to follow these disciplines into higher education or careers are thought not to be following a 'real' job.

Managers in business often ridicule the intuitive thinker and belittle ideas that come from unexplained sources. The Right Brain thinker is labelled as emotional, illogical and often dangerous because they only use their gut reaction, and don't really think things through.

In recent years we have come to understand a lot more about the mysteries of the Right Brain. During this research we have also discovered that this could be the beginning of a new and better way of thinking. Using the whole of our brain rather than just part of one side could open up billions of new opportunities.

This research into how the brain operates has also grasped

the attention of many of the business gurus who write about how things should be in the world of work. If we look at the results of what has been achieved by our business leaders to date, who have primarily operated using the left side of their brain, it is not such a wonderful record of achievement. During the 80s we saw the rise of accountants running companies – organisations being governed by balance sheet management. What has been ignored by many corporations is the creative and feeling aspects of business and creative growth.

I am not saying that we should all now swing the other way and abandon logic, structure and analytical process. What needs to be advocated for the future is a more balanced brain activity which allows us to explore different methods and processes in new and exciting ways. More creative and intuitive thinking needs to be introduced into our own working styles and our education. You will not find intuitive studies included in an MBA course yet but maybe things will change.

Fortune 500 recently conducted a survey in North America, of the top 100 executives and asked them what they rated as their most valuable attribute. The answer was almost unanimously intuition, but they were all reluctant to acknowledge this publicly because it wasn't considered to be what top executives should value highly. What shareholders and employees wanted was logic, strategic thinking and financial skills. Feelings, imagination and sensitivity are not readily seen as the qualities for hard-headed businessmen.

What of the future? If the decline in manufacturing and production-type activities continues, with an increase in service industries, we need to urgently consider new ways of thinking and working. The old ways of running a production industry will not easily transfer to a service business. The skills required to maintain successful output from a foundry, which is highly reliant on machinery, or the skills required to manufacture a litre of petrol are firmly routed in the left brain.

Our future business growth seems to be more and more within the service sectors and more and more concentrated on people. We hear continually that corporations need to take more account of their human resources. This will never be achieved if we continue to rely on the left-brain dominance of our business world. What must develop is a more balanced approach to how we use our brain. We need employees who know how to work smarter not harder.

To develop yourself successfully you need to be able to draw on all your potential and utilise *both* sides of your brain. This balance should exist naturally because it produces the best results and will mean greater productivity and effectiveness in whatever field you work in.

The Right Brain is able to assimilate a mass of information all at once, using your five senses and without any conscious effort it will come up with a solution. When you say 'I've got a feeling about something,' this feeling is coming from your Right Brain. Usually your dominant Left Brain will over-rule your feeling with logic, and persuade you that your feeling must be wrong. If your left brain doesn't succeed in this activity you will probably find a left-brained colleague or boss who will certainly convince you that this flash of inspiration can't possibly be of any value.

This type of brain power is often referred to as feminine intuition and not generally held in high esteem. From my experience I have found that women are more attuned to using their Right Brain but they usually lack the confidence to stand by their right-brain ideas in the midst of a male-dominated left-brain business world. Some young and creative thinking men are also having problems convincing their less creative superiors that their flashes of inspiration have any worth.

What you need to understand is how you can utilise your Right Brain more and learn to trust this intuition, be more receptive to your feelings and not worry about having to rationalise ideas that come to you during a moment of intuition. What follows in this chapter are some exercises to help you feel more confident in this new way of thinking and to extend your powers of right-brain activity. It will give you greater insights into how you think and an opportunity to explore something that naturally you should feel quite comfortable with.

If you are discouraged by views that some of the exercises are impractical or over the top remember that this is your well-tuned Left Brain trying to take control. You may at times, especially at the start, have to suspend your logical and critical reasoning and continue in a blind act of faith.

Many people believe that creative thinking is the prerogative of the intelligent. Edward De Bono, one of the early leaders in the field of creative thinking, believes that everyone is capable of this type of thought process and that there are only two blocks to successfully developing a more active Right Brain. The first is intelligence, because you convince yourself that there is a more logical way of achieving a result. The second is arrogance, which prevents you from using many of the recognised techniques because you think they are foolish or beneath you.

Left and right brain activities

Left Brain	*Right Brain*
Verbal	Non-verbal
Analytical	Holistic
Literal	Spatial
Linear	Musical
Mathematical	Imaginative
Logical	Spiritual
Controlled	Dreaming

How do you think?

Although your brain is a very powerful organ it is also very efficient and this efficiency can lead you into bad habits. The brain likes to utilise what is already stored as a starting point for any activity and this will present an option, which at face value may be OK but really it is just the same old solution that you have always used. From your earlier analysis of your weaknesses you will now understand that this solution may actually draw on what is really one of your weaknesses. By understanding more about how you think, you can stretch your brain to use parts that are not commonly called upon to work. Extending your creativity is all about you using more and more of your brain power and harnessing more of your potential. Don't worry that you may over tax this great machine because at present you are probably only using about 10% of its capacity

259

and the more you use your brain the more it grows to accommodate the extra activity.

Now to understand more about how you think or use your brain. If you can understand more about this process you will be able to take more control over how it works. The starting point is your five senses which are the focal point for what you experience, how you think and how you feel. Your senses tell you all you know, they are your avenues for communication. Your brain then interprets what you see, hear or touch in so many different ways and in so many different ways from the person next to you. From your senses come your understanding, your experience and your consciousness. Thinking is about how you manipulate these inner records that are stored in the brain.

Like most things in life you will have a preference for using one or more of your senses. Research has shown that most people favour using sight or visualising, followed by hearing. Touch and smell are less dominant. Here are a collection of phrases that will give you some clues to your preferred way of sensing.

Visual
'She has a blind spot.'
'Show me.'
'It appears to be.'
'We don't see eye to eye.'
'Please shed some light on it.'
'I've been looking into this.'
'It looks OK to me.'
Auditory
'We're on the same frequency.'
'That rings a bell.'
'It comes over loud and clear.'
'She turned a deaf ear.'
'He described it word for word.'
Feeling
'How do you feel about that?'
'Don't lose touch.'
'We must keep in contact.'

'Hold on a minute.'
'He got a warm welcome.'
'Her response was rather frosty.'

Other clues to your thinking style will be evident in the way you speak. Visual thinkers will generally speak quickly and at a high pitch as the pictures flash through their brain. They can often experience being tongue tied as their brain works faster than their lips. Auditory thinkers will usually speak in a clear voice sometimes with their head held at an angle as if they are listening to something.

ACTION

The following exercise will give you an opportunity to discover which senses may be your most dominant, and also to develop a sense that you don't use too much.

Gentle brain toning

Sit in a quiet place, one where you will not be interrupted by anyone or anything. Remember that this is important and needs your full attention.

Close your eyes, relax and imagine a very special Christmas morning that you have experienced either as a child or as an adult. Picture the room, the walls, windows, door, fireplace, Christmas decorations, the tree, the presents, any other object or people that are with you on this special day – parents, children, friends, family, pets. Visualise the room in all the detail that you can recall. Now add the Christmas sounds, maybe carols, excited screams of children, a log fire crackling in the grate. Stay with your picture and concentrate on this wonderful day. Remember how you were feeling. Touch the chair you are sitting in. Remember the feel of the wrapping paper as you open your presents. Feel the warmth from the fire or the cold as you go outside for a walk. Next try to remember the Christmas smells from the cooking in the kitchen or the mulled wine as you toast your friends. Stay with your picture for as long as you can adding more and more detail as your eyes wander around the room and your memory recalls this happy day.

This exercise demonstrates how you can control your thoughts which can bring enormous practical benefits to your life and your career. You can decide what you want to remember, what to imagine, what to dwell upon and what to ignore. You have great power over how your brain works. You do not have to let it run ahead of you controlling your every thought.

Positive thinking

The most beneficial aspect of this process of brain toning is the skill of positive thinking. Our visualised thoughts are often fleeting and rather vague, we are not encouraged to have rambling thoughts about nothing in particular. Day dreaming is considered to be a waste of time and this is because we are all brain-washed to applaud the rational workings of the Left Brain.

One mental process which we are all very good at is worrying. We can all very easily lie awake at night and imagine all sorts of disastrous things that will happen when your boss discovers X. . . . These worrying skills have little value in your working life but they come flooding in all too often. Imagine how your life could change for the better if you could learn to control these worries and direct all that mental energy to more positive activities.

Thinking positive thoughts has two strong effects on you. One is that you can use your mental energy in a more beneficial way. Secondly, it has a physical impact on the working of your body. There is an improvement in your blood circulation and breathing rate, in fact your whole metabolism works more efficiently. All this, just from recalling a pleasurable memory from the past.

Once you have mastered the skill of recalling past memories (just like your wonderful Christmas morning) you can use this skill to imagine future events. If you have a difficult task ahead of you, one that you have been putting off for a while, you can use these positive thinking skills to imagine the best results rather than worry about the worst.

How organised is your brain?

The left side of the brain is extremely organised and efficient at arranging the information it stores, much like a filing system. This organised efficiency can have drawbacks which lead the brain to follow tried and tested routes of thought which are great for left-brain thinking but hamper creative thought. The right side of the brain prefers a more chaotic approach. Creative thinking, or what Edward De Bono calls lateral thinking, requires a style that breaks out of the accepted patterns of the Left Brain.

De Bono has devised a number of techniques which help to bombard the brain with many different stimuli from very different perspectives. These are explained on pages 105–17 together with other more accepted techniques including Brainstorming and Mind-Mapping. These techniques will encourage the brain to explore new ways of working and the more practice and the more varied the techniques, the better.

To these techniques I want to add further ideas which encompass some of the more recent thinking about creative brain power. They are simple ideas to encourage a different way of thinking.

Reframing

This is a technique for upsetting your existing brain patterns. It can change just about anything you face in your career. There are two ways in which you can reframe situations. One is reframing the context or setting of the situation. The other is reframing the content of something that is troubling you.

Reframing requires you to imagine a different setting or content which will place the situation in a positive light and enable you to see different aspects. This technique can be useful when dealing with a difficult personal situation, say with a figure of authority. Imagine this figure in a different context and maybe add a little humour, think of him or her conducting very mundane jobs which can break the aura of control and power. See this person making an enormous gaffe at an important social gathering, like slipping on a banana skin.

This technique will challenge your brain to use new avenues of thought. Your reframing does not have to be rational or true, all it has to achieve is a confused arena for the exploration of new ideas.

Metaphor thinking

This is a simple technique which has proved to be valuable in many situations. Ideas are generated by linking the problem with something that has no connection with the issue being considered. If your business deals with inanimate objects use metaphors from nature or the animal kingdom. If you deal in concepts use metaphors with concrete images.

This technique can also be extended to help you when you are trying to explain difficult and complex ideas to a new audience. I use metaphors extensively when making presentations. I have a collection of slides of everyday objects, usually with a little humour added, which help to tell a simple story about a complex issue. These simple and striking images stay in people's minds. They may forget the words you have spoken but the image will remain and this will help them to recall the concept. They often say afterwards 'I still remember that picture of . . . .'

Questioning

People who are more practised in using the right side of their brain usually ask excellent questions. They are able to explore and challenge in a very creative way. I'm sure you have been in meetings when you have heard someone ask a question and you have thought 'Why didn't I think of that?' You can practise asking good questions and therefore receiving excellent answers by using a questioning style that is more open. Most people tend to rely on closed questions which only solicit single word responses. The following is an example of a closed question, to which the only reply is yes or no. 'Did you like our new colour range?' By rephrasing this into an open question, a more helpful answer is ensured. 'What did you think of our new colour range?' This would prompt a reply like 'Great, but I would have liked more choice in the range of blues.'

Open questions are simple to construct. Just remember that they all start with one of these words: **What? Why? When? Where? How?** This simple technique of using open questions will literally open up a wealth of new information.

Using dream power

Even the most left-brained male accountant spends a significant part of his day in right-brain activities. However he is probably unaware of this because it takes place when he is asleep! While sleeping everyone dreams for several periods every night. Dreaming is a right-brain activity and right-brain thinkers tend to recall their dreams more readily. Left-brain thinkers dream as well, but they forget them instantly.

Dreaming plays a vital part in keeping your mental activities healthy and in good order. The process involves the brain in searching, classifying and rearranging information that has been collected from our consciousness during the day. Our understanding of dreams may be vague but there is more and more evidence to support the view that dreams do have a very significant part to play in our thinking process. This is because dreams are so often connected to issues that are related to the present. During our dreams we are able to explore and connect with feelings and information from the past. Also dreams are always honest, there is no rose-coloured view of yourself in your dreams.

To make more of your dreams you need to be able to control them, so that you can recall your dreams more effectively *and* use them to help you solve problems. You can control your dreams by telling yourself before you go to sleep that you need to solve a particular problem. You must do this just before going to sleep, when you are in a relaxed state (this is known as your alpha state and will be explained in more detail below). You also need to train yourself to be able to recall your dreams on waking, and to interpret their meaning in relation to the issue you wanted to solve. It is important that you have pen and paper handy by the bed or a tape recorder so that you can record your ideas as soon as you wake.

If you find it difficult to recall your dreams you will probably not be able to solve your career block overnight by using this technique. Like any skill you will need to practise it. Start by recalling your dreams on a regular basis before you pass on to the stage of giving specific instructions about problem issues. This may be a very new area of exploration for you so progress slowly, have patience and remember that your rational left brain is bound to put up some barriers. Also, our Western culture places an extremely low value on dreaming so you will meet many sceptics who will attempt to persuade you into thinking this is 'mumbo jumbo.'

Are you ready to practise some creative techniques?

The previous pages have bombarded you with a torrent of techniques and new ideas. Hopefully you are slightly confused and don't really know where to go next. Remember that confusion is one of the required states for creative thinking but you now need to learn how to harness this confusion.

The first golden rule is that you need to make time available to practise these new techniques, especially if you have a strong preference for left-brain thinking. If you are your own boss it is much easier to set aside time for practise and exploration. If you are part of a traditional corporate structure your employer is less likely to appreciate you spending time doing what might appear to be nothing. The time you set aside needs to be away from your usual environment, if possible, and in surroundings that are conducive. This will really depend upon you and your own preferences.

Personally, I am at present exploring the time I spend swimming. Recently I have been advised for medical reasons to take up swimming on a regular basis. My first reaction to this was hostile but gradually over the months I have changed my feelings. My hostility was mainly due to my fear of placing my face underwater but I have had to overcome this fear as part of my improved swimming style. Swimming with my head erect was not helping my back problem. My fear was faced first by purchasing a pair of very good goggles and then by observing the style of other swimmers. I practised and have gradually mastered a technique which allows me to swim underwater for the first time in over forty years. Swimming underwater is a new experience for me which is different from anything I've known before, and I am beginning to use these brief moments to suspend my thought processes and see what emerges.

You don't always have to make time completely in isolation from your normal daily activities. Some people use their journey to and from work as space to think. Others switch their mind when they are doing mundane or routine tasks, like taking a bath or shower or doing the washing up.

Once you are committed to making time available to explore and practise these new techniques of creative thinking you need to be in the right frame of mind. That means you need to be in a mental state that is conducive to right-brain activities. You are most receptive to creative thoughts when you are relaxed. When your brain is in a relaxed state it is producing very distinctive wave patterns known as alpha waves. These waves operate at a very low frequency and are associated with access to your subconscious. Being in a relaxed state can produce many benefits for your mental and physical health, as discussed previously.

ACTION

To achieve a relaxed state you must first concentrate on physical relaxation. Find a quiet place with no distractions. Get into a comfortable sitting or lying position. Breath deeply and slowly. Learning to control your breathing can have a very calming affect in any situation and is an excellent technique to master. Now concentrate on all parts of your body in turn, imagining that every part is feeling heavy. Don't forget all areas of your hands, feet and especially your neck and face, which can hold a great deal of tension. If you find this exercise difficult you may want to use a relaxation tape or some music to help you focus your mind.

When your body feels in a pleasant state you need to focus your attention on your mind which may still be working overtime, perhaps wondering if you will achieve a pressing deadline. Take your mind away from the worries of your daily life, and travel to a place that you have really enjoyed in the past. Maybe a beach, or a field by water, or a mountain side – anywhere that brings back pleasant and tranquil memories. Spend some time making your selection because this will become your own very special place, and you will be spending a lot of time here in the future. This place is to become your own very special retreat where nobody can interrupt you or bring you anything to worry about. It will be your place for creating ideas and solving any problem that blocks your growth.

At first you will find that this process takes a while, but with practise you should be able to call up your special place quickly and at any time. You may find it more convenient to practise just before going to sleep, and then again before you get up in the morning. But to really grasp the techniques correctly you need to set aside a specific time during the day – a moment that will not be pushed aside by fatigue or a hectic morning schedule.

The power of your imagination

So far I have only referred to the power of your imagination in passing or as part of other techniques but it needs to be understood that your imagination is a mighty, powerful asset in creative thinking. Some of you may believe that you have a poor imagination or maybe no imagination at all. This is not true, we all have imagination. What may be true in your case is that it has been allowed to wither or become comatosed. With a little gentle exercise you can awaken this very powerful asset.

During your relaxation exercise you were using your imagination when you pictured your special place. When you did the Christmas Day exercise (on page 261) to explore your senses you were using your imagination again.

ACTION

Now let us see if you are ready to apply your imagination to a real LIFE situation which is facing you at the moment. Take an issue that is taxing you right now. To begin with you may feel that you want to concentrate on something relatively small. Prepare yourself by getting into a relaxed state and finding your special retreat. Now imagine what it would be like if the problem had gone away, if it had been solved. How would you feel, how would people react? How would they behave? Stretch your imagination to see, feel, hear, smell and touch the new situation.

By doing this exercise in your imagination you are creating new ideas, you are forming a new reality and this is where creative thinking begins, this is where change starts.

Expanding your right-brain activity is, I am convinced, the way forward for the future. From recent experience I am amazed at how quickly individuals have developed through exploring these techniques. Also, when people begin to understand how the brain works in more detail they become aware of situations when they have used the right side of their brain unknowingly in the past. This for many is the eye opener which helps them to understand why they are constantly at loggerheads with their boss, who is completely unreceptive to any form of creative thought. He or she will demand total logical explanation of how something will happen. The right-sided thinker will find this difficult because he or she knows that what they are proposing to their boss is right, but not why it is right nor how it will work. What usually happens is that the right-brain thinker struggles to provide logical explanations, but the demands from the boss become more and more unreasonable and the creative thinker becomes so frustrated that they stop contributing their brain waves. They stop using their creative brain power and stagnate.

This is such a waste of potential but at present it is happening to a frightening degree. Corporations are just neglecting the brainpower they have for the future. Hopefully this chapter will help you to overcome some of the negative blocks within your own situation and provide ideas for what is such an exciting new way of thinking.

EPILOGUE:
REACHING THE END

You have now successfully passed through the final phases of career management. Congratulations! Your reward is ownership of a powerful set of tools and techniques that can assist you through any career issue. Some you may want to use immediately or perhaps have even started to use, others will lie dormant for a while.

It is now vital to contract with yourself to return to the career management model in six months' time. This will refresh your memory and help you to monitor which phase you are in. The real test of successful career management is to know which phase of the career model you are in at the moment. Once you have worked through the model for the first time you will generally stay in the fourth phase, but from time to time you will need to return to the other phases as you face different career, or even life, issues.

From this book you will have gained an insight into the process of career management and an understanding about the commitment of time and effort that is required. Without this commitment nothing can be achieved, but to make it means a valuable investment in your future.

A word about professional career management support

At some point in your career you may want to invest in professional career management support.

Gradually its value is being recognised at various levels. Corporations are developing strategies which embrace the concept throughout their culture. Michael Howley, from the University of Surrey, wrote an article recently in the *International Journal of Career Management* entitled 'Career Management for Today's MBAs', in which he stressed the need for impartial outside advice when it comes to consideration of career matters.

My own post and telephone enquiries grow constantly as more and more people are facing critical issues relating to their careers, and these are all from people who are currently employed.

Sound investment

One of the most difficult hurdles in career management is concerned with cost. Organisations are becoming more enlightened and recognise the value of this service. Individuals still find it difficult to grasp the true value of this type of investment. Michael Howley believes that all executives, including MBAs, will have to change their attitudes. In 1992 it costs about £6,500 to study for an MBA. It seems illogical that individuals are not prepared to invest much smaller sums in gaining professional support to ensure they are maximising this asset, and gaining valuable insights and understanding of the corporate arena.

In the area of cost, individuals need to have a deeper understanding of the true value of professional services, and to begin to see them more as valuable and vital investments.

Finding professional help

If you want to find a professional career counselling service, some addresses can be found in the Resources Guide at the end of this book. The British Association for Counselling (BAC) can also provide contacts. Personal recommendation is a very sound method.

Before seeking professional assistance in this field try to do the following:

1. Work out what it is you are really looking for.

2. Clearly understand the type of service that is on offer.

3. Check the qualifications of the consultant/counsellor.

4. Find out if they work from a counselling framework. If so, which one (this can be checked with the BAC)?

5. How long will each session last?

6. What are the costs and methods of payment?

7. Ask if you can speak to other clients.

8. The first session should be without charge or obligation.

9. Avoid hard-pressure selling.

10. Counsellors of any type can only advertise facts about their services. Wild claims of success are not allowed.

11. If you are in any way uncomfortable or have doubts, look for someone else.

The greatest value of professional help is in the area of confidentiality. Within the four walls of a career counselling office anything can be explored with no fear of judgements being made, careers being jeopardised or conclusions being wrongly attributed. Nothing is passed on to another person. An individual can explore alternatives fully, voice options, ventilate anger, express fears, take risks, try out new ideas and prepare strategies of action in the safe knowledge that the discussions will have no repercussions within their organisation.

This opportunity to 'dump' a lot of issues is invaluable, and for many is a very positive experience. As problems come into the light so they can be identified and viewed in perspective. This alone often makes them less threatening.

Professional career counselling is purely based on counselling skills linked to a knowledge of careers, work, organisations, cultures and people, and should not be confused with mentoring, which was discussed in Chapter 11, or outplacement.

Career counselling is about enabling and empowering people to make their own decisions. It is not about giving advice! Advice is something which can be right or wrong and has little to do with counselling. Advice embraces the views of another person, usually about a subject that has little effect on the person giving the advice. By contrast counselling is about working with people to help them find their own solutions and take charge of their own decisions.

BOOK LIST

Career management

The Age of Unreason
Charles Handy (Hutchinson)

Build Your Own Rainbow
Barrie Hopson and Mike Scally (Lifeskills Ass.)

Creative Thinking and Brainstorming
J Geoffrey Rawlinson (Gower Business Skills)

Everyone Needs a Mentor
David Clutterbuck (Institute of Personnel Management)

Great Answers to Tough Interview Questions
Martin John Yate (Kogan Page)

How to be Headhunted
Yvonne Sarch (Business Books)

How to Find the Perfect Job
Tom Jackson (Piatkus)

Job Hunting for Women
Margaret Wallis (Kogan Page)

The Job Promoters
R Meredith Belbin (Heinemann Professional)

Managing Change
Colin Carnall (Routledge)

Managing Your Own Career
Dave Francis (Fontana)

Networking and Mentoring – A Woman's Guide
Dr Lily M Segerman-Peck (Piatkus)

Networks
Tim Heald (Coronet)

Smart Moves
Godfrey Golden and Andrew Garner (Blackwell)

What Colour is Your Parachute?
Richard N Bolles (Ten Speed Press)

Your Ideal Job or Next Career
Richard N Bolles (Ten Speed Press)

The Right-Brain Manager
Dr Harry Alder (Piatkus)

Assertiveness

Assert Yourself
Robert Sharpe (Kogan Page)

Assert Yourself
Gael Lindenfield (Thorsons Publishing)

Beating Aggression
Diana Lamplugh (Weidenfeld Paperbacks)

Getting Past No
William Ury (Business Books)

Getting to Yes
Roger Fisher and William Ury (Business Books)

A Guide to Assertiveness
Paddy O'Brien (Industrial Society Press)

How to Develop a Positive Attitude
Elwood N Chapman (Kogan Page)

Successful Self-Management
Paul R Timm (Kogan Page)

When I Say No, I Feel Guilty
Manuel J Smith (Bantam)

Marketing yourself

Hype: The Essential Guide to Marketing Yourself
Andrew Crofts (Hutchinson Business Books)

The Influential Manager: How to use company politics constructively
Lee Bryce (Piatkus)

Marketing Yourself
Dorothy Leeds (Piatkus)

The Perfect CV
Tom Jackson (Piatkus)

Personal Power
Philippa Davies (Piatkus)

Self presentation

Better Business Writing
Maryann V Piotrowski (Piatkus)

Body Language
Allan Pease (Sheldon Press)

High Impact Business Presentations
Lee Bowman (Business Books)

Power Speak
Dorothy Leeds (Piatkus)

Presenting Yourself: A Personal Image Guide For Women
Mary Spillane (Piatkus)

Presenting Yourself: A Personal Image Guide for Men
Mary Spillane (Piatkus)

Your Total Image
Philippa Davies (Piatkus)

Counselling

Counselling and Psychotherapy, Is it for Me?
Hetty Einzig (British Association for Counselling)

277

Counselling Skills
Ray Woolfe (Scottish Health Education Group)

Dealing with Difficult People
Robert Cava (Piatkus)

50 Activities for Developing Counselling Skills
Roy Bailey (Gower)

Gestalt Counselling in Action
Petruska Clarkson (Sage)

Personal Problems at Work
Hetty Einzig and Richard Evans (British Association for Counselling)

Practical Counselling and Helping Skills
Richard Nelson-Jones (Cassell)

Principles of Counselling Series I and II
Francesca Inskipp and Hazel Johns (Alexia) Tapes available from British Association for Counselling

Training in Counselling and Psychotherapy
Isobel Palmer and Denise Chaytor (British Association for Counselling)

Transactional Analysis Counselling in Action
Ian Stewart (Sage)

Starting your own business

Going Freelance
Godfrey Golzen (Grafton Books)

Starting Your Business
(Which? Books, Consumers' Association)

Start and Run a Profitable Consulting Business
Douglas A Gray (Kogan Page)

Starting a Business
Richard Hargreaves (Heinemann)

Starting a Business on a Shoestring
Michael Syrett and Chris Dunn (Penguin)

Miscellaneous

Creative Thinking
Michael LeBoeuf (Piatkus)

Holistic London
Kate Brady and Mike Considine (Brainwave)

Introducing Neuro-Linguistic Programming
Joseph O'Connor and John Seymour (Mandala)

The Managerial Woman
Margaret Hennig and Anne Jardim (Pan Books)

Mind Power
Christian H. Godfroy with D R Stevens (Piatkus)

The Right Brain Manager
Dr Harry Alder (Piatkus)

Thinking Course
Edward de Bono (BBC Books)

Women Mean Business
(Everywoman)

Women Mean Business
Caroline Bamford and Catherine McCarthy (BBC Books)

The Celestine Prophecy
James Redfield (Bantam Books)

RESOURCES GUIDE

CAREER COUNSELLING/MENTORING/COACHING

Jon Nixon, Tree House, Blackheath Way, West Malvern,
WR14 4DR
Tel: 01684 576245

Mike Vincent, M & E Change Consultancy, 68 Marsden Rd,
Kingsway, Bath BA2 2LL
Tel: 01225 400268

Macwhinnie Ass. 27 Percival Drive, Harbury, Leamington
Spa, CV33 9GZ
Tel: 01926 614707

Jeremy Clare, 3 Chestnut Close, Amersham, Bucks HP6 6EQ
Tel: 01494 432980

PERSONAL COUNSELLING

John Towler, CJT Partners, Thatched Cottage, Ibsley Drove,
Ringwood, Hants BH24 3NW
Tel: 01425 653299

Child & Associates, 83 South St, Dorking, Surrey RH4 2JU

CAREER COACHING AND TRAINING

E. W. Training, 50 Webbs Rd, London SW11 6SF
Tel: 0171 585 2816

IMAGE AND PRESENTATION CONSULTANTS

Esra Parr, House of Colour, 25 Parke Rd, Barnes, London
SW13 9NJ
Tel: 0181 255 7280

INTERIM MANAGEMENT

Barton Interim Management, 30 Nottingham Place,
London W1M 3FD
Tel: 0171 486 8563

Executive Interim Management, Devonshire House, Mayfair
Place, London W1X 5FH
Tel: 0171 629 2832

Russam GMS Ltd, 48 High St North, Dunstable,
Beds LU6 1LA
Tel: 01582 666970

NEURO-LINGUISTIC PROGRAMMING (NLP)

International Teaching Seminars, 73 Brooke Rd,
London N16 7RD
Tel: 0181 442 4133
www.nip-community.com.

SELLING STYLES

The LIFO® (UK & Eire) Organisation, Clark House,
Milborne Port, Sherborne, Dorset DT9 5EB
Tel: 01963 251107

PROFESSIONAL ASSOCIATIONS

British Association for Counselling, 1 Regent Place, Rugby,
Warwickshire CV21 2PJ
Tel: 01788 578328

Association for Counselling at Work, Eastlands Court, St Peter's
Rd, Rugby, Warwickshire CV21 3QP
Tel: 01788 335617

British Psychological Society, St Andrews House, 48 Princess
Rd East, Leicester LE1 7DA
Tel: 01533 549568

Institute of Directors, 116 Pall Mall, London SW1Y 5ED
Tel: 0171 839 1233

Institute of Personnel and Development, 35 Camp Rd,
Wimbledon, London SW19 4UZX
Tel: 0181 971 9000

WEBSITES

www.jobsunlimited.co.uk
This is a job search website provided by the Guardian Media
Group.

www.jobsearch.com
This site is the largest source of IT vacancies in the UK.

www.topjobs.co.uk
Although this site is relatively new, it is already Europe's most
visited website for management, professional and technical
jobs. It provides a service whereby you can register your
search criteria and it will e-mail you when jobs appear on the
site that match your requirements. Features world leading
companies.

www.qti.co.uk
This is the website for the Employer's Index. It provides
access to over 235 top employers interested in recruiting
graduates.

www.highflyers.co.uk
This recruitment site describes itself as looking for the cream
of the crop for top city jobs. Take the hype with a pinch of
salt!

www.jobsite.co.uk
Over 4,000 vacancies for IT, computing, science, engineering,
commercial, management, professional, healthcare and
education.

www.prospects.csu.ac.uk
The official publishers of Higher Education careers guidance.

INDEX